BLACK & WHITE

An Intimate, Multicultural Perspective
on "White Advantage" and
the Paths to Change

STEPHEN DORSEY

NIMBUS
PUBLISHING
— NIMBUS.CA —

Nimbus Publishing Limited
3660 Strawberry Hill Street, Halifax, NS, B3K 5A9
(902) 455-4286 nimbus.ca

Printed and bound in Canada
NB1598

Editor: Whitney Moran
Cover inspired by Charley Maria Dorsey
Cover design by Jenn Embree
Interior design by Rudi Tusek

Library and Archives Canada Cataloguing in Publication

Title: Black and white : an intimate, multicultural perspective on "white advantage" and the paths to change / Stephen Dorsey.
Names: Dorsey, Stephen (Author of Black and white), author.
Identifiers: Canadiana (print) 20210375981
    Canadiana (ebook) 20210382821 | ISBN 9781774710364 (softcover)
    ISBN 9781774710524 (EPUB)
Subjects: LCSH: Dorsey, Stephen (Author of Black and white) | CSH:
    Black Canadians—Biography. | CSH: Black Canadians—Social
    conditions. | LCSH: Racism—Canada. | LCSH: Canada—Race
    relations. | LCSH: Privilege (Social psychology)—Canada.
Classification: LCC FC106.B6 D67 2022 | DDC 305.800971—dc23

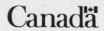  

Nimbus Publishing acknowledges the financial support for its publishing activities from the Government of Canada, the Canada Council for the Arts, and from the Province of Nova Scotia. We are pleased to work in partnership with the Province of Nova Scotia to develop and promote our creative industries for the benefit of all Nova Scotians.

For Charley and Kingston.

To my brother Chris. My story is our story.

Love. Love. Love.

I was inspired to write this book in Toronto, on the traditional territory of many nations including the Mississaugas of the Credit, the Anishnabeg, the Chippewa, the Haudenosaunee and the Wendat peoples, and now home to many diverse First Nations, Inuit, and Métis peoples. I acknowledge that Toronto is covered by Treaty 13, signed with the Mississaugas of the Credit, and the Williams Treaties, signed with multiple Mississaugas and Chippewa bands.

Contents

Prologue

A Global Reckoning;
A Personal Awakening

THE YEAR OF THE GLOBAL PANDEMIC WILL ALSO BE REMEMBERED AS A WATER-shed moment in the history of the civil rights movement—2020 was a historical milestone as the continuing fight for equality by Black people and people of colour around the world rose to a level not seen since the 1960s in the United States.

The sixties were a transformative era for America. Martin Luther King Jr. and other civil rights leaders—including the incomparable and courageous John Lewis (who almost lost his life in the first of three marches he led from Selma to Montgomery, Alabama, in 1965)—inspired millions to mobilize around non-violent civil disobedience to seek equality under the law for Black people across America. The crowning achievements of the movement came in two forms: the Civil Rights Act of 1964, which prohibited discrimination on the basis of race, colour, religion, sex, or national origin, provided for the integration of schools and other public facilities, and made employment discrimination illegal; and the Voting Rights Act of 1965, which introduced federal oversight to prohibit racial discrimination in voting via voter suppression laws, such as the requirement to pass literacy tests in order to vote.

And then, nearly sixty years later, on May 25, 2020, George Floyd was killed. This very public murder of an unarmed Black man by a Minneapolis police officer sparked a global reckoning on the issue of anti-Black racism and has supercharged the Black Lives Matter (BLM) movement in the US, Canada, and around the world—most visibly sparking worldwide protests, marches, and a flood of social media activity that has seen hundreds of millions of global citizens engaged.

Mr. Floyd had been stopped by police outside a convenience store for allegedly trying to pass a counterfeit twenty-dollar bill. The encounter with police escalated when Floyd became agitated (noting claustrophobic anxiety) when an officer tried to put him in the back of a squad car. He was then pulled out of the car and several officers wrestled him to the ground, leading one officer to place his knee on Mr. Floyd's neck. The officer would keep his knee there, pressing down, for nearly nine minutes. The officer continued to restrict

Mr. Floyd's airway even as Mr. Floyd begged for his life—saying many times, "I can't breathe." Minutes later, George Floyd's life force was extinguished, for all the world to witness.

The irrefutable video evidence of a Black man being killed by police was, for many non-Black people, the straw that broke the camel's back—an inflection point that (by choice or by circumstance) could not be ignored, and which demanded reflection. This led many to direct action, and Black Lives Matter organizations offered a relevant rallying point. Millions chose to join BLM-led protests around the world, while others showed their support for the movement via social media.

Like many Black people, it took some time before I was able to make myself watch the video of Mr. Floyd's murder. I was hesitant because I wasn't sure if I was in the right frame of mind to handle the moment—or whether I ever would be—and needed to get myself mentally prepared for the pent-up anger I knew would be ignited. When I did finally watch the footage, I was struck by the casualness of it all. While he had his knee pushed into Mr. Floyd's neck, the police officer showed no emotion—he even had one hand casually tucked in his pocket as Mr. Floyd begged for his life. I wondered what he was thinking while slowly killing another human being, as if the public murder of a Black man were just another day at the office. It all seemed psychopathic. I was horrified.

As a mixed-race Black man, I experienced a range of emotions from that moment on. Having one foot in both the white and Black worlds, I live with perpetual internal conflict. Even though witnessing violence is not an uncommon reality in today's media-saturated world, it was shocking to watch a man be killed in front of my very eyes. I felt such sadness hearing George Floyd call out for his mother, and that feeling morphed into anger at the senselessness of his killing. In the hours and days that followed, I reflected on what this incident and the reaction to it—both my own and the public's—meant. I was heartened to see so many people engaged in similar reflection, and that gave me hope that perhaps change was in the air—that this moment in history was a tipping point, and that real change was possible.

This glimmer of hope was validated when, in April 2021, the officer who killed George Floyd was found guilty of second-degree murder and, that following June, sentenced to twenty-two years in prison. It was a very rare example of a police officer being held accountable for the murder of a Black man in America. A poignant added dimension to the trial was the fact that the Minneapolis police chief—Medaria Arradondo, the first ever Black man to hold the position—testified against the officer, stating that his restraining methods were "certainly not part of [Minnesota Police] ethics or values."[1] It

---

[1] "Police chief says Chauvin's actions weren't proper policy," The Lead, *CNN Politics*, cnn.com/ videos/politics/2021/04/05/chauvin-trial-police-chief-george-floyd-lead-vpx.cnn

was a powerful statement and a break from the norm. The lived realities the Black community had decried for ages—fear of being targeted by the police, outright discrimination in the health, education, and employment sectors, and other societal disadvantages due to bias and prejudice—were now being recognized and addressed as a *real* issue by the white majority. This populice acknowledged that the killing of Black people by police was not a series of individual, tragic events but part of a much larger, ingrained system of anti-Black racism. The response of white allies did not feel like window dressing this time, but serious and purposeful, spurred by a desire for deeper under-standing, especially by those who self-identify as progressives.

∞

My race duality has given me a unique perspective on both the Black and white experience in Canada. I grew up in a white family, in white neighbourhoods, and attended schools with only a handful of Black students and people of colour. Even though I was immersed in all aspects of white society, the colour of my skin defined my racial identity. It still does. No matter the fact that I am 5o percent white, I am seen as Black man. For most of my life, I gave little time to thinking about my Blackness and what that meant to me, or what it meant to others. I preferred instead—unconsciously, I believe—to lean into who I was as a human being, to see myself simply as Stephen Dorsey: someone others would describe as smart, open-minded, kind, idealistic, and empathetic, with an infectiously happy and charismatic disposition. To paraphrase Martin Luther King Jr., I wanted to be judged *not by the colour of my skin but by the content of my character*.

Life has a way of creating moments that just happen to you. Whether you are prepared to navigate them successfully is largely determined by when they come into your life, who you are as a person at that time, your abilities, and your desire to engage in the moment or not. For decades, my brother, Chris, and I had many conversations about our difficult experiences growing up Black in a white world. Those discussions became more frequent in 2020, when both of us expressed that perhaps *this* was the moment to share our story more broadly, to get the negativity out of our systems once and for all.

In the days following the killing of George Floyd, my phone rang off the hook and emails flooded in. Family, friends, acquaintances, colleagues, and community leaders were checking in—the majority of them white. They gen-uinely wanted to know how I was feeling about everything. They wondered how they could help; what they should do or say. Some worried their good intentions may be perceived negatively or that they might make a mistake wading into the discourse. A few even wanted me to understand, have me reaffirm for them, there was no chance I thought they were in any way racist or held racist views. "Stephen, you know I'm not racist, right?" Of course, I understood their insecurities and empathized as to why they felt a need to ask. In uncertain times, everyone wants to know where they stand and, perhaps even more importantly, how they are viewed by society at large and by those close to them.

They were looking for safe harbour in a confusing time. Many non-Black people were introduced to terminology that was foreign to them, words like "systemic racism" and "anti-racist" forcing them to reckon with where they fit into the equation as allies; how to make change without taking up space; how to care for the Black people in their lives, and the larger Black community, without coming across as ignorant or disrespectful or, at worst, racist. They were also confronted with truths that required them to answer fundamental questions as to where they stood on important issues, such as the calls to defund the police. Their answers to these questions informed what they should or would do about it, and how. These times made it impossible for most to continue to sweep the anti-Black racism issue under the carpet or ignore the discourse altogether. And for some, trying to understand new terminology around the issue caused great anxiety, not only because of a lack of understanding but because of what it said about who they were. For many, I expect this feeling was destabilizing.

For most of the people who reached out to me, I was their closest connection to the Black community; many of the people I know have no other Black friends. It was in some ways overwhelming to field all this inbound energy, especially since I was also trying to manage my own emotions and understand how I felt about the reckoning. It seemed odd that, all of a sudden, I also found myself in a position to speak on behalf of an entire race—at least initially, within my network of friends, family, and colleagues. I took the time to reflect on the moment and did my best to provide insight and direction in a manner that would be helpful.

I kept my advice simple. They should speak from their hearts, in a genuine and authentic way, the same way they would about other matters in their lives that affect them profoundly. They should not let their fear of making mistakes stop them from trying. It was inevitable that some with good intentions would misstep. Some wanted, for example, to discuss the merits of joining others on social media in changing their profile picture to the black box image, a symbolic gesture intended to show solidarity with the BLM movement. My view was that this was a personal choice that should be driven by their own moral and ethical beliefs, and that their "statement" would be understood in the proper light by those who mattered. It wasn't a gesture I was motivated to make. In my view, so many people were doing it that it felt to me like a commoditization of support for the movement. But if it gave others comfort to do it, I didn't think it was my place to judge them.

Much like what we saw during the civil rights movement of the 1960s in the United States, many non-Black citizens in Canada expressed their desire to be part of the conversation and, at a minimum, to further explore their own personal ideals around the meaning of change. As diverse as Canada is, it's clear there are many different starting points of awareness and understanding for those who want to be allies in the fight against systemic racism, and different degrees of ability and motivation to take specific steps of action. A monolithic approach.

As I watched the many protests in the streets across Canada in the summer of 2020, I saw many non-Black citizens joining in, demanding change in support of the BLM movement, marching arm-in-arm with Black people, standing at the barricades. This moment in history challenged some white allies in other ways. As you may have experienced in your own circle of friends, many did not feel compelled to march in the streets but instead took the time to reflect on where they stood in all of this. Even as a Black man, I found myself more aligned to this approach—probably because I have a foot in both the Black and white worlds, and because my platform as a marketing and communications professional allows me to have greater public impact.

Many tried to make sense of the racial tumult—how it would affect their lives. Through hundreds of exchanges, I could feel the wheels turning as people worked toward their own understanding of anti-Black racism, refining their thinking about the depth of the issue and its negative impact on generations of Black people in this country. I would characterize another segment of the white population as simply *unaware* of the social, political, and cultural movements shaking up the world they live in. From #MeToo to #idlenomore to #BLM. For whatever reason—age, or socio-economic or cultural background—they were ignorant to the issues.

Some were distracted and unaware by choice; others simply walked through life oblivious of the tempest around them. Some in this latter group of white Canadians were just beginning to grapple with the basics of the anti-racist dialogue thrust upon them. It's understandable, given the speed with which the reckoning on race became topic number one around the globe—even, for a time, overshadowing the once-in-a-century pandemic gripping the world. Many North Americans struggled to make sense of an issue they may have never before given much thought. It's easy to understand how this could be unsettling for some, especially if they were learning for the first time that they had some responsibility for the injustices at play, simply because of their whiteness. The realization that their apathy toward the issue of systemic racial inequality—whether by taking an apolitical stance or due to their express support of the status quo—somehow made them complicit proved destabilizing and even painful.

What became most evident to me, however, was an almost universal need to build bridges of understanding between Black and white Canadians. A need to inform and educate so that hopefully, in due time, we can arrive at some level of consensus to achieve real change.

∞

An incident in my own life further validated this need for education. In July 2020, the owner/operator of the local Home Hardware store in my Toronto neighbourhood posted a message on his marquee that read, *All Lives Matter. Be Safe. Be Kind.* A neighbourhood resident took a photo, shared it on social media, and the post quickly went viral. Print media also picked up the story. The store owner had, without understanding, bought into the misguided rhetoric that an appropriate response to Black Lives Matter is to counter with "All Lives Matter." As Daniel Victor explains in *The New York Times*[2], "the statement—particularly in a social media hashtag—is not seen as a Kumbaya sentiment but as a way to remove focus from the specific grievances of black Americans." Rather than acknowledging the reality: that, historically and systemically, Black lives have *not* mattered, saying "All Lives Matter" "would suggest...that all people are in equal danger, invalidating the specific concerns of Black people."[3] As you can imagine, the backlash was immediate, with lots of angry posts, including calls to boycott the store, which had been in business for more than eighty-five years. Within twenty-four hours, the owner resigned from the Roncesvalles Business Improvement Association board (where he had served for twenty-plus years) and had taken down the offending message and replaced it with a Black Lives Matter statement.

This incident caused much discussion and debate in our neighbourhood and generated many opinions; some called the owner a racist while others defended him as a pillar of the community with "no racist bone in his body." I wanted to fully understand the situation and see if this could be a learning opportunity. I had many questions, so I called the owner. We had an interesting fifteen-minute discussion, which quickly revealed to me that he was unaware of the big-picture realities of racism in our society, and of the recent uprising in consciousness and energy around anti-Black racism. I wanted to know more, so I told him I would meet him in person to continue the conversation.

The next day, I met with him at his store. We knew each other casually from the 'hood, as I often shopped there, and he was a regular sponsor of the local organization where I serve as a volunteer board member. I had no desire

---

[2]   "Why 'All Lives Matter' Is Such a Perilous Phrase" by Daniel Victor. *The New York Times*, July 15, 2016. nytimes.com/2016/07/16/us/all-lives-matter-black-lives-matter.html

[3]   *Ibid.*

to pile onto the debate without context, or to solely take my cues from the social media vitriol and apologist comments. I wanted to simply understand his actions.

I asked him if he was a racist. He said no. "I was taught by my father to respect all people," he added. I asked him if he understood the difference between not being a racist and being *anti-racist*. He said no, so I took the time to provide an explanation.

I asked him if he understood what was meant by *anti-Black racism.* He said that someone had just explained it to him the day prior, but he had no clue about the broader issues or the real impact of racism on the daily lives of Black people.

I asked him how he came to decide what words he was going to put on his marquee that day. "I just wanted to share a positive message with the community, and 'All Lives Matter' sounded inclusive and positive."

"So, of all the words you could have picked, that is what you chose?" I asked him. "Yes," he responded.

He also reiterated his public position, that he had no intention to hurt anyone and that there had been no malice behind his action. He said he now recognized and understood why people were upset at what he'd done.

I asked him how he could be so out of the loop in a world filled with twenty-four-hour cable news, newspaper articles, and online media. He told me he worked twelve hours a day, went home every night to have dinner, and that he and his wife mostly focused their discussions on their family—their children and grandchildren—and plans for holidays and family get-togethers. He hardly went online, and barely read a paper or watched the news.

In short, his family did not often discuss what was happening in the world around them; they were comfortable in the bubble of their immediate life. Hard to imagine for many of us, but I expect it's more common than we think.

I asked him if he understood what was meant by *white privilege.* "Not really," he answered.

I did my best to explain it to him. I pointed out how different things were for white people compared to Black people. I explained that his white privilege enabled him to remain in a bubble of blissful unawareness with no real negative consequences (until now), while Black people and other visible minorities had no such luxury, as they were impacted by racism in their daily lives. He acknowledged that this accurately reflected his reality.

In the ten-plus years I shopped at his store, I'd never seen an employee from a visible minority. I asked him why he had never hired a Black person. He said that most of his employees had been with him for a very long time, that he had hired some of his own children over the years, and that not one Black person had ever applied for a job in all the years he has been running his business.

As one of a handful of Black residents in my neighbourhood, I realize it's not an impossibility. But what is clear is that Black people continue to be discriminated against in the workforce. On the issue of pay alone, data published in 2020[4] shows that Black men in the US (similar data is just starting to be collected in Canada) make $0.87 for every dollar earned by a white man. It's even worse for Black women, who on average make $0.63 for every dollar earned by a white man. And that's if they even secure the job. In 2017, researchers at Northwestern University, Harvard, and the Institute for Social Research in Norway concluded that, on average, "white applicants receive 36% more callbacks than equally qualified African Americans."[5]

The Home Hardware owner also told me he accepted full responsibility for, and the consequences of, his mistake. He understood that some would choose to stop shopping at his store, that he could lose his franchisee rights, and that in time, he may lose his business. He understood that this could all happen and that he would be solely responsible. He told me he would be taking steps to become more aware, to learn and listen (he was grateful for our conversation), and to find ways to do his part to effect change. For my part, this conversation helped me feel more anchored and, in having heard his version of the story, I gained my own understanding of the situation. Ultimately, proof of his truthfulness and sincerity will be judged by his actions.

If we want white people (including people who are well-meaning but unaware, like this store owner) to be part of the change, should we not try to provide these potential allies with an on-ramp to do so? How will burying them in shame and scorn lead to the progress we seek? Outrage or "cancel culture" (ostracizing and vilifying people who have been deemed to have said or done the "wrong thing"), as exemplified often on social media, leads to more division, and this negative feedback loop impedes progress. Division does not lead us, as a society, to positive change.

Like many of you, I'm angry. But it's what we do with our anger that will ultimately make the difference. Anger for the sake of anger does nothing to achieve progress. Turning that anger into motivation to bring people closer together, to attempt to find common ground: this seems a more productive approach. I think we are also at a time where the broader reckoning and introspection have set the stage for this possibility.

The reality is that white people today still control the levers of power, so eliminating systemic racial inequality will require the support of the white majority. This includes white Canadians who are in positions of authority and

4   "Black Workers Still Earn Less than their White Counterparts: Employers can examine their policies to root out inequities" by Stephen Miller, *SHRM online*. https://www.shrm.org/ResourcesAndTools/hr-topics/compensation/Pages/racial-wage-gaps-persistence-poses-challenge.aspx

5   Study: Anti-Black hiring discrimination is as prevalent today as it was in 1969" by German Lopez. *Vox*. vox.com/identities/2017/9/18/16307782/study-racism-jobs

who have the power to affect the corporate and government policy changes we need. At the other end of the spectrum, it includes the average white citizen who is willing to stop normalizing the racist behaviours of others by calling out racism when they see or hear it. Everyone has a part to play. And that includes people like me.

In the weeks and months that followed George Floyd's murder, my perspectives on anti-Black racism and the Black Lives Matter movement were elevated to the national stage. A week after publishing my op-ed about the All Lives Matter incident, I was invited on CBC Radio's *Metro Morning* for an interview with host Gillian Deacon, and shortly thereafter, I was called out by a fellow member of the Black community in an op-ed in *MacLean's* who noted, "Dorsey is wrong: our emotions do not impede progress." It was a mischaracterization of what I had written. I subsequently published another op-ed in the *Globe and Mail* in October 2020, calling for the elimination of "white advantage"—a term that I believe is more accurate and accessible than "white privilege."

My "moment" had arrived. I decided that I could play a part in the change by bridging difficult conversations between Canadians of all stripes—Black, white, French, English—and I would do so by writing a book. A book that would encompass my thoughts on the BLM movement from my unique perspective, and my ideas on what the change we need and want could and should look like. It would be interspersed with stories of my lived experiences dealing with racism—many stories that had been bottled up deep inside since childhood.

I was ready. I hoped others were ready too.

Chapter One

All in the Family

IN 1969, THE SUMMER OF LOVE, MY FAMILY MOVED INTO A NEWLY BUILT HOUSE in the middle-class neighbourhood of Longueuil, a suburb of Montréal. For my mother, Carmen, this was a dream come true—something she never would have envisioned just a few years prior. Born in 1936, she was raised in abject poverty in Montréal's working-class neighbourhood of Sainte-Marie, located in the shadow of the Jacques Cartier Bridge. Her father, my grandfather Conrad, grew up in the even poorer neighbourhood of Faubourg à m'lasse (Molasses suburb) just next door, in the exact spot where the iconic Molson brewery and Radio-Canada towers still stand today. His home at 4 Molson Terrace, once the estate home of the Molson family, had been converted into a tenement building when the brewery expanded and the affluent Molsons moved uptown.

Legend has it that at one time, Faubourg à m'lasse residents would go down to the Montréal port and collect the "liquid sugar" (molasses) that dripped out of containers as they were unloaded from the ships. In the early 1960s, the entire Faubourg à m'lasse neighbourhood was razed—including twelve grocery stores, thirteen restaurants, about twenty factories—and five thousand residents were evicted to make way for the new Radio-Canada towers, a parking lot, and a brewery expansion.[1] Its poor citizens were left to find housing they could afford on and off the island of Montréal. (Interestingly, there are plans underway today to re-imagine this neighbourhood for the twenty-first century as the Molson brewery and Radio-Canada relocate. Although plans do envision some affordable housing, the reinvention of this old neighbourhood will probably trigger another cycle of gentrification in which many lower-income citizens will be pushed out for a more affluent citizenry.)

My mother's family, the Moores, had, at most, a grade-school education. They were white French Canadians descended from English Protestant immigrants from Dover, England: sailors, who landed and settled on Île-d'Orléans, just a few kilometres east of Québec City, in the 1670s. Through marriage, they integrated into the French Catholic community and, over generations, made their way south to Montréal; they had made the move in search of opportunity but instead found themselves at the precipice of homelessness.

---

[1]   "Faubourg à m'lasse," Wikipedia (n.d.). wikipedia.org/wiki/Faubourg_à_m%27lasse

During and after the Second World War, my mother, her four siblings, and her parents lived in a two-room walk-up apartment. The tiny space was the back room of an actual apartment only accessible via outdoor, wooden stairs. It had once been a stable, a relic from when horses were the city's main form of transportation. Over the years, my mother often shared with me the details of the social ills that affected her family, including her father's alcoholism and how on payday, she and her mother were often forced to search for him in local taverns to ensure he did not spend his entire meagre income on booze. During the cold Montréal winters, they burned newspaper to try to keep warm and also used it to wrap their feet, stuffing the one pair of shoes they each owned, summer shoes not meant for the harsh winter weather.

In 1951 a housing shortage on the island of Montréal pushed them out, and my mother and her entire family moved across the bridge to the south shore of the St. Lawrence River. In search of cheaper accommodations, they landed in the even poorer suburb of Ville Jacques-Cartier, where future leaders of the FLQ (Front de libération du Québec), the militant arm of the Québec separatist group, would famously plan their terrorist plots in the late 1960s. Ville Jacques-Cartier would be amalgamated into Longueuil in 1969, but when my mother's family arrived it was open farmland, where people staked claim to a small plot of land and built ramshackle housing from whatever materials they could find—including sheet metal salvaged from abandoned railcars and wooden pallets discarded in and around the Port of Montréal. The town had no sewer system and the homes no electricity, running water, or indoor toilets. In French, Ville Jacque-Cartier was known as a *bidon ville*. A shanty town.

∞

My mother was married at seventeen to her boyfriend, Leo, a white man a year her senior, and that same year she gave birth to my half-brother, Peter. She and Leo had met at a local diner and fallen in love dancing to the jukebox. He was a nice boy, handsome, and danced well. He had a nice family and a nice home—things my mother did not have. My mother really wanted to leave the family home as she had become the breadwinner, working in small factories, including Bond LaSalle, where she helped sew men's suits. Her father was never home—always off drinking away the little money he made.

But it was young love, and eventually Leo's "other" interests got in the way. By the time my mother was twenty, the marriage had ended.[2] A young mother

---

[2] I would meet Leo decades later in my teens when he moved to Vancouver to start a flooring business. I liked him. He had married a woman named Ginette a few years after divorcing my mother and they'd had a son, Luc, who, through our shared brother, Peter, became another dear member of my family. The half-brother of my half-brother!

with no education and little money, her opportunities for a better future were limited. After her divorce, my mother moved back in with her parents and siblings and found work in a series of factories on the south shore and was expected to, once again, bring money home for the family. My grandmother watched Peter during the day. Around 1960, when my mother was in her early twenties, she decided she could make more money—and have some more fun—by going to across the bridge to downtown Montréal to find work in bars and restaurants with her best friend, Réjeanne. She had to borrow money to buy clothes to look the part. My mother was very beautiful—her beauty only surpassed, she admits, by her naïveté about the ways of the world and men, having been sheltered as a young girl by her mother within the Catholic norms of the times.

After Prohibition and the Second World War, Montréal had truly become one of the most cosmopolitan cities in North America, attracting people from across the United States and Europe. Foreign workers from around the world arrived to plan and begin construction on Expo 67, which would become one of the most successful World's Fairs of all time. New, modern office towers were going up all around the city (the new home of Radio-Canada/CBC included), and Montréal's modern Métro system became a reality. The city's club, cabaret, and restaurant scenes were exploding, especially on and near Sainte-Catherine Street, the city's main drag, and my mother found herself at the centre of it all. Everyone was in on the action, from legitimate businesspeople to infamous, colourful figures from Montréal's underworld—some of whom my mother worked for at Hôtel LaSalle (the Calypso Bar) at Drummond and Sainte-Catherine, and later at the Tap Room at Peel and Sainte-Catherine.

My mother recalls the routine vividly. They worked until the bar closed and then she and her girlfriends would go to restaurants to eat and drink till dawn. Places like Da Giovanni, Schwartz's Deli, Dunn's, and bars like Casa Loma and the Copacabana, where they danced all night to live orchestras. She particularly loved the Esquire Show Bar, a swing, jazz, soul, and R&B club on Stanley, south of Sainte-Catherine, that featured lots of great musicians, including many Black artists from the US. A legendary Montréal nightclub of the era, featuring a round bar with an elevated stage in the centre, it was a favourite haunt for the city's restaurant and bar staff.

On the day Kennedy was shot in 1964, my mother met my biological father at the Tap Room bar where she worked. He was a tall, good-looking, charismatic Black man who had moved to Montréal from upstate New York. His charm offensive included telling my mother he was a professional accountant, that he had played college football, and, I expect, whatever else he needed to say to sweep her off her feet. Interestingly, my mother once told me she'd had no pre-conceptions or biases regarding engaging in a relationship with a Black man, even though interracial relationships were still quite taboo at the time. It wasn't an issue that she or any member of her family had ever considered. Perhaps because there were so few Black people in Montréal at that time, and because her family was so concerned with surviving everyday life, race was not something they'd ever consciously had to think about. From my mothers' perspective, my biological father was simply a good-looking guy she wanted to spend time with.

One thing led to another, as they say, and just weeks after she met my father, my mother became pregnant. They moved in together and in March 1965 my brother, Chris, was born. But their partnership quickly deteriorated. Within a few short months, my father's true identity revealed itself: he was a man unable to work and take care of a family. My mother packed up Chris and moved back in with her parents. Shortly thereafter, she found out she was pregnant again, and on March 17, 1966, I was born, just a year and six days after my brother. My mother was now a single mother of three boys—two toddlers and a teenager—two of whom were Black. Needless to say, an unusual situation for a young, white, French Canadian Catholic woman in 1960s Québec.

My mother continued to work. In the beginning, we all lived together at my mother's parents' house, but by the time I was two and Chris was three, my mother began to board the two of us. We first stayed during the week with family friends who lived nearby and spent some weekends with my mother. I have only vague memories, mostly of playing with those cool futuristic spaceships from the popular sci-fi show *Thunderbirds*. My half-brother, Peter, was fourteen or fifteen by then and he spent a few months at a Catholic boarding school before returning to live full-time at the family home.

About a year later, Chris and I boarded at a big stone home on Chambly Boulevard in Longueuil (blocks away from the home we would move into less than two years later). The home was run by a Mrs. Silverstone who boarded the children of single mothers who had to work to provide. Decades later, my uncle Robert recalled coming to visit us with my mother one day; he was sickened to see me sitting on the front steps by myself, covered in scratches and bruises, my clothes messy and soiled. Luckily, I don't remember why. This was the reality of our young lives for nearly two years. Chris and I had only a part-time mother and family, and no real home to call our own.

∞

In 1968, my mother met the man who would become my stepfather at the restaurant where she worked near Longueuil. She felt an instant connection and fell hard for him—love at first sight. A white, French-speaking immigrant from Belgium, his European background, in her mind, meant he was sophisticated and educated: he was someone from the old country They were inseparable from the moment they met. He had immigrated to Canada just two years before to work on refurbishing the Fortress of Louisbourg—an eighteenth-century French fortress on Nova Scotia's Cape Breton Island—as a skilled slate-roofing tradesman. The contract had fallen through upon his arrival to Canada, so he had decided to make his way to the south shore of Montréal to find work. He subsequently met someone who became his business partner in an aluminum sales and installation company, through which he'd made enough money to establish himself in Québec. When he bought a house at 385 Pelletier Street, a newly developed area of Longueuil on what had recently been farmland, he asked my mother to move in with him.

My brother and I, four and three at the time, were too young to form any real memories of first meeting our stepfather or of moving into the house as a family. My mother remembers move-in day because of how happy she felt, knowing all her children would be together under one roof, in a proper home, with all the middle-class comforts she had only ever dreamed of. As she tells it, there was little time to rejoice that day as my stepfather sat her down for an important conversation. He wanted to discuss the "story" my mother would share with their new neighbours. While he did not tell her outright what he wanted her to say, he made his intentions crystal clear: the neighbours were not to know that Chris and I were her biological children.

That day, the next-door neighbour, Lise, invited my mother over for coffee and a chat. They had an amicable conversation about their lives and their families. When she returned home, my stepfather was waiting, anxious to know what had been discussed. She simply told him she had made up a story on the spot—that in fact, they had adopted me and Chris to give us an opportunity at a better life. With the deceitful deed done, she tried to put it out of her mind.

From the day we moved into that house as a family, Chris and I just accepted that we were, in fact, adopted. This was the narrative shared by our parents with neighbours, friends, and anyone else who asked. My mother and stepfather never actually sat us down to tell us which orphanage we came from, who our birth parents were, or to offer any insights as to our ethnic background. Nothing.

When I was around five years old, I came across boxes of old photos stored away in our basement—photos of my very young mother getting married to a white man who was clearly not my stepfather. It was years later that I connected the dots—that the man in the photos was my half-brother Peter's father, Leo—but at that time, I had no idea my mother had ever been married to someone else and I was confused, thinking my stepfather was perhaps Peter's biological father. I searched and searched but found no photos of myself or Chris as babies. It seemed our lives had only begun when we moved into our new home.

Over time, this adoption narrative became part of our realities. It was how we identified ourselves and how our neighbours and friends, all of them white, came to know us. In their eyes, I expect, my parents were amazing people who went against the norms of the time to open their home to two little Black orphans, and they were more than happy to accept the goodwill that came their way because of it.

In April 1970, my sister, Elizabeth, was born. A cute little baby who transformed into a beautiful little girl, she had a big smile and was full of joyful energy—the way she remains to this day. Being closest to her in age, I was the one who watched out for her, helped her get dressed, walked her to the school bus, and made sure she got to class. I indulged her, sitting at her little table to partake in elaborate tea parties with her favourite dolls. Loving moments like these created a close bond between us that endures to this day, despite the challenging realities that drove a wedge between us for a time.

∞

Things continued for our family of five at Pelletier Street, with my stepfather working and spending time at restaurants, bars, brasseries, and taverns. He would usually get home between seven and eight o'clock at night for family dinner—all of us kids having to wait that late to get fed. My mother took care of us but was primarily responsible for making sure the home was managed to my stepfather's liking—ready to entertain any visitors my stepfather would invite over to "impress." My siblings and I helped with our many assigned chores around the house, went to school, and played outdoors for hours on end—street hockey, soccer, riding our bikes, and skateboarding. As far as we knew it, our lives were no different than anyone else's.

In 1976 Montréal was set to host the Summer Olympics. I was ten years old, and the city felt alive with energy and possibility. One day that summer, a day like any other, my mother, Chris, Elizabeth, and I were chatting at the kitchen table. We were having a regular conversation when my mother just blurted it out.

"You're not adopted. You're my children. I'm your real mother."

I can't recall having much of an emotional reaction to the news, but my brain began working overtime to uncover the hints I had unconsciously ignored. Interestingly, it was just recently, in 2020, that my mother, at age eighty-four, shared the details as to how our origin story, the Big Lie, had gone down back in 1969. I asked her if she thought the neighbours had really bought her story. She had no idea. But I believe they knew the truth, because if anyone looked beyond our skin colour, it was obvious my brother and I were related to our mom.

Back at the table in 1976, my mother also told us about our biological father—that he was alive and living on the island of Montréal, about a twenty-minute drive away. After the initial shock of learning that our mother was our real mother and that we had a biological father somewhere out there—somewhere nearby!—our identities were completely flipped upside down. We needed to make sense of this monumental news and gain a better understanding of who we really were. As you can imagine, Chris and I had a lot of questions. But that was the end of the discussion. My mother and stepfather never asked us if we were interested in connecting with our father or learning more about him or about our Black cultural roots. It was a dead end. The topic was closed. My stepfather was angry that our mother had told us the truth, that she had broken the seal of the Big Lie. It was one of the few times I ever saw my mother defy my stepfather. It was a lot to process, but suddenly it explained many things for me—for one, how our stepfather had treated us over the years under "his" roof.

I was too young to intellectualize all of this then, but as an adult I would come to comprehend how the Big Lie had come to be and why. Even as a young person just approaching my teens, I would realize that my stepfather was full of shit, and stop taking what he said at face value. I started silently questioning his views of the world, how he saw and spoke about others, and I felt a deep sense that something was wrong with the way he treated my mother. Even if I didn't have the words to express it yet, his misogyny and control over my mother had been obvious for years.

The truth is, my stepfather could not abide people knowing he'd married a woman who had slept with a Black man. There were a few reasons for this: one, it was the 1960s, and we lived in a very Catholic province that saw interracial unions as taboo; two, my stepfather had an enormous ego, and his Belgian heritage trumped his ability to transcend the prejudices and biases he had carried with him from his home country.

Belgium's colonial history with racism and bigotry is well documented, including the genocide committed against more than 20 million Black people in the Congo under the reign of King Leopold II in the late nineteenth century. My stepfather's upbringing and heritage had led him to believe that Black skin signified the lowest caste of human beings—barely human. King Leopold II's own words convey this mindset most clearly:

> Evangelize the niggers so that they stay forever in submission to the white colonialists, so they never revolt against the restraints they are undergoing. Recite every day—'happy are those who are weeping because the kingdom of God is for them.' Convert always the blacks by using the whip. Keep their women in nine months of submission to work freely for us. [...] Teach the niggers to forget their heroes and

to adore only ours. Never present a chair to a black that comes to visit you. Don't give him more than one cigarette. Never invite him to dinner even if he gives you a chicken every time you arrive at his house.
–King Leopold II of Belgium, 1883

Given the world he came from and the attitudes he brought to Canada with him, it would be untenable for my stepfather to have to explain that his wife had conceived children with such an inferior being. It must have conflicted him deeply when he suddenly found himself the head of a multiracial household, responsible for two Black kids. But while I understand the context, I still can't fathom his decision. As a father of two young children—my son, Kingston, is five and my daughter, Charley, is nine—I can't imagine being asked by anyone, much less my life partner, to disown my own children. I would choose death first.

∞

While all this was happening in my own home, I also experienced what I call "bully prejudice," the type of everyday bigotry most are familiar with. Verbal racist attacks by children who have been indoctrinated (unconsciously in many cases) by parents and guardians with varying levels of prejudicial, racist, and white supremacist world views. Racism transcends language, so when I was young, the verbal abuse I experienced came from both French- and English-speaking kids. I remember being called nigger and *salle negre* ("dirty nigger") mostly by kids I didn't know at the local park or in the schoolyard.

I remember when the mini-series *Roots*, starring LeVar Burton and based on the famous book by Alex Haley, came out in 1977. The series was a significant cultural moment celebrated universally, as it was the first time the story of slavery had been told from the Black perspective (retracing the author's family ancestry) and shown on prime-time television. A record-breaking audience of 130 million tuned in. But I hated it. Not because it wasn't good TV or because the story wasn't important, but because it added fuel to the racist taunting. On the Monday following the airing of the first episode, I got off the school bus and heard my friends and others calling out at me, "Hey, Toby"—the name given to Burton's character by his slave master. Others called me Kunta Kinte, the character's African name. Everyone joined in for days. All I wanted to do was disappear.

When I reflect on the hundreds of incidents of racist taunting I experienced in primary school, I realize that I simply thought, *this is normal*. The kids with glasses got picked on; the overweight kids got picked on. The colour of my skin was, according to the other kids, my weakness—a symbolic weakness for others to exploit. It wasn't a racial attack. At least that's how I processed it at the time: they were just kids picking on another trait that was different.

Perhaps that's the reason I just moved through it all, leveraging the innate skills I had to make it through each day with as little negativity as possible. When confronted with challenges in the schoolyard, I could talk my way out of sticky situations, run away (I was a fast little kid), or one of my bigger friends would step in to diffuse the situation. In later years, I would learn to harness my diplomatic talents and communication skills to navigate the adult world in a similar fashion.

∞

We lived for ten years in that house in the suburbs in what must have looked, from the outside, like an idyllic place to grow up. But that couldn't have been further from the truth. On the surface, our neighbourhood was a typical suburban community, with parks, a public pool, an ice rink, and sports fields. When we first moved into our small home, there weren't even any fences between homes; they slowly went up over the years as homeowners could afford the privacy. It was the early 1970s, and it seemed everyone was becoming more affluent. People were buying new cars, boats, and motorcycles and customizing minivans, and of course, building pools in their backyards. Being in the construction business, my stepfather had an in-ground swimming pool built in our backyard—the first of its kind in our town. For my siblings and me, it should have been magical.

My stepfather and his business partner were just like the characters played by Danny DeVito and Richard Dreyfuss in the 1987 movie *Tin Men*: door-to-door salesmen and shameless hustlers. It was all an elaborate grift. My stepfather once bragged about how he and his partner convinced a farmer and his wife to spend $5,000 (equivalent to $40,000 today—an outrageous amount) on aluminum siding for their farmhouse—something the couple never really needed or wanted. The money they made selling and installing these types of products was obscene, and these practices would eventually be regulated by consumer protection laws.

As he tells it, my stepfather was the set-up man (the immigrant mentee learning the ropes from the master), and his partner played the big boss from the "home office" in Montréal. As a native Québécois, my stepfather's partner understood that many rural farmers literally kept their savings in hard cash under their mattresses, not trusting the banks controlled by the anglos. My stepfather drove the shiny new luxury car of that year—possibly a Cadillac— chauffeuring his partner, who sat in the back seat. When they spotted the right targets—unsuspecting peasant farmers with little formal education—he stepped out to speak to them. He told them the president of the company was in town, that they were driving around looking for the perfect showcase home for that year, and their farmhouse had been selected. Imagine that! He would then ask the couple if they would like to meet the company president (his partner, who had remained in the car for full effect) and when the couple bit, my stepfather's partner was invited inside for coffee and a chat. Even before they sat down, my stepfather planted a red, $50-dollar bill in the home. They asked to tour the very modest farmhouse and, as if by chance, the "president" reached down to pick up the bill. He handed it to the man and noted he had just found it on the floor. Trust sealed. Using these unscrupulous practices, my stepfather and his partner managed to prime the pump of their business with enough cash to grow it into a somewhat more legitimate enterprise. Time and karma, however, would eventually catch up to them both.

I share this story of my stepfather because it says a lot about who he was fundamentally: a man of little moral integrity who was singularly focused on his own needs and wants, with no regard for how his actions negatively affected others. In our years under the same roof, he also revealed his bigoted and racist attitudes through the way he spoke of others, in the manner in which he treated Chris and me, and the misogyny he displayed toward my mother. In some ways, he was like Archie Bunker, the bigoted and chauvinistic "master of the house" on the '70s TV show *All in the Family*, a ground-breaking series that reflected the prevalent attitudes of the time. I was a big fan because it resonated with me. Even though I was young, I instinctively understood how the show deliberately shone a light on the idiocy of racism.

Archie Bunker's bigotry stemmed from a lack of education, a narrow understanding of the complexities of society, a basic fear of the "other," and his comfort with the patriarchal social norms that had been passed on to him. Even in his misogynistic treatment of his wife, Edith, you never felt Archie was driven by a purposeful intent to harm. Unlike Archie, my stepfather's actions were driven by a willful desire to oppress and control those he perceived as less-than, and to satisfy his large ego. He was a skillful predator, using his intellect to manipulate those around him. He treated my mother like a servant, offering only fleeting moments of the love and care she craved. He preyed on the knowledge that my mother was fearful of returning to the socio-economic realities of her past—to a life of poverty for her and her children.

In 1970, when Elizabeth was born, Peter moved out; he was only sixteen years old. In later years, Peter shared that he was asked to leave by our step-father as it was "for the best," noting that our stepfather had made it clear he didn't want my brother around. Peter was old enough to question him and push back, and our stepfather would have none of that under his roof. Peter quit school in grade nine and moved to a rented apartment above a bakery—the same bakery we visited every Sunday morning to buy bread and baked treats.

Being only four years old at the time, I wasn't sure why my brother wasn't living with us anymore, and so I just accepted things as they were.

∞

My brother Chris and I enjoyed playing sports with our friends in the neighbourhood. I particularly loved street hockey and seemed to have a natural talent. I was also a diehard Montréal Canadiens fan. I'd often imitate my favourite players, like Jean Béliveau, Guy Lafleur, and the legendary goalkeeper Ken Dryden. I was a very small child, but I was up for physical battles against kids of any size.

When I expressed an interest in playing ice hockey, I remember my stepfather abruptly telling me it was a bad idea because Black people had weak ankles and were not suited for the sport. That was the end of the conversation. There was no room to question my stepfather on anything. I just had to accept his will as the way. It was a big blow for a kid in Montréal to not be allowed to play ice hockey, but my dream had ended before it even started.

In 2014 I had the opportunity to meet and chat with P. K. Subban, a Black hockey phenom from Toronto who had made it big, on and off the ice, with my Habs in Montréal. It was a thrill. I couldn't help wondering at the time how things could have been different for me and other kids of colour if there had been more high-profile Black players like P. K. in the league back in the 1970s—people to look up to, who could inspire us and make hockey a seemingly accessible sport for Black youth.

My stepfather often spouted his views on Africans: how they were lazy and uncivilized; how many had immigrated to Belgium and made a mess of his country. In 1976, when I was ten, he would even go so far as to use the African boycott of the Montréal Olympics as a scare tactic to avoid having to take my brother and me: he suggested we'd be targeted if we went anywhere near the Olympic events being held just a few kilometres away. It was very disappointing to miss out on this once-in-a-lifetime experience, especially when all our neighbourhood friends raved about the experience.

In 1971, at the ages of five and six, my brother and I signed up for a newly formed "inter-city" soccer league. Chris and I would go on to play at the highest competitive level in Québec until we were thirteen and fourteen. Interestingly, my stepfather did show some support for our soccer careers. He encouraged us to join a private club, Vasco da Gamma, the only one of its kind in the province at the time. But it turned out he had his own motive. As one of its major funders, he used his influence to shape the soccer club, including lobbying for the style of uniforms we would wear. They just happened to be modelled on the uniforms for the Belgian national team, the Red Devils. I remember wearing a uniform he had brought back from Belgium to a meeting; I was made to stand on a table to showcase it for other parents. Like the monkey to the organ grinder. He got his way.

My brother and I would go on to play hundreds of matches during our eight-year run with the club. In all those years, and despite how interested my stepfather seemed in the prestige of the club itself, he and my mother only attended one match to lend their support. Our wins, trophies, and the MVP accolades we accumulated were never celebrated; our stepfather would not allow the spotlight to shine on anyone but himself. It's one of the reasons that today I prioritize time and attention when it comes to my children, as I believe that is what they most crave, and what will stay with them for life.

∞

We were a foodie family, and the love of cooking and eating was central to our daily lives. My siblings and I learned to cook at a very young age, and we each developed a joy for food. My stepfather was happy to teach us about the epicurean lifestyle—about wine, cheese, and the etiquette of dining. With the good, though, always came the bad. He was a tyrant at the dinner table, requiring all of us to adhere to a very strict set of manners when eating. We each had to hold our fork and knife a certain way, rest our hands on the table—not our elbows!—and chew with our mouths closed at all times. If any of us boys stepped out of line, we would get a heavy flick on the ear. My stepfather had large hands with huge fingers. On many occasions, it took all the strength I had to hold back my tears. Crying would only make things worse. If you were on his bad list, you'd be the one sitting next to him on his favourite side—his right—where he could reach you in the blink of an eye.

He only did this to us within the sanctuary of his own home, of course, because no one was around to stop or correct him. I came to understand later that my stepfather was, in fact, a coward. He had a lot of bravado when no one was watching. In fact, for most of his life, when things didn't go right for him, he would cut all ties with friends and acquaintances, pull up stakes, and move, choosing to try to reinvent himself rather than address his own shortcomings and adjust his behaviour.

But things often got worse. If my stepfather deemed that you were eating "like a pig," his punishments would escalate. He would grab your plate and some newspaper and he'd walk you downstairs to the unfinished basement; there, he'd have you eat the rest of your dinner off a dirty piece of newspaper on the floor, alone in a pitch-black room. Just recalling this memory brings back horrible feelings. I didn't realize it at the time, but it also started to create a distance between me and my mother. Why was she unwilling to protect me? Why didn't she come to my rescue? All I wanted was for her to take me in her arms and tell me I was safe and loved. Even today, the gap of trust and love with my mother has never fully healed.

The same basement was eventually transformed into a large bedroom shared by Chris and me. It was our own space, where we could retreat from the chaos. As "Irish twins," born one year and six days apart, we were very close, and as my big brother, he looked out for me. Chris asked me recently if I remembered having to stay in the basement on occasion when my parents would be hosting dinners or parties upstairs. I had not remembered this, but once he said the words, memories flooded back.

My stepfather would often entertain at the house, as he loved showing off his stuff. The new car in the driveway (he changed cars every couple of years, it seemed), his Rolex watch, the fully stocked home bar and beer fridge, the latest TV set and stereo system, the in-ground swimming pool (kept resort-clean by me and Chris), his European dishes, art, and more. It was a Hollywood set meant to impress, a statement conveying success. He was known for carrying a wallet overflowing with money and came home with thousands of dollars in cash every Friday evening. He bought fancy clothes and jewelry for my mother to show off her off. It was all part of the image he wanted to convey to the world.

Decades later, my mother remined me about David, a business associate of my stepfather's who was Jewish. "The Jews like me," my stepfather was fond of boasting. Chris confirmed that we had never met this David, and that during his many visits we had been instructed to stay downstairs and out of sight. I'm still not sure whether David even knew we existed, but I do remember the negative feelings this stirred within me—that we were either not important or that we were a secret not to be revealed—hurtful feelings that added to my growing sense of separation from my "parents" within my own home.

One of my few happy memories of this time was our family's annual summer holiday, a month-long trip to Maine. But my parents also took many holidays without Chris and me. They went to Belgium several times—sometimes during the Christmas holidays or our summer breaks, when we could easily have come along.

I remember a woman named Madame Lampron, the mother-in-law of one of my parents' friends, coming to take care of us at our house, sometimes for weeks. She was a lovely little old lady with a bad-fitting wig and false teeth. We would ask her to pop out her teeth for us, which made us laugh. She was a warm and kind person. I remember one Christmas opening the little gifts she had for us: a chocolate bar, a hockey puck, and her legendary knitted underwear. Imagine that! A fond memory was her letting us stay up past midnight on New Year's Eve to watch the traditional *Bye Bye* show on CBC that featured one of my all-time favourite comedians, Dominique Michel.

All the while, my parents were in Europe enjoying themselves. No phone calls, nothing. We were never taken along to meet my stepfather's relatives in Belgium because, as it turns out, we did not exist.

There were numerous other occasions when Chris and I were "tucked away" at a camp here and there while our mother, stepfather, and Elizabeth went on holiday together or hosted my stepfather's relatives in our home. It was a well-orchestrated deception that, luckily, my brother and I were mostly oblivious to at the time. This was all we knew. We had no way of knowing that we were being treated as less-than, and even if we had, this was an era when kids still feared their parents and other authority figures. You did as you were told. It was still "normal" to get smacked on the hand by your teacher at school or be spanked hard by your parents. My mom chasing us with a wooden spoon is a vivid and weirdly funny memory. Times have changed.

∞

My stepfather was not a physical abuser. He did enjoy his flicks on our ears and the occasional spanking (one hard slap with his large hands was enough), but he was a master of psychological abuse and manipulation. As the years went on, he began to exhibit bipolar-like behaviour, and Chris and I often found ourselves in his crosshairs during one of his moods. I remember him making an effort to take us boys fishing with a local friend when we were vacationing one summer in Maine. The large fishing boat, which had about fifty people onboard, reminded me of the vessel in *Jaws*. As soon as we were out on the water, our stepfather became unhappy at being there with us. His negativity made the entire afternoon a chore rather than something fun we could enjoy together.

Chris took the brunt of the abuse, with seemingly endless flicks on his ears for not "eating properly." But mostly it was psychological. Our stepfather was fond of calling my brother "Gaston Lagaffe," referring to a European cartoon of the 1950s and '60s whose titular character is known for being lazy and of limited intelligence, always messing up in his role as an office worker. He would waste no opportunity to remind my brother, who was still a young boy, why he was saying or doing something wrong—through a barrage of verbal aggression intended to make Chris feel that he was good for nothing. It was purposeful and mean. (He didn't know it then, but my brother's eventual global professional success would, in part, be fuelled by a drive to prove my stepfather wrong—a big and well-deserved *fuck you*. Amen to that.)

I observed what triggered my stepfather and did my best to avoid attracting his attention. But I was not to escape unscathed. Like many young kids, I went through a period where I wet my bed—except for me, it lasted a long time. By the time I was nine, my mother took me to the doctor to see if there was something physically wrong with me, but it turns out my bedwetting was physiological. My stepfather, meanwhile, had made his own diagnosis. I was just lazy and couldn't be bothered to make the effort to wake up and go to the bathroom. He had the cure, and decided to take matters into his own hands.

First, he thought humiliation would do the trick, so he made me wear diapers. These were the kind of cotton diapers held together with a safety pin, but since I was nine, it was a very large safety pin that would dig hard into my side. For this reason, it seemed to exacerbate the issue rather than fix it. Often, in the middle of the night, I would wake up suddenly with my diaper soaked. Not wanting to be found out, I'd quietly make my way downstairs to the laundry room and tuck the diaper into the laundry basket. When my stepfather realized his humiliation tactic was not working, he tried to shame me publicly instead, by having my diapers hang outside on the clothesline for all to see. And to ensure there was no confusion, he would tell anyone passing by that they were mine.

I still wet the bed. So he took his punishment even further.

One Saturday morning he woke me up very early, led me to the bathroom by the arm, and instructed me to strip down and get in the tub. Minutes later, he showed up with a big industrial white bucket filled with my dirty diapers. The smell of ammonia was overwhelming. He placed the bucket under the tap and turned on the cold water. He handed me a large bar of Sunlight soap (I can still recall the smell) and ordered me to hand-wash my diapers while he towered over me and screamed obscenities, telling me how lazy I was and how ashamed I should be.

My hands became red from the cold water, and the more I cried, the more he yelled at me. I would twist each diaper dry and then hang them on the clothesline in the backyard. This experience was difficult to process then and is still difficult to recollect today. I can't imagine how anyone, especially a parent, could purposely traumatize their child in such a brutal manner.

To this day, it remains unclear to me why someone with my stepfather's racial biases would decide to take in and raise two Black kids. It has always been confusing to try to understand his cruelty towards me and my brother. Was he simply an abuser who was further motivated by the racist and bigoted views he held, or did his racist and bigoted beliefs inspire his abusive behaviour? Whatever the truth, Chris and I faced the harsh realities of racism early in our formative years from inside our own home, within our own family. Not only did this have negative effects on our childhood, but it also affected us as adults, impacting how we trusted people and viewed the world around us.

∽

In 1978 our suburban life as we knew it started falling apart. The economy was tanking as the world was in the grip of a global recession, the political climate in Québec had created a mass exodus of English-speaking Québecers to Ontario, and my stepfather's business was going bankrupt. There is a photo

I still have, taken of me at Christmas that year, twelve years old, when my world was imploding all around me. I recognize the look on my face; I knew that bad things were on the horizon.

For reasons still unclear to me (and apparently to my mother as well), my stepfather came home one day and announced he was selling his business, selling our home, and we were moving across the country to Victoria, British Columbia. It was a bombshell. I did not understand why he would choose to move our family to an English-speaking city when he spoke essentially no English—a foolish plan for someone who made his living in sales. My mother spoke some basic, conversational English, but only Chris and I were fully bilingual, having done all our schooling in English.

I remember a conversation Chris and I had with my mother at that time. She was trying to reassure us that things would be okay. "We don't have a big family, but we've got each other, and we'll always stick together," she assured us.

Months later, in March 1979, just one week before my thirteenth birthday, I remember pulling away from our house in our big car, leaving behind all our friends and the only home I had ever known, anxiety for the unknown rising with every kilometre west. I could never have predicted the major life changes that would befall my brother Chris and me just one year later.

Chapter Two

Canada's Mythology on Race

IN THE SPRING OF 2021, AS I WAS DEEP INTO RESEARCHING AND WRITING THIS book, I realized my mood was changing. I could feel the anger building within me again, spurred by the growing chatter all around me. The reverberations of the racial reckoning of 2020 were still making themselves known; the conviction of the police officer who killed George Floyd dominated media headlines and caused many of us to reflect on what had changed—and what hadn't—over the past year. And then in late May, a national story broke that had Canadians, once again, confronting the ugliness of their country's history.

Unmarked graves were found in the small British Columbia town of Kamloops. It is believed to be the final resting place of 215 Indigenous children who attended a government-mandated, church-run Indian Residential School—part of a system that, for over one hundred years (from the late 1800s to 1996), saw Indigenous children, some as young as four years old, forcibly taken from their parents, their communities, their cultures. The policy objective of the IRS system was to "kill the Indian in the child." It was another of Canada's dirty secrets—one well known in Indigenous communities, where survivors' stories had been told for decades. But in June 2021, the majority of Canadians, hidden behind the veil of white advantage, were forced to look this despicable truth in the eye for the first time. Polls released following the discovery of the mass grave in Kamloops revealed that a staggering two-thirds of Canadians had, until that moment, known "nothing" or "very little" about Indigenous Residential Schools.[1]

Despite this sad reality, it was heartening to see so many people from coast to coast to coast react with genuine sadness for the Indigenous children lost, and with empathy for their mourning communities. Across the country, vigils were held; church steps overflowed with children's shoes, people hung orange T-shirts in their windows, flags hung at half-mast. But as saddened as we all

---

[1] "Until remains of 215 children found in Kamloops, two-thirds of Canadians say they knew just a little—or nothing—about residential schools" by Steve McKinley, *Toronto Star*, June 15, 2021. thestar.com/news/canada/2021/06/15/two-thirds-of-canadians-knew-just-a-little-or-nothing-about-residential-schools-before-kamloops-discovery-survey-suggests.html

were, Indigenous leaders warned us that the horrific news of the 215 was just the tip of the iceberg: there were more terrible truths to come. First Nations leaders demanded an inquiry, a task force, federal funding to search the sites of every former residential school in Canada. The government's position was that there was already adequate funding in place through the Truth and Reconciliation Commission.

A few weeks later on June 24, 2021, using ground-penetrating radar, the Cowessess First Nation uncovered unmarked graves near the site of the former Marieval Indian Residential School in Saskatchewan. The remains of as many as 751 souls were buried there. That same day, the Canadian government pledged to substantially increase its funding to allow Indigenous communities to search former residential school sites for mass graves of Indigenous children.

Compounding these newly unearthed truths about Canada's racist past was the fact that they were revealed in the weeks leading up to Canada Day. Despite the wave of heightened awareness rippling out across the country, some Canadians reacted to the news of the unmarked graves with a knee-jerk defensiveness that, for me, was exasperating. These were people whose first instinct was to assert that that the horrors of the past had no impact on the present. If I had to hear one more person say, "That's not my Canada," I was going to scream, "It IS your fucking Canada." The generational trauma of residential school survivors is real and palpable. Making light of Canada's ugly truths comes across as lazy and uniformed. Callous comments like, "Why am I being blamed? I wasn't around then" only added to my growing angst. My instinct was to confront every person directly on the issue, but instead, I leaned on good friends to talk it out with, and used my negative emotions as fuel for my writing.

While I can relate to feeling proud of what a great country Canada has become and could still be, I believe that to be a true ally you need to understand that not everyone has had the same experience as you and your ancestors. To put it plainly, a lot of bad shit has happened in Canada, particularly to BIPOC (Black, Indigenous, and people of colour) and some of it continues to this day. Acknowledging these truths doesn't mean you love your country any less. Recognizing your country's capacity for greatness and the ways in which it falls short means you're holding it to a higher standard.

In the summer of 2021, Indigenous leaders across the country called for a boycott of traditional Canada Day celebrations and asked Canadians to instead reflect and remember all those who had suffered or been killed within the Indian Residential School system. Everyone was welcome to join in this day of mourning as they saw fit. There was a growing movement across the country to #CancelCanadaDay because in recognizing Confederation, the day has never been celebratory for Indigenous peoples. And yet all around me, I heard people complain about how they felt pressured to not celebrate Canada Day and, specifically, to set aside their celebratory fireworks displays.

I was thankful, though, to find that some people were being more thoughtful. My friend and neighbour, Katie, emailed me ahead of going up to her cottage for the Canada Day weekend—a getaway on the traditional territories of the Wahta Mohawk First Nation near Lake Huron. She wanted my opinion before sending an email she had drafted to her fellow cottagers, asking them gently to consider not putting on a fireworks display this year. I suggested she email the chief of the Wahta Mohawk Nation, Chief Philip Franks. He replied right away and generously thanked Katie for her efforts to educate her neighbours. He noted that "as a sign of respect it would certainly help relationships if there were no fireworks celebrations. I do understand some may regard this as cancel culture (as recently coined), but really, whose culture was cancelled?" No one was trying to cancel anyone. Allies were simply trying to respectfully acknowledge that many people around us were experiencing pain and trauma, and that by toning down our own celebrations we could, in a small way, lighten their burden and demonstrate some empathy.

I saw the actions of those who were pushing back as yet another example of reactive bullshit. I was tired of dealing with it. But my analytical brain was still ticking. Where did this reaction come from? I needed to know. The more I thought about it, the more I realized that this deflective reaction is symptomatic of a much larger issue: the preference of some citizens to live in the world of *mythology*—that is, the *story* of what they believe their country to be, and not the reality—its "inconvenient truths," to quote the writer Thomas King. Skipping over the ugliness is easier, but it mostly serves those who benefit from the injustices their ancestors, or even they themselves, may have had a hand in perpetuating.

∞

Canada's "national sport" is to compare itself to the United States. At the very core of our Canadian identity is a sort of internalized tally; we note our positive differences from and overall superiority to our neighbours to the south, particularly when it comes to democratic principles and racism. Many find comfort in rallying around our national constructs of multiculturism and the Charter of Rights and Freedoms. But although these institutions were intended to ensure a just society, they're not the full story.

The reality is that slavery was legal in British North America until 1834 (Canada became a federation in 1867), embraced within a colonial framework of oppression and exploitation. The history of slavery in what is now Canada spans two hundred years, going back to when France began colonizing North America as New France in the seventeenth century. This territory initially comprised of the coasts of Newfoundland, the entirety of Prince Edward Island, Nova Scotia and the coasts of New Brunswick, the St. Lawrence River, and the Gulf of Saint Lawrence. It later expanded to include a much larger territory, encompassing the entire region of the Great Lakes, southern Ontario, northern regions stretching to and past Hudson Bay, and a large region of what is now the Midwest United States, stretching down to Louisiana (until it was ceded in 1717).

In May 1689, after several requests, and considering the success of the slave trade in the West Indies and New England, the King of France authorized the importation of Black slaves to New France "to improve the labour and economic condition of the colony."[2] Slavery became official in 1709 when Jacques Raudot, the administrator of the territory at the time, issued an ordinance "confirm[ing] the servile statuses of both enslaved Africans and Indigenous people within the colony."[3] In one fell swoop, the ordinance made all slaves held in New France chattel under colonial law. Colonists now owned them outright.

Slaves were brought mainly from the colonies of the French West Indies—Martinique, Guadeloupe, and especially San Domingo (today's Haiti). In what is now Canada, most were assigned to menial tasks, as domestic help, stable boys, and cattle breeders in the cities of Québec, Trois-Rivières, and Montréal. The reality is that Black slaves in Canada were treated as badly as those in the United States. In our own country, according to *The Canadian Encyclopedia*, many enslaved Black people were subjected to cruel and harsh treatment by their owners. Some Black slaves were tortured and jailed as punishment, others hanged or murdered. Enslaved Black women were often sexually abused by their masters. Families were separated when some slaves were sold to new owners.[4]

∞

Punishment was used to discourage disobedience and to affirm the dominance of the slave master. Even though slavery was never widespread in New France, in terms of the number of Black people affected, thousands versus millions in the US—it had long-term, systemic negative impacts. And most importantly, this doesn't erase the reality that white ownership of Black bodies was considered to be the natural order of things, and Canadian ancestors condoned and benefited from slavery.

---

[2]   *The Colonial Denizen: A Proposal to Move Beyond the Politics of Recognition toward a Politics of Responsibilities* by Deanne Aline Marie LeBlanc (PhD thesis, Political Science, University of British Columbia, March 2020), 132.

[3]   *Ibid.*

[4]   "Black Enslavement in Canada" by Natasha L. Henry, *The Canadian Encyclopedia*. thecanadianencyclopedia.ca/en/article/black-enslavement

Although much of the history of the oppressed and disadvantaged was never written but rather passed down orally from one generation to another, and was often suppressed by the powers that be, some stories have managed to survive time and obscurity. Marie-Joseph Angélique was a twenty-nine-year-old slave originally from Portugal (most likely brought to that country as a slave from Africa) who, by 1734, was living in Montréal. That year, she was accused of having set fire to her master's house while attempting escape—a fire that spread rapidly and destroyed more than forty homes and the city's Hôtel-Dieu hospital. It remains unclear whether or not she was guilty of the crime (she maintained her innocence and only confessed under torture), but either way, as a poor Black foreign slave she was an outcast, and therefore "made an ideal scapegoat for the crime."[5] Furthermore, as with all slaves, "she had no rights that white society would respect." Angélique was found guilty and sentenced to be tortured—her legs crushed in a a Medieval device called a brodequin—executed by hanging, and her body burned. Her story is but one example of the cruel treatment thousands of Black slaves experienced in Canada—most of their stories lost to history because they were not even considered to be human.

The French ceded the territory of today's Canada to the British in 1763 as result of France's 1759 defeat at the Plains of Abraham in Québec City and their overall defeat in the Seven Years' War (1756–1763). But in this change of colonial hands, slavery simply continued under new masters. There exists, from this era, public evidence of slave auctions—examples like this notice in *The Royal Gazette and Nova Scotia Advertiser* from September 7, 1790:

> Sales at Auction by William Millett, At His Auction Room, on Thursday next, the 9th Inst, at 12 o'clock. About Two Tons of Ship Bread, A few Barrels of Mess Pork, Indian and Rye Meal, Some Household Furniture, A stout likely Negro Man, And sundry other Articles.[6]

Not surprisingly, the Black man is for sale as a commodity—as property. However, this occurrence in late eighteenth-century Nova Scotia *may* be a surprise to many Canadians. The reality is that many Black families living in North America today are descendants of people whose value as human beings was once reduced to that of chattel. But this isn't the story we've been told.

The myth of Canada as a haven for American slaves fleeing bondage was unfortunately just that—a myth. As James W. St. G. Walker writes in his 1985 book, *Racial Discrimination in Canada: The Black Experience*, "It's estimated

---

5   "Marie-Joseph Angelique" by Afua Cooper, *The Canadian Encyclopedia*. thecanadianencyclopedia.ca/en/article/marie-joseph-angelique

6   Excerpt from *Racial Discrimination in Canada, the Black Experience* by James W. St. G. Walker. The Canadian Historical Association, Historical Booklet No. 41, 1985.

that nearly 100,000 slaves made their way north to Canada over several decades in the late 18th and early 19th century via the 'underground railroad' but their hope for justice and equality were dashed soon after they crossed the border." Southern Ontario was a popular destination because of its vast border with the US, and so was Nova Scotia, especially for Black Loyalists—the estimated three to five thousand former slaves who escaped bondage by fighting for the British in the American Revolutionary War (1775–1783), under the promise of protection, freedom, and land grants in Canada.

Upon arriving in their new home in 1783, however, most Black Loyalists experienced widespread discrimination. They found themselves having to compete for jobs and land with European immigrants (mainly from Ireland, Scotland, and England) who were arriving in droves, and were faced, once again, with overt racism.

In reaction to Black Loyalist settlement in eastern Canada, the city of Saint John, New Brunswick, for example, amended its charter in 1785 to specifically exclude Blacks from practicing a trade, selling goods, fishing in its harbour, or becoming freemen; these provisions stood until 1870.[7] Meanwhile in Nova Scotia, land and supplies granted to Black Loyalists were often only distributed after many freed slaves were forced to build temporary shelters in the woods, known as "pit houses," with dirt floors and only a firepit for heat. When they finally did receive their land, it was located far outside of town on rocky, infertile soil, making farming nearly impossible.

These realities left a discriminated and disenfranchised people "free" but with no systems in place to allow them to provide for themselves. Most had little choice but to take any available work for much lower wages than whites. During the region's economic downturn in the late eighteenth century, many newly landed white Loyalists saw Black people as a threat to their own livelihoods and this manifested, as fear often does, in violence against the emerging Black communities in the region.

One such explosion of racially motivated violence took place over ten days in Shelburne County, Nova Scotia, in July and August 1784—an event now known as the Shelburne Riots. A mob of about forty white men began attacking and demolishing a Black preacher's house; their rampage escalated, resulting in the destruction of twenty additional Black homes, ultimately running the families out of town. These attacks lasted for ten days until calm was eventually restored by the authorities. The riots firmly established Shelburne as a white, segregated town.

Many Black people began to relocate to other parts of the province, but a mass exodus occurred when more than one thousand accepted the offer

---

7   "Arrival of the Black Loyalists: Saint John's Black Community" Archived Heritage Resources, May 19, 2011, the Wayback Machine.

of permanent deportation to Sierra Leone on the African continent. In 1790, Thomas Peters, a Black Loyalist representing hundreds of Black families, had travelled to England to petition the government for his people's long-promised land grants. During his voyage he met Granville Sharp, a passionate abolitionist who had helped initiate the court case that ended slavery in England. Sharp and his associates created the Sierra Leone Company, whose work was to return Black Loyalists and freed slaves to their homeland. On January 15, 1792, nearly ten years after their arrival in Nova Scotia, roughly twelve hundred free Black people left Halifax on a fleet of boats, bound for a new colony in Sierra Leone: Freetown.

Similar tensions were still simmering in the United States. In 2021, I learned of "Black Wall Street," the moniker given to the main street of Tulsa, Oklahoma's Greenwood district, a thirty-five–square block area that was one of the most thriving and prosperous Black communities in America. Emergent in the early 1900s, the area saw Blacks and whites segregated from one another, but with such a large Black population, this led to what the Oklahoma Historical Society calls "a nationally renowned black entrepreneurial center."[8] The district was home to about two hundred Black-owned registered businesses, including hotels, restaurants, grocery stores, beauty salons, movie theatres, a bank, as well as medical, legal, and real estate offices.

Not unlike the Shelburne Riots in Canada over a century before, Black Wall Street was attacked in 1921 by a large, hate-filled mob of white residents from a neighbouring district—an incredibly violent event known today as the Tulsa Race Massacre. The heavily armed mob burned down the entire business district and more than twelve hundred homes. Hundreds of residents were killed—some fighting to protect their families and property; others as they were attempting to flee for their lives.[9]

Later generations of Tulsans knew little or nothing of this ugly chapter in their history—and most Americans were completely unaware of it—as the massacre was covered up, was never taught in schools, and the little information available labelled the horrific attack a "race riot"—implying that the Black people targeted and murdered were at least partly responsible for their fate. And of course, no white person was ever charged with murdering Black citizens during the Tulsa massacre. Many of the victims are believed to be buried in mass graves in the area.

This lack of information was all to do with maintaining the mythology around who was to blame. At the time, businessmen and politicians "real-

---

8   "Greenwood District" by Hannibal B. Johnson, Oklahoma Historical Society (n.d.). okhistory.org/publications/enc/entry.php?entry=GR024

9   "What the Tulsa Race Massacre Destroyed" by Yuliya Parshina-Kottas et al., *The New York Times*, May 24, 2021. nytimes.com/interactive/2021/05/24/us/tulsa-race-massacre.html

ize[d] fairly quickly that they had a huge PR problem with the massacre,"[10] as Tulsa wanted to retain a more positive image as the oil capital of the world. As a result, newspaper reports of the day were altered decades later as the records were transferred to microfilm, and some official government reports were destroyed to hide the truth. A series of conflating events in the 1990s— including the Oklahoma City Bombing and the seventy-fifth anniversary of the Tulsa Race Massacre (promoted by Black city leaders)—led reporters to pay much more attention to the rumours of mass graves. This eventually led some members of the press to write more widely on the matter.

Unfortunately, Tulsa was not an isolated incident. Violence occurred in other cities across America, especially during the late nineteenth and early twentieth centuries, in cities like Chicago (1919), Memphis (1866), New Orleans (1866), and Atlanta (1906) to note but a few.

From my vantage point, it seems like most Canadians are more familiar with the post-slavery Black experience in America rather than that in Canada. The Emancipation Proclamation of 1863, an executive order by President Abraham Lincoln that declared that "all persons held as slaves" within the rebellious states "are, and henceforward shall be free," did not actually end slavery in the United States due to the many provisions, exceptions, and loopholes used by various states. It was not until the 13th Amendment was passed by the Senate on January 31, 1865, that slavery was officially abolished in the United States.

From 1865 to 1877, following the Civil War, the United States went through an era known as Reconstruction, the broad goal of which was to bring the South back into the Union while protecting the rights and safety of newly freed slaves. The US government therefore enacted a series of equity policies and provided military protection and enforcement, ostensibly giving Black Americans rights as full citizens and supporting their participation in main-stream society, with access and representation in institutions and systems— especially at the state and local levels in southern states, where opposition to emancipation continued to be widespread.

In 1867 not a single African American in the South held political office, but within three or four years "about 15 percent of the officeholders in the South were Black—a larger proportion than in 1990."[11] Unfortunately, due to much political turmoil and intense opposition from politicians and lobbyists in the American South, the federal government clawed back key economic and social supports established under Reconstruction; most notably, it withdrew federal troop protection of Black people in the South. As a result, much of the progress achieved by Black people during Reconstruction began to collapse in the southern states after 1877.

---

[10] "How the Tulsa Race Massacre Was Covered Up" by Alexis Clark, *History.com*, January 27, 2021. history.com/news/tulsa-race-massacre-cover-up

[11] *Abraham Lincoln and the Second American Revolution* by James M. McPherson, (1992), Oxford University Press, p. 19.

What followed was "a new racial system...resting on the disenfranchisement of Black voters, a rigid system of racial segregation, the relegation of African Americans to low-wage agricultural and domestic employment, and legal and extralegal violence to punish those who challenged the new order."[12] An era commonly referred to as "Jim Crow," which "institutionalized economic, educational, and social disadvantages for many African Americans," remained in place in the United States until 1965.[13] In addition to legal discrimination, Black Americans—especially in the South—were subject to racially fuelled intimidation and violence by white supremacist organizations (including the Ku Klux Klan), by ordinary, racist white citizens, and by various levels of law enforcement. For nearly a century post-Reconstruction, thousands of Black Americans would be murdered simply for being Black—many lynched in hate-fuelled public spectacles, some of which were even attended by gleeful children, caught up in the experience as if enjoying a fun day at the fair. Imagine that.

The Civil Rights movement of the twentieth century began to make strides in America in the 1950s and achieved important milestones in the 1960s, under the leadership of Dr. Martin Luther King Jr. and with support from President Lyndon B. Johnson. The Civil Rights Act of 1964 outlawed discrimination based on race, colour, religion, sex, national origin, and later, sexual orientation and gender identity. The Voting Rights Act of 1965 prohibited racial discrimination in voting. Though some progress was achieved by the Civil Rights movement—exemplified by individual breakthroughs by Black Americans in the worlds of sports (Muhammad Ali, Arthur Ashe, Wilma Rudolph) and entertainment (Sidney Poitier and Diahann Carroll)—it did not solve the issue of systemic anti-Black racism in the United States.

∞

Although Canada's history following the abolition of slavery in 1834 differs from that of the United States, the impact on Black people and other racialized communities in Canada was no less harmful or long-lasting. Post-slavery, Black people in Canada lived within a segregated society. They found themselves alienated from a majority white population both legally and socially.[14] The Government of Ontario, for example, set up separate schools for Black children in the early 1840s, and in 1850 passed the Common School Act, allowing trustees to demand separate schools for Black children—even against the

---

12 "The end of Reconstruction" by Elliott Rudwick, *Encyclopedia Britannica*. britannica.com/event/ Reconstruction-United-States-history/The-end-of-Reconstruction

13 "Jim Crow Laws." *Wikipedia*. wikipedia.org/wiki/Jim_Crow_laws

14 "Racial segregation of Black people in Canada" by Natasha L. Henry, *The Canadian Encyclopedia*, May 27, 2019. thecanadianencyclopedia.ca/en/article/racial-segregation-of-black-people-in-canada

wishes of Black parents. When parents fought against segregation, the courts upheld the practice unequivocally. Ontario was not alone in its approach to segregation in education. Nova Scotia instituted similar segregation laws for the Black population depending on the county—including full segregation of Black students in separate Black schools, such as in Halifax, and, when the population density of Black people in a particular area did not warrant a separate school, outright refusal of access to public schools. The last segregated schools closed in Ontario in 1965, while in Nova Scotia this did not happen until 1983.[15]

In the early twentieth century, discrimination in Canada's higher-education system prevented Black people from attending many prestigious Canadian universities. This included, in some cases, banning access to medical schools. Dalhousie University, Queens University, and McGill University (whose founder, James McGill, according to the institution's own newspaper, "enslaved Black and Indigenous people and used the wealth he accrued from their exploitation to fund the university,")[16] passed various policies to restrict Black people from attending their medical schools, creating numerous barriers to admission, and even banning Black students from interning in Canadian hospitals, which meant Black students, should they somehow manage to be accepted, had to complete this important part of their training in the United States.

More broadly, discrimination against Black people extended to housing and home ownership (restricting where Black people could live or own a home or land); they were forbidden by law to buy or rent homes in neighbourhoods of their choice. Common in the early twentieth century in Vancouver, for example, were land titles with covenant clauses to prevent the sale or rental of property to Black people and other racialized groups. Deeds dating back to at least 1928 and as late as 1965 stated,

> That the Grantee or his heirs, administrators, executor, successors or assigns will not sell to, agree to sell to, rent to, lease to, or permit or allow to occupy, the said lands and premise, or any part thereof, any person of Chinese, Japanese or other Asiatic race or to any Indian or Negro.[17]

And of course, Black people and other racialized groups aspiring to professional careers (even if they had been able to secure credentials) like medicine, finance, and law, faced similar targeted discrimination.

---

15 *Ibid.*

16 "Erased by the administration: James McGill was a slave owner" by Sepideh Afshar, *McGill Tribune*, February 18, 2020. mcgilltribune.com/opinion/erased-by-the-administration-james-mcgill-was-a-slave-owner-18022020

17 "Racial Segregation of People in Canada." *The Aeolian*, October 8, 2020. aeolianhall.ca/racial-segregation-of-people-in-canada-housing-and-employment

∞

The attitudes of leaders, past and present, often determine how a society treats its people. In 1910, Prime Minister Sir Wilfrid Laurier made clear his perspective on Black people in Canada in this pronouncement: "We see in the United States what grave problems may arise from the presence of a race unable to become full members of the same social family as ourselves."[18] This positioning of the white race as superior to all others is the kind of white supremacist attitude that remains at the root of Canada's systemic racism today. In this example, the most powerful person in the country has pronounced to all non-whites that they have no future in his nation simply because of the colour of their skin. If you, as a Black person, heard this kind of rhetoric from the leader of your nation, how would you develop a sense of self-esteem, let alone a desire to achieve?

In 1911, as part of an effort to limit the immigration of Black people to Canada, Prime Minister Laurier passed an Order-in-Council that effectively banned Black people from entering the country for an entire year, because "the Negro race...is deemed unsuitable to the climate and requirements of Canada."[19] The order, which passed in August 1911 and was repealed in October of that year (it was never put into effect), along with other forms of harassment and fear tactics during that era, kept many Black people away from Canada.

But some would not be dissuaded, believing they could forge a new and better life here despite the obstacles. Between the years 1908 and 1912, over one thousand Black people migrated north from Oklahoma, escaping the segregationist policies of the state, and settling in Saskatchewan and Alberta.[20] These Black pioneers (many of them farmers) also became cowboys and contributed as early settlers—yet their story has been largely forgotten until just recently.

The man responsible for enforcing Canada's immigration policies at the time was Superintendent of Immigration W. D. Scott, who made his white supremacist views crystal clear:

> The negro problem, which faces the United States is one which Canadians have no desire to share. It is to be hoped that climatic conditions will prove unsatisfactory to those new settlers, and that fertile lands of the West [Canada] will be left to be cultivated by the white race only.[21]

18 Excerpt from *Racial Discrimination in Canada, the Black Experience* by James W. St. G. Walker. The Canadian Historical Association, Historical Booklet No. 41, 1985.
19 "Order-in-Council P.C. 1911-1324—the Proposed Ban on Black Immigration to Canada" by Eli Yarhi, *The Canadian Encyclopedia*, September 30, 2016. thecanadianencyclopedia.ca/en/article/order-in-council-pc-1911-1324-the-proposed-ban-on-black-immigration-to-canada
20 "Diplomatic Racism: Canadian Government and Black Migration from Oklahoma, 1905–1912" by R. Bruce Shepard, *Great Plains Quarterly*, 3.1: Winter 1983: University of Nebraska Press.
21 Excerpt from *Racial Discrimination in Canada, the Black Experience* by James W. St. G. Walker. The Canadian Historical Association, Historical Booklet No. 41, 1985.

Soon after, in August 1914, Canada entered the Great War. Despite the institutional segregation and daily discrimination they were forced to endure on home soil, Black Canadian men, like their American cousins, felt a responsibility to fight for the country they called home. But before they could join the fight in Europe, Black Canadians first had to fight to for the right to enlist in what was dubbed the "white man's war."[22] Though Black men were willing to die for their country, the Canadian military still denied them. This April 1916 quote from Major-General W. G. Gwatkin, chief of the general staff of the Canadian militia, says it all:

> The civilized negro is vain and imitative: in Canada he is not impelled to enlist by a high sense of duty; in the trenches he is not likely to make a good fighter; and the average white man will not associate with him on terms of equality.[23]

Despite pushback from military leaders and a desperate need for soldiers, Black men would eventually be permitted to fight alongside white soldiers in the First World War. The first large Black military unit in Canadian history, the No. 2 Construction Battalion, known now as the "Black Battalion," was formed in Pictou, Nova Scotia, on July 5, 1916. They were tasked with non-combat support roles and hard labour, including building roads, railway tracks, and bridges, defusing land mines, removing the wounded from the battlefield, and digging and building trenches. Despite facing continued discrimination throughout the war, they served with distinction in France.

When white soldiers returned home from the war, they were honoured as heroes, but the Black soldiers from No. 2 Battalion would not be properly recognized for their service until 1982[24] after much lobbying by Senator Calvin Ruck,[25] a long-time civil rights activist in Nova Scotia and only the third Black man ever appointed to the Senate. I would venture to guess that most Canadians today have little to no knowledge of the military sacrifice made by Black people in this country—whether during the First or Second World War, or going all the way back to 1812—when Black men fought for the British. I myself only became aware of this rich history during my research for this book.

---

[22] "'They fought to fight': How Black Canadians battled racism to serve the country" by Maham Abidi, *Global News*, November 11, 2019. globalnews.ca/news/6147380/black-canadians-soldiers-world-war-racism

[23] Excerpt from *Racial Discrimination in Canada, the Black Experience* by James W. St. G. Walker. The Canadian Historical Association, Historical Booklet No. 41, 1985.

[24] "'They fought to fight': How Black Canadians battled racism to serve the country" by Maham Abidi, *Global News*, November 11, 2019. globalnews.ca/news/6147380/black-canadians-soldiers-world-war-racism

[25] "Calvin Ruck" by Niko Block, *The Canadian Encyclopedia*, March 10, 2021. thecanadianencyclopedia.ca/en/article/calvin-ruck

As in the United States, Black people in Canada continued to push forward on all fronts to create new opportunities for themselves and their families within a society that worked incredibly hard to keep them disadvantaged—in many cases, via discriminatory policies and laws shored up by the power of the court system. In James W. St. G. Walker's revealing 1985 book, he lays bare the truth about Canada's racist history: "Racial discrimination was not contrary to Canadian law," he says. This was exemplified, he explains, by the "Supreme Court of Canada's 1940 judgement that found no fault with the Montréal Forum tavern for refusing to serve a black man."[26] The ruling had disastrous ripple effects, in that it allowed private businesses to discriminate in the name of *freedom of commerce*.

Here's what happened: on a summer evening in 1936, Fred Christie, a Black immigrant from Jamaica, and two friends (one Black and the other a white French Canadian) had gone to the York Tavern, which was attached to the Montréal Forum. As a season ticket holder, Christie had visited the venue before without issue. This time, however, staff refused to serve the three men because Christie was Black. Christie sued, taking his case all the way to the Supreme Court of Canada, which ruled that the York Tavern was within its rights to refuse to serve people based on race.

In its majority ruling, the justices noted that "in refusing to sell beer to [Christie], the [York's] employees did so quietly, politely and without causing any scene or commotion whatsoever."[27] If there was blame for the unfortunate events, Justice Rinfret claimed, it lay squarely on Christie's shoulders, since he "persisted in demanding beer after he had been so refused and went to the length of calling the police, which was entirely unwarranted by the circumstances."[28] This case remains a perfect example of state-sanctioned discrimination in Canada, where, once again, the blame for systemic racism was placed squarely on the victim. It wasn't until 1975, nine years after I was born, that Québec enacted its Charter of Human Rights and Freedoms, which finally prevented taverns from discriminating on the basis of race.

Having been refused opportunity and excluded from participation in institutions controlled by the white majority for centuries, many Black people began to create their own institutions—schools, churches, and businesses—within their own communities across North America. This began in the late 1800s and continued as Jim Crow laws spread in America. Sadly, discriminatory

---

[26] Excerpt from *Racial Discrimination in Canada, the Black Experience* by James W. St. G. Walker. The Canadian Historical Association, Historical Booklet No. 41, 1985.

[27] "Fred Christie Case" by Eric Adams, *The Canadian Encyclopedia*, April 5, 2018. thecanadianencyclopedia.ca/en/article/fred-christie-case

[28] *Ibid.*

policies and exclusions were upheld in Canada through much of the twentieth century. Perhaps the most well-known is that of Viola Desmond.

Viola Desmond was a successful Black entrepreneur from Halifax, Nova Scotia, who had studied to become a professional beautician and owned her own salon, Vi's Studio of Beauty Culture. She eventually opened the Desmond School of Beauty Culture to mentor young woman.[29] In 1946, after purchasing a movie ticket and taking a seat, she was removed from the Roseland Theatre in New Glasgow for sitting in a whites-only section. Existing laws were used to sanction her for breaking the unwritten rules of segregation.

Ms. Desmond was charged with tax evasion for failing to pay the full tax on a main-floor movie ticket—a difference that amounted to *one cent*. After her release from jail, she unsuccessfully fought the charges all the way to the Supreme Court of Canada. Ms. Desmond was no stranger to discrimination; she had not been allowed to attend the beauty school in Nova Scotia because she was Black, and so had received her training in Montréal and the United States. She was successful in spite of the systemic racism that pervaded Nova Scotia and Canada, but she would not see true justice for her arrest in her lifetime. She passed away in New York in 1965.

On April 15, 2010, the first Black Lieutenant-Governor of Nova Scotia, The Honorable Mayann Francis, granted Desmond a posthumous free pardon, the first ever to be granted in Canada. In 2018, Viola Desmond became the first Canadian woman, and the first person of colour, to have her face on Canadian currency. That same year, Canada named her a National Historic Person. It is safe to say that only now, over half a century since her death, Viola Desmond is being truly recognized for the role she played in challenging systemic anti-Black racism.

∞

As unaware and unknowledgeable as many Canadians are about our country's history of anti-Black racism, the legacy of racist policies against other racialized communities has also remained in the shadows of mainstream history. When I started digging, it seemed there was no end to the examples I could find. One of the most egregious was the story of Canada's treatment of the Chinese in the late nineteenth century.

In the early 1880s, Canada turned to Chinese workers for cheap labour, most famously to complete some of the western sections of the Canadian Pacific Railway, noted to be the "most dangerous and difficult."[30] Thousands of Chinese had come to Canada looking for opportunity and to escape the

---

[29] "Viola Desmond" by Russell Bingham, *The Canadian Encyclopedia*, January 27, 2013.
[30] "Legacy of Hate: Chinese immigrants encounter prejudice and violence as they settled in Canada," *Canada: A People's History*, CBC. cbc.ca/history/EPISCONTENTSE1EP11CH3PA3LE.html

impacts of economic downturns and political change in their home country—a large majority arrived from the port city of Guangzhou—while others came up from California, having being lured there by the gold rush. In total, more than fifteen thousand Chinese railway workers were brought to Canada that decade to lay the CPR tracks through the Rocky Mountains.[51]

Before I started writing this book, I knew very little about nineteenth- and twentieth-century Chinese Canadian history. It was never taught to us in school. My only real basis for understanding the connection between the Chinese and Canada's national railway came from watching a *Heritage Minute* on the subject, a sixty-second video produced by not-for-profit Historica Canada and released in 1992 that describes how Chinese workers were used to dynamite tunnels to make way for the railroad, taking on extra risk for extra pay. The narrator of the story, a grandfather telling his personal story to his grandchildren, conveys the most poignant moment of the story when he tells them, "They say there is one dead Chinese man for every mile of the track."

Once Chinese labour was no longer needed, the Canadian government instituted policies intended to marginalize the growing community of nearly fifteen thousand Chinese immigrants, disadvantaging the former railway workers and their families in every manner possible, including restricting their access to top-tier jobs in medicine and law, and preventing them from applying for government jobs or exercising the right to vote. In 1885, in an attempt to limit further Chinese immigration—which was occurring at a rate of about four thousand per year—the Canadian government introduced the Chinese Immigration Act and enacted an ever-increasing head tax for every Chinese immigrant entering Canada—a policy that lasted until 1923 and that, at its height, amounted to $500 per person ($7,500 today).

The head tax was removed with the passing of the Chinese Exclusion Act in 1923, which banned all Chinese immigrants from entering Canada until its repeal in 1947. (Total restrictions on immigration to Canada based on race, however, would not be fully repealed until 1967.) It's estimated that thousands of Chinese families were able to reunite in Canada after 1947, some of whom hadn't seen each other in over twenty-five years.

We were reminded during the COVID-19 pandemic that bias and prejudice against American and Canadian citizens of Chinese heritage still exists in certain corners of civil society. In 2020, there were some who wanted to blame China—and, by association, any East Asian person—for the spread of COVID around the world. Many took out their pandemic-related frustration and anger on those of Chinese heritage, using a variety of harassment tactics, including

---

[51] "History of Canada's early Chinese immigrants." *Library and Archives Canada*, April 19, 2017. bac-lac.gc.ca/eng/discover/immigration/history-ethnic-cultural/early-chinese-canadians/Pages/history.aspx

violence. In fact, according to a 2021 study from the Center for the Study of Hate and Extremism at California State University, San Bernardino, the rate of hate crimes against Asians in sixteen of the largest cities in America rose by 164 percent between 2020 and 2021.[32] This particular flame was fanned in part by President Donald Trump, who repeatedly and publicly referred to COVID-19 as the "Chinese Virus" throughout the early days of the pandemic.

At a time when we really needed to come together as a society to battle a common enemy (the virus), these racist attitudes only served to further divide us, adding yet another dimension to the discourse on systemic racism that had been sparked by the Black Lives Matter movement and the George Floyd murder.

Digging even deeper into history, the stories of South Asian discrimination provided even more context to Canada's challenges with race.

∞

In May 1914 the *Komagata Maru* arrived in Vancouver, British Columbia, with 376 passengers from India—mostly Sikh men as well as a few women and children. A Singaporean businessman, Baba Gurdit Singh, had privately chartered the vessel. While aware that Punjabis were not welcome to immigrate to Canada at the time, he "wanted to challenge the continuous journey regulation with the hope of opening the door for immigration from India to Canada."[33]

An estimated five thousand South Asians had previously settled and built a community in Vancouver, so the passengers hoped to begin their new lives there. Before they could dock, local authorities used all kinds of legal tactics as well as force to stop the passengers from even stepping off the ship. In what would become a standoff of over two months, passengers nearly starved to death as the ship languished in the harbour. The ship was finally forcefully taken by police, the military, and customs officers and ordered to return to India.

Upon arrival in India, the exhausted passengers were met by British authorities who accused them of rebellion against the Commonwealth. A riot ensued, during which more than twenty passengers were shot and killed and many others imprisoned. In Canada, immigration discrimination targeting South Asians (through eligibility quotas and voting rights restrictions, for example) would not be removed until 1967. In 2016, 102 years after the incident, Prime Minister Justin Trudeau offered a full apology in the House of Commons on behalf of the Government of Canada. He said, in part:

---

[32] "Anti-Asian hate crimes surged in early 2021, study says" by Josh Campbell, *CNN News*, May 5, 2021. cnn.com/2021/05/05/us/anti-asian-hate-crimes-study/index.html

[33] "Komagata Maru" by Hugh Johnston, *The Canadian Encyclopedia*, August 31, 2021. thecanadianencyclopedia.ca/en/article/komagata-maru

The passengers of the *Komagata Maru*, like millions of immigrants to Canada since, were seeking refuge and better lives for their families. With so much to contribute to their new home, they chose Canada and we failed them utterly. As a nation, we should never forget the prejudice suffered by the Sikh community at the hands of the Canadian government of the day. We should not and we will not.[34]

In 1942, less than thirty years after the *Komagata Maru* incident, and following the bombing of Pearl Harbor by the Japanese military on December 7, 1941—the event that pushed the US to declare war on Japan—the Canadian government began the process of detaining and repossessing the homes and businesses, including more than twelve hundred fishing boats, of more than twenty-two thousand Japanese Canadians living in the province of British Columbia. These Canadian citizens were seen by the white Canadians who ran the government as enemies of the state. Within mere days of America's declaration of war against Japan, the Canadian Pacific Railway fired every single Japanese Canadian employee. Other industries would soon follow. The government went so far as to confiscate radios from Japanese Canadians, out of fear they would be used for illegal communication. In 1943, the Government of Canada would sell all the seized property without the owners' consent.

Japanese Canadians were uprooted from their homes. Many were separated from their families and sent to livestock-processing barns in Vancouver's Hastings Park to be photographed and documented before being sent to "camps" throughout the province's interior, where they were detained legally under the War Measures Act. To add insult to injury, detainees were made to work at the camps to pay for the cost of their own internment. To remain together, some families offered to leave the province, taking work in Alberta and Manitoba on sugar beet farms. However, "those who resisted and challenged the orders of the Canadian government were rounded up by the RCMP and incarcerated in a barbed-wire prisoner-of-war camp in Angler, Ontario." [35]

David Suzuki, a second-generation Japanese Canadian and one of Canada's pre-eminent science broadcasters and environmental activists, was sent to an internment camp with his two siblings and parents when he was six years old. He recounts how his family—all of whom were born in Canada—were dispossessed of their home, their small dry-cleaning business, and their rights, and then sent to an internment camp in interior British Columbia. In his later

---

[34] *Ibid.*

[35] "Internment and Redress: The Japanese Canadian Experience" by Masako Fukawa, *Japanesecanadianhistory.net.* japanesecanadianhistory.net/wp-content/uploads/2018/02/Secondary-Guide-Complete.pdf

years, he reflected in a video produced by Library and Archives Canada on how Canada had failed to live up to its democratic ideals.

> I became deeply disturbed that Canada boasts of being a democracy and guaranteeing freedom of movement and speech and treating all Canadians as equals...It's easy to talk about all of our grand ideals and what we guarantee when times are easy; it's only when times are tough that those ideals are very, very important. If you can't guarantee those ideals when times are tough, what's the point of having such ideals? If we can't live up to those ideals of equality and freedom for all, then we simply have no right to call ourselves a democracy.[36]

Ian Mackenzie, Deputy Prime Minister of Canada during the Second World War under Prime Minister Mackenzie King, pandered to anti-Japanese sentiment in British Columbia. At his 1944 nomination meeting, he declared to his constituents: "Let our slogan be for British Columbia: 'No Japs from the Rockies to the seas.'"[37] As British Columbia's senior cabinet minister, Mackenzie would have a key role in the government's decision to inter Japanese Canadians for the duration of the war. It was not his first act of racist policy.

Earlier in his political career as a Member of the Legislative Assembly of British Columbia in 1922, Mackenzie won unanimous approval for a motion to amend the British North America Act (the precursor to Canada's constitution), permitting the province to deny Asians the right to acquire property or engage in provincial industries. "Economically," he asserted, "we cannot compete with them; racially we cannot assimilate them; hence we must exclude them from our midst, and prohibit them from owning land."[38] Two years later, Mackenzie urged Ottawa to halt Japanese immigration in order "to guarantee a white red-blooded Canada."[39]

At the war's end in 1945, the Canadian government gave Japanese Canadians the choice to be deported to Japan—which, for many, as first- or second-generation Canadians, was a foreign land they had never visited—or to be relocated east of the Rocky Mountains. Not until 1949 would Japanese Canadians be reinstated as full citizens, allowed to vote and to move back to British Columbia if they chose to do so. Interestingly, of the tens of thousands of Japanese

---

[36] "In Reflection" by David Suzuki. youtube.com/watch?v=WWdPN0pI1ig

[37] "Japanese Interment: British Columbia wages war against Japanese Canadians." *Canada: A People's History*, CBC. cbc.ca/history/EPISCONTENTSE1EP14CH3PA3LE.html

[38] "MACKENZIE (McKenzie), IAN ALISTAIR (John Alexander)" by Patricia E. Roy and Peter Neary. *Dictionary of Canadian Biography*, vol. 17, University of Toronto/Université Laval, 2003. biographi.ca/en/bio/mackenzie_ian_alistair_17E.html.

[39] *Ibid.*

Canadians detained, "not one was ever charged with an act of disloyalty."[40]

In 1988, more than forty years after the internment camps were closed, the Government of Canada formally apologized to Japanese Canadians for their unjust forced internment and announced reparations of $21,000 for each of the thirteen thousand surviving victims, plus an additional $36 million to fund community programs and establish a race-relations foundation. Just months earlier, the US government had apologized to more than one hundred and twenty thousand Japanese Americans, announcing the Japanese-American Internment Compensation Bill, admitting the mistake, acknowledging Japanese Americans' loyalty to their country (many served in the US military during the Second World War), and offering restitution of USD $20,000 each. President Regan spoke of the need to restore honour and reaffirm "Equal justice under the law."

∞

When it comes to Canada's most pervasive, long-standing mythologies, the whitewashed narrative of Indigenous peoples is its most disgraceful. Having been educated in the 1970s and '80s, my foundational understanding of Indigenous peoples in Canada was rooted in purposeful deception, obfuscation, a blatant disregard for the truth, and a lack of acknowledgement of the true cultures and histories of the peoples who had lived in this part of the world since time immemorial.

What I learned can be summed up like this: Europeans discovered North America and encountered "savages." They traded with them (admitting they took advantage by exchanging worthless trinkets in exchange for valuable land and furs), learned from them how to survive on the land (the original inhabitants shared their knowledge of hunting, farming, portaging in canoes and more), used them to help fight wars against their enemies (noting that the savages were fierce warriors), and, eventually, generously provided these original inhabitants with reservations—land on which they could continue to live their less-civilized lives amongst their own. We were taught about how treaties had been negotiated—with the inference that they were fair, mutually beneficial, and agreed to freely by Indigenous peoples—to allow for trade, hunting, fishing, and settlement by the ever-growing European settler population.

We were also taught about of some of the infamous "warrior tribes" that inhabited central Canada, like the Mohawk and Iroquois, and the clothing they wore (moccasins, headdresses made of feathers), the weapons they used (bow and arrow and tomahawk), and even their practice of scalping. I also

----

40 "Government apologizes to Japanese Canadians in 1988." CBC Archives. cbc.ca/archives/government-apologizes-to-japanese-canadians-in-1988-1.4680546

remember learning about Louis Riel, the nineteenth-century Métis leader, the narrative being that, in the words of Sterling Lyon, who became the premier of Manitoba in 1977, "he was a traitor and deserved to hang."[41]

And of course we were taught the basics about the "Eskimos" in Canada's North—now legally and respectfully referred to as the Inuit—and how they hunted seals and polar bears, had sleds pulled by dogs, and built igloos to live in. I remember being mesmerized by the old National Film Board videos we watched in the school gymnasium on occasion, including *Tuktu and the Snow Palace* (1967), which depicted an Inuit community's nomadic life in the North—including the construction of an igloo!—a life so foreign to me it could have been from another planet.

Does this sound familiar?

Like millions of other schoolchildren in the nineteenth and twentieth centuries, I had been fed the dominant version of history: the Euro-centric, white version of Indigenous History on the North American Continent. I was also influenced by what I consumed on TV and at the movie theatre—especially the depiction of Native Americans. Indigenous peoples were portrayed by the Hollywood propaganda machine as savages: uncivilized, uneducated, bloodthirsty, violent people looking to kill all white men and rape and steal their women. The white hero, a toxically masculine cowboy depicted by actors like John Wayne, came to the rescue with the cavalry behind him, ready to squash the Indian threat and save the day. As it turns out, most of the history we were taught was from an uneducated, ignorant, and racist perspective that largely ignored the rich history and contributions of Indigenous peoples and, most egregiously, omitted the many injustices and damages inflicted upon them for centuries by European settlers.

When I moved to British Columbia in 1979 at the age of thirteen, it was the first time I witnessed Indigenous traditions first-hand—most notably the amazing art created by the many First Nations in the region, including the Haida. It was all around us, in the amazing totem poles in Beacon Hill Park, in Emily Carr's paintings, in the intricate carved mask at the Royal British Columbia Museum, and in beautifully patterned fabric art like the world-famous Cowichan sweaters. Before then, I had no idea these creative expressions by Indigenous peoples in Canada even existed.

Beginning in my high-school years, when I began to pay more attention to the world around me, people often openly expressed how they were tired of

---

[41] "Louis Reil's trial from 135 years ago continues today with competing cultural stories" by Alberta Braz, *The Conversation*, June 16, 2020. theconversation.com/louis-riels-trial-from-135-years-ago-continues-today-with-competing-cultural-stories-and-icons-133049 https://theconversation.com/louis-riels-trial-from-135-years-ago-continues-today-with-competing-cultural-stories-and-icons-133049

hearing "Indians" complain about Canada. "They don't even have to pay taxes"; "We give them money for nothing"; "We pay for them to go to school." At that time, I didn't know whether what they were saying was accurate or not, and I didn't take the time to dig deeper to uncover the truth. It turns out it was a lot of nonsense, rooted in a lack of knowledge or understanding.

For most of my twenties and thirties, I had been singularly focused on my career. I lived and worked abroad for nearly a decade, including stints in Seville, Spain, Brisbane, Australia, Kingston, Jamaica, and Seattle, Washington—with little time spent thinking more deeply about the societal challenges affecting Canada. Everything changed in 2008 when, at the age of forty (two years following my return to Canada from Seattle, where I'd lived and worked for six years), I was selected to participate in the Governor General's Canadian Leadership Conference (GGCLC). The goal of this quadrennial conference is to bring together "Canada's emerging leaders from business, labour, government, NGOs, education, and the cultural sector" with the goal of "broadening their perspectives on work, leadership, their communities, and their country."[42]

The two-week event included a two-day kick off plenary in Banff, Alberta. Participants were then divided into study groups of about fifteen and sent to all corners of Canada to experience and observe community-based leadership. I was lucky to be awarded my number-one choice: the Yukon—a territory I had never visited before. I was driven by an interest in better understanding the Canadian North and learning more about the Indigenous nations in the region. After ten days in the field, all participants would fly to Ottawa for a two-day closing plenary, where we would present our observations to fellow conference participants, the chair, and the Governor General of Canada, who at that time was Michaëlle Jean, the first ever Black person to hold this position.

I was excited for the opening plenary because it was in the amazingly beautiful town of Banff, but also because of the incredible lineup of scheduled speakers: Rick George, Suncor CEO and the conference chair (who sadly passed away too young in 2017); Michaëlle Jean; Jim Balsillie, the then high-flying CEO of Research In Motion (BlackBerry); Ms. Hanson Chan, a member of the Legislative Council of Hong Kong; Dr. David Foot, the celebrated economist and author of *Boom, Bust & Echo*; former Premier of Alberta Peter Lougheed (with whom I'd have a great chat about Pierre Trudeau); Sheila Watt-Cloutier, a Nobel Peace Prize–nominated Inuit environmental activist, and several others. But of all the presentations, it was the address by Phil Fontaine, then Chief of the Assembly of First Nations, a national advocacy organization representing more than 900,000 people from 634 First Nations in Canada, that would have the most profound impact on me.

Chief Fontaine began his speech by acknowledging he had been invited to

---

[42] *The Governor General's Leadership Conference.* leadershipcanada.ca

speak to us about leadership but had decided that instead, he was going to share with us his personal residential school story. I knew a little about residential schools only because in just a few days (June 11), the Government of Canada was scheduled to formally apologize to Indigenous peoples for the country's Indian Residential School system, and its enduring painful and tragic legacy.

Chief Fontaine began his story, taking us back to his youth, which he spent in Sagkeeng First Nation on the Fort Alexander Reserve in Manitoba. You could sense that something heavy was coming. The room of around three hundred people went silent. Back in 1990, in a CBC interview with Barbara Frum, Chief Fountain had provided some details of the physical, psychological, and sexual abuse he and his classmates had experienced at the Fort Alexander Residential School. But this would be the first time he would go into such detail publicly, and the first time I would bear witness to such a testimony.[43]

As Chief Fontaine revealed his traumatic experience, I felt tears streaming down my face. I was overcome with sadness. It was a devastating and horrific story—one which stirred deep seeded memories of my own. Near the end of his testimonial, he told us that this abuse against Indigenous children had gone on for over two hundred years, that it had only ended in the late twentieth century. When I heard those words, the sadness I felt turned to shame and anger. I felt an overwhelming need to leave the room. I walked out of the hall and into the dark Banff night. It was unusually cold for early June, and the crisp air acted as kind of a buffer, keeping me from exploding in rage.

I was ashamed. I'd always thought of myself as someone who walked through life in a state of awareness, someone who soaked up knowledge and had a deep love of history. How could I have missed this? How could our government and educators have kept this truth from us? I thought back on my world travels as a young man, when I'd proudly displayed the Canadian flag on my backpack, a cheerleader promoting the greatness of my country. I recalled many conversations from decades earlier. In 1988, when working and living in Australia, I'd often explained to my Australian friends how much better we treated *our* Indigenous people compared to how they treated the Aborigines. How we gave them money to build their communities, how we paid for their education, and how our laws freed them from having to pay taxes. I'd regurgitated the dribble that had been fed to me in school, and by the Canadian government.

What I was just now starting to understand, standing outside the room in which Chief Fontaine had told us his devastating truth, was that much of what we'd been taught was a smoke screen; behind it were centuries of broken promises, outright discrimination, and attempted genocide. My anger was

---

43 "Phil Fontaine's Shocking History of Physical and Sexual Abuse." CBC Digital Archives. cbc.ca/archives/entry/phil-fontaines-shocking-testimony-of-sexual-abuse

focused on Canadian leaders who for generations had a hand in discriminatory policies and laws that sanctioned the abuse so many Indigenous people
had suffered. I was angry at all those who preached the virtues of religion but
instead used their "God-given" moral authority to inflict such cruelty upon
other human beings—particularly vulnerable children who were taken by
force from their families.

I took some time to compose myself outside as best as I could, and rejoined
the conference. That evening, I had the privilege to meet and have a chat
with Chief Fontaine at the beautiful Stoney Nakoda Resort. I thanked him
for sharing something so deeply personal with all of us and let him know
that his story had had a profound impact on me. I promised to learn more
about the issues affecting Indigenous peoples and to do my part as an ally.
What struck me most about Chief Fontaine was how approachable he was;
how comfortable he was around people. He had managed to overcome the
darkness of his past to become an inspirational leader to his people and to
those Canadians who were open to learning and understanding.

The next day, still fresh from Chief Fontaine's profoundly moving speech,
my study-group colleagues and I flew to the Yukon, landing in the territorial
capital of Whitehorse. Our first working session early the next morning was
at the Yukon legislature, attended by officials and members of the media. We
sat facing a panel of four people, one of whom was an Indigenous woman. Our
host welcomed us and noted he wanted to introduce a special guest. Millie, an
Elder of the Selkirk First Nation, had contacted him the day before and asked
to join the meeting. She had heard some "important" people were coming,
and she had a message she wanted to share with us.

Millie spoke softly but with intent. She began by telling us that, just the
day before, her brother had died. He had recently received a big cheque, the
latest installment in the broader self-government agreement (SGA) that had
been reached between federal and provincial governments and the Selkirk
First Nation in 1997.[44] Millie and her brother were survivors of residential
schools. He had turned to alcohol to deal with the demons that continued to
torment him, and ultimately his drinking led to his death.

Millie described the widespread depression that settles into her community
each year as the leaves turn and the geese fly south, for that is when, in her
words, "me and the other children were rounded up in cattle trucks and taken
away." She went on to describe how military-style trucks would come to take
the children away to residential school, and how parents and Elders had no
way to stop it from happening. Many would never see their children again. It
was a heartbreaking story, and again I found myself in tears.

---

[44] At the time of writing, eleven of the fourteen First Nations in the Yukon have successfully negotiated SGAs.

Imagine if instead of the happy first day of school that most parents experience each year, cattle trucks rolled down the streets of your neighbourhood and armed law enforcement officers snatched up all the kids and took them away—leaving you there with no legal right to stop them. It's not hard to imagine how this would cause irreparable harm to the mental health of those parents and to an entire community.

That's what happened to more than 150,000 Indigenous families over a century. That feeling of loss and helplessness has had profound negative effects for many generations. To help us understand, Millie spoke of the Indigenous philosophy of the Seven Generations, which underscores how decisions made today—the good and the bad—will have an impact seven generations into the future. She used this philosophy to explain how the traumatic past experiences of her people continue to negatively impact them today. And finally, despite the injustices they have suffered, Millie ended by speaking of forgiveness and the need to get her people well again.

Millie's powerful personal testimony had a profound impact on our journey through the Yukon. We thought of her often over the next ten days as we engaged with other Indigenous peoples across the magnificent territory. The truths shared by Chief Fontaine and Millie did more to help me better understand the challenges facing First Nations than any textbook ever had.

But what happens when the history of this country, as written by colonizers, is built into the physical landscape? Street names, statues, monuments, memorials to the white men whose names are found in every corner of Canada are a constant reminder that their crimes, no matter how heinous, do not overshadow their contributions to the story that is Canada. Recently, there have been calls by BIPOC leaders and allies to remove monuments erected in honour of Canadian leaders whose actions, taken in the name of colonialism, attempted to eradicate racialized communities. Some called for the statue of Egerton Ryerson (one of the primary architects of Canada's residential school system) to be removed from the Ryerson University's main campus. It was eventually toppled by protesters in June 2021, and the university is currently undergoing an official renaming process. Others argued for the removal of the many statues across Canada dedicated to the memory of Sir John A. Macdonald, Canada's first prime minister, a vocal white supremacist who unleashed the full power of his government in an attempt to wipe Indigenous peoples from their traditional lands.

Macdonald, too, was an architect of the Indian Residential School system in Canada. He championed aggressive policies to remove Indigenous peoples from their lands to make way for European settlers and for the cross-country railroad, relegating them to small plots of undesirable land the government called "reserves." He legalized the arrest of Indigenous peoples caught off reservations without permission, claiming, "We have been pampering and coaxing the Indians...we must take a new course, we must vindicate the position of the white man, we must teach the Indians what law is."[45]

For the Plains First Nations peoples living on the Canadian prairie, life became even more arduous with the near-complete decimation of the bison population. A primary food source, bison also provided materials for clothing and shelter, but the local population had been over-hunted by white settlers on both sides of the border. The decimation of the Indigenous population on the plains was also accentuated by the spread of European diseases like smallpox, brought to their lands by colonial settlers.

Macdonald saw this unfortunate situation as an opportunity. The Canadian government would "starve Indigenous communities in order to forcibly relocate them onto squalid reserves overseen by dictatorial Indian agents—clearing the plains for settlers."[46] This policy purposefully imposed starvation-level food rationing upon Indigenous peoples who were now dependent of the government for food because they could no long farm or hunt, forcing them into signing treaties with unfavourable terms. But Macdonald clearly was in charge, and therefore in control of the narrative. In 1882, MacDonald told the House of Commons, "I have reason to believe that the agents as a whole... are doing all they can, by refusing food until the Indians are on the verge of starvation, to reduce the expense."[47]

For centuries, Indigenous peoples have been victimized by the Canadian government through treaties signed and breached, oppressive, genocidal policies (made law with the passing of the Indian Act in 1867), the institutional attempted genocide of the Indian Residential Schools system, and the pervasive and deeply rooted indifference of law enforcement in relation to Missing and Murdered Indigenous Women and Girls (MMIWG).

It would not be until 2016 that the federal government would establish a commission to thoroughly investigate the systemic MMIWG issue, with a report calling for action tabled in June 2019. The report, *Reclaiming Power and Place*, revealed "persistent and deliberate human and Indigenous rights violations and abuses [as] the root cause behind Canada's staggering rates of

---

[45] "Sir John A Macdonald Fact Sheet" by Social Healing and Reconciliatory Education (SHARE) research group, Queen's University. educ.queensu.ca/sites/webpublish.queensu.ca.educwww/files/files/JAM%20Fact%20Sheet.pdf

[46] "Here is what Sir John A. Macdonald did to Indigenous people" by Tristan Hopper. *The National Post*, August 28, 2018. nationalpost.com/news/canada/here-is-what-sir-john-a-macdonald-did-to-indigenous-people

[47] *Ibid.*

violence against Indigenous women, girls."[48] In June 2021, the government finally announced a path forward—albeit, a thin list of short-term priorities, which many critics decry as being "too broad, with no dollars attached and no clear timelines—to address the 231 recommendations detailed in the report."[49] Disappointing, to say the least. Potentially fatal, if you are an Indigenous woman or girl in this country.

One can draw a clear line from the legacy of the residential school system to the Sixties Scoop, a period during which "Aboriginal children were seized by child welfare authorities and taken from their homes and placed, in most cases, into middle-class Euro-Canadian families"[50]—some even sent abroad to be adopted. Although this practice didn't begin in the 1960s, this period marked a drastic increase in Indigenous children being adopted out of their communities. It's estimated that twenty thousand Indigenous children were victims of this practice over a period of nearly two decades. The long-term effects are wide-reaching, including loss of cultural identity, cultural alienation, low self-esteem, frustration, and feelings of shame, loneliness, and confusion.

Today, this type of government policy "intervention" continues in a different form. Based on federal government census data from 2016, 7.7 percent of children under age fourteen in Canada are Indigenous, yet 52.2 percent of Indigenous children under fourteen are in foster care. Imagine if more than 50 percent of all white children in Canada and the US were taken from their families and made wards of the government? The white majority would never allow it; if this were the reality for white children, the government would have enacted policies that addressed the root causes. However, rather than look inward, many Canadians find it more comfortable to point to how the United States has mistreated the Native American population. A relentless stream of discriminative state and federal government policies worked to eradicate Native American belief systems, languages, and cultures, while others, like the Indian Removal Act, signed by President Jackson in 1830, were intended to control and, more specifically, eliminate Indians all together.

With the passing of the Indian Removal Act, the American government began forcibly relocating tribes—including members of the Cherokee, Muscogee, Seminole, Chickasaw, and Chocktaw nations—from their traditional territories along the eastern coast to what the US government called Indian Territory: reserved lands in eastern sections of present-day Oklahoma. This

48 *Reclaiming Power and Place: The Final Report of the National Inquiry into Missing and Murdered Indigenous Women and Girls.* National Inquiry Volume 1A. mmiwg-ffada.ca/wp-content/uploads/2019/06/Final_Report_Vol_1a-1.pdf

49 "Long-awaited national action plan on MMIWG falls short, critics say" by Jill Macyshon. *CTV National News*: Manitoba, June 2, 2021. ctvnews.ca/politics/long-awaited-national-action-plan-on-mmiwg-falls-short-critics-say-1.5454171

50 "Sixties Scoop." Indigenous Foundations, UBC. indigenousfoundations.arts.ubc.ca/sixties_scoop

forced relocation, known as the Trail of Tears, is estimated to have resulted in up to six thousand deaths. And lest we forget, over a period of nearly three centuries the American Army was responsible for countless massacres of Native Indian peoples. This is exemplified by the 1864 Sand Creek Massacre in the Colorado Territory, during which Colonel John Chivington led a massacre of at least 150 peaceful Cheyenne and Arapaho, about two-thirds of whom were women, children, and infants. Scalps and other body parts were taken by Chivington and his men as trophies. In defense of his actions Chivington stated,

> Damn any man who sympathizes with Indians!...I have come to kill Indians, and believe it is right and honorable to use any means under God's heaven to kill Indians....Kill and scalp all, big and little; nits make lice.[51]

We cannot ignore the atrocities committed by our neighbours to the south, but as Canada's true history begins to reveal itself in the twenty-first century, we as Canadians must reckon with our own despicable record.

I've heard some Canadians express their concern that we are "cancelling" our history in favour of political correctness. But what we are experiencing is, in fact, a long-overdue redressing of the incomplete history of our nation. If someone is to be revered, for example, for having connected our nation from sea to sea by rail, should they not also be held accountable for the thousands of deaths that occurred as a result of the policies they championed? If a convicted murderer donated $1 billion to charity, would they not still be a murderer? Would they have hospital wing named after them in honour of that donation? Of course not.

History in Canada and the United States has always been written by those with the power—mostly white men who had an agenda to advantage themselves and to ensure their historical legacy. What they didn't count on was that the truth would not stay buried forever. The May 28, 2021, discovery of the unmarked graves in Kamloops provided tangible proof to all Canadians of what Indigenous leaders and residential school survivors have been telling us for years. The cruelty shown to those young souls will never be fully known, their found remains giving us a mere glimpse of the depths to which some will go to satisfy their need for power and control over those who are different than them, and the lengths they will go to in order to bury those truths.

---

[51] "Sand Creek Massacre." *Wikipedia.* wikipedia.org/wiki/Sand_Creek_massacre

It's easy to feel overwhelmed. But to move toward change, Canadians must commit to taking purposeful steps to unlearn the false narrative of "Canada," a story that has been propagated for more than 150 years, and one into which we've all been indoctrinated. We have to let go of the mythology of Canada's history as a safe haven, a welcoming mosaic of multiculturalism. It's due time for us to each acknowledge the truths of our nation's darkest chapters and seek a true and full understanding of the systemic inequality that diminishes the ideals we espouse and threatens our very democracy.

Because there is no Canada without an inclusive history—one that accurately reflects who we truly are as a nation and that sets the foundation for how we move forward positively, together.

Chapter Three

White Advantage

I HAD MANY CONVERSATIONS ABOUT RACE WITH MY WHITE FRIENDS IN 2020. Some wanted to talk about the Black Lives Matter movement and how I felt about its global spread. Was I feeling hopeful? Should they? Others wanted to share their perspectives on, and understanding of, race relations and its impact on them and their families. Some seemed perplexed at the amount of anger and civil unrest—the street marches and the polarizing discourse on social media and among friends and neighbours—while others wondered aloud about the severity of racism in Canada as opposed to the United States. A recuring situation emerged when the topic of "white privilege" was raised: people were defensive. Common refrains like "I've worked hard for everything I have" and "I came from nothing and built my business from the ground up" were enough to show me that we had a communication problem.

It's only in recent years, since the rise of the Black Lives Matter movement, that the term "white privilege" has become common in our lexicon. The term was coined by Peggy McIntosh in her essay "White Privilege: Unpacking the Invisible Knapsack," which first appeared in *Peace and Freedom* magazine in 1989. From her perspective as a white academic, Ms. McIntosh noted fifty "privileges" that "attach somewhat more to skin colour privilege than to class, religion, ethnic status or geographic location,"[1] meaning that each of these privileges represented an instance in which skin colour is the *most important* factor in determining the treatment of individuals. And yet, in North America, the term "privilege" is most often understood to confer *class advantage*, meaning that the higher a person's class status, the more opportunity available to them. A "privileged upbringing" is, therefore, afforded by financial means and through proximity to power and influence. I believe it is this understanding of the concept of *privilege* that prevents many people from recognizing themselves *as* privileged. And because people don't see their own privilege, they tend to push back or become defensive when the term "white privilege" is suddenly attributed to them.

What is really being discussed, though, is what I call "white advantage": racially biased institutional and systemic policies that have given white Cana-

---

[1] "White Privilege: Unpacking the Invisible Knapsack" by Peggy McIntosh, excerpted from *The Heart of Whiteness: Confronting Race, Racism and White Privilege* (City Lights, September 2005). admin.artsci.washington.edu/sites/adming/files/unpacking-invisible-knapsack.pdf

dians (and Americans) unearned advantages at the expense of non-whites. Simply by being white, society advantages you and, in turn, your Blackness or non-whiteness disadvantages you in large and small ways that fundamentally affect your very existence. As former US president John F. Kennedy said in 1963, "The rights of every person are diminished when the rights of one [person] are threatened."

In my efforts to bridge the gap of understanding with the people I engaged with, I shared a simple metaphor to illustrate the reality that Black Canadians have experienced for centuries. Imagine the 100-metre Olympic final. Usain Bolt is still the fastest man in the world, and the field is stacked with seven other world-class racers who are white. Race officials, the majority of whom are also white, and who have the power to make and change the rules, have unilaterally decided to stagger the start in favour of the white athletes. Bolt is set in his blocks at the start line. The rest of the racers are moved up to the 10- to 30-metre lines. The gun goes off. Even the fastest man in the world could not overcome the "advantage" given to the white athletes. And he's a 1-in-7-billion superstar. Such are the real-life inequalities Black Canadians face in nearly every aspect of their lives, including education, job opportunities, and housing—simply because of the colour of their skin.

One of the advantages of whiteness McIntosh details is this: "If I should need to move, I can be pretty sure of renting or purchasing housing in an area which I can afford and in which I would want to live."[2] This is not something most white people have ever had to consider. But for Black people, being turned away or prevented from buying or renting a home in a location of their choice is a much-too-familiar experience. I've lived it myself.

In the early '90s, I moved back to my hometown of Montréal to live with my white girlfriend. We began a search for the perfect apartment. Every day we perused the classifieds, circled places of interest, and set up in-person appointments. Old school. When we showed up to meet the landlord, we'd inevitably be told that the apartment in question had just been rented. After nearly a dozen similar rejections, we finally found a hospitable landlord, but the discrimination we had experienced was difficult to process. I was disappointed but not surprised based on the racism I had faced in my formative years, but for my girlfriend, it was a shocking revelation; this was the first time she had encountered racial discrimination by association.

Today, white advantage continues to be prevalent in our society; it manifests in unearned advantages that many white people are unaware of and find difficult to understand. And because these advantages are ubiquitous, they have been baked into our social institutions—systems built by white people, for white people, to advantage white people. Everywhere I turned in 2020, I

2   *Ibid.*

heard people discussing *systemic anti-Black racism* and observed many white people having difficulty understanding what was really meant by it—or, just as often, not wanting to believe it was real. The irony is that this difficulty to understand, or to believe in, the existence of systemic anti-Black racism is *itself* a symptom of white advantage.

Those who experience white advantage have never had to burden themselves with the work of fully understanding the foundational constructs (many built upon prejudice) of the institutions that guide our society today. But this work is crucial. The white majority's awareness and acknowledgement of these truths is key to progress. It's also important to understand that white advantage resulting from systemic racism is separate from the racist behaviours of individuals. It's easier to point out, and in turn ostracize, individual racists in our midst by shaming them publicly; it's much more difficult for white people to recognize the racism ingrained in the systems of public and private institutions, which is where the greatest harm is rooted.

The most important thing to understand about systemic racism is this: the same systems built to advantage white people, by their very existence, disadvantage Black people. This includes the laws that govern our rights as citizens in our democracy, and the policies and processes that direct our police and judicial systems, our educational, health, and welfare systems, and our workplaces. Some of these inequalities have more severe impacts because of their intergenerational nature, such as the policies that once prevented Black people from aspiring to higher education and professional careers—some of which remained in place well into the second half of the twentieth century.

For example, it wasn't until 1965 that Black students were able to enroll in the Queen's University medical school, a ban enacted in 1918 and not "officially repealed" until 2018. And they were not alone. Medical schools at McGill, Dalhousie, and the University of Toronto also either excluded Black students outright or placed restrictions on their admission."[3] These policies had severe, long-lasting impacts, because even once these discriminatory policies were finally removed, the impact on future generations remains, adding to the seemingly insurmountable generational wealth gap between white and Black people—which, studies show, is just as wide as it was in 1968.[4]

For centuries, Canada and the US have been controlled by white men who have shaped the systems and institutions in ways that advantage themselves. Essentially, it's a club to which only those with white advantage can ever

---

[3]   "When Black medical students weren't welcome at Queen's" by Wendy Glauser, *UniversityAffairs. com*, universityaffairs.ca/features/feature-article/when-black-medical-students-werent-welcome-at-queens

[4]   "The black-white economic divide is as wide as it was in 1968" by Heather Long and Andrew Van Dam, *The Washington Post* online, June 4, 2020. washingtonpost.com/business/2020/06/04/economic-divide-black-households/

belong. Many of these foundational societal systems—from the educational systems that groom young people for the workforce to the private and public workplaces that provide opportunities to achieve financial independence—have, for centuries, been exclusionary to non-white people. These facts are indisputable, but as with climate change, some are prone to disregarding the scientific evidence because it doesn't fit into their ideology, or their view of how society serves *them*. People have been known to twist themselves into knots to confirm their own biases. From a Black perspective, this refusal by many white people to accept the reality that systemic anti-Black racism is real is tantamount to refusing to agree that water is wet: we can see it, we can feel it, it has always been so. It is a problem of perception.

But perhaps this should not be so surprising in an era of "alternative facts." In 2020, we saw many public figures and organizations push back against the reality of systemic anti-Black racism, some finding refuge in the very institutions and systems whose priorities should have been to protect us from inequality, discrimination, and harassment. Police services across North America have been at the centre of this debate. For many white citizens, the police are an institution for good, while in the BIPOC community, which experiences greater instances of police violence and historically has a much higher rate of incarceration, the police are mostly seen as an oppressive and dangerous institution—a reality I will explore in greater depth in Chapter Six.

Perhaps no political figure has been more egregious than Donald Trump, the denier-in-chief, who continued to publicly deny the existence of systemic racism. When asked about the reality of systemic racism in America during a roundtable discussion on public safety in Kenosha, Wisconsin—the site of the recent police shooting of Jacob Blake—he stated simply: "I don't believe that."[5] This is the same president who doubled down on his Make America Great Again mantra, which became a dog whistle to those harkening back to an America that was *only* great for white men. As we know, the past wasn't "great" for members of the LGBTQIA+ community, for women, for Indigenous peoples, or for the millions of Black people enslaved for nearly four hundred years. Knowing the data supported the existence of systemic racism, Trump chose to ignore the massive national protest of the Black Lives Matter movement that saw millions take to the streets across America and around the world.

Other politicians took their cues from Trump's intransigence, including the premier of Québec, François Legault, who, along with his ministers, still refuses to acknowledge the existence of systemic racism in the province. Legault went so far as to suggest that admitting to its existence would be

---

5   "Trump's visit to Kenosha 'not about unifying that community,' NAACP president says" by By Meg Wagner, Mike Hayes and Melissa Macaya, *CNN*, January 18, 2021. edition.cnn.com/us/live-news/kenosha-jacob-blake-09-01-2020/index.html

"an attack against the people of Québec." I wondered which *people* he was referring to. But I could write a whole chapter on Québec—and I have. More on that later.

Loosening the grip on these systemic levers of power has been an ongoing struggle. Generational efforts sparked by the civil rights leaders of the mid–twentieth century continue with today's Black Lives Matter Movement—and they're still fighting for the same things: equality rights (the right to freedom and liberty), access to education and jobs, and protection from a discriminatory criminal justice system and systemically racist police forces. However, there is hope that we have arrived at a moment in history where there is a collective desire for real change.

Of course, some accommodations have been made in the past due to societal pressures and untenable realities, most notably the abolishment of slavery (in 1834 in British North America and in 1865 in the US), and the various minority rights that were enshrined and judicially protected within the Canada's Charter of Rights and Freedoms (Constitution Act of 1982). I have a copy of the Charter proudly displayed on the wall in my office. It is inscribed with a personal note from former Prime Minister Pierre Elliott Trudeau, in response to a letter I wrote him in 1999.

The Charter, of which Trudeau was one of the chief architects, was devised to grant every Canadian equal protection under the law no matter their race, ethnicity, religion, or cultural background. Fundamental to the Charter is the concept that everyone is entitled to the same benefits provided by laws or government policies. Importantly, the Charter also makes accommodations to account for differences, such as race and ethnicity, and law-making that promises equality by improving the conditions of those who have been historically disadvantaged because of those differences. These accommodations are what is what is meant by "equity measures"—changes to the systems that drive our many public and private institutions. In short, the Charter is powerful in its protection of minority rights, which are a cornerstone of modern, progressive democracies. The work that must now be done is the *reform* of the systems guided by the core principle of equality enshrined in the Charter. In many cases, this will require equity measures that work to level the playing field so equality is possible.

Despite the Charter, the institutions in our civil society have not been fundamentally re-engineered to effectively acknowledge or consider the lived experience of non-whites. The same is true in the United States. The US Declaration of Independence of 1776 states: "We hold these truths to be self-evident, that all men are created equal, that they are endowed by their Creator with certain unalienable Rights, that among these are Life, Liberty and the Pursuit of Happiness." We know this declaration of equality did not apply to Black men (and women), who would be deemed property for another century. The space between the ideals of a nation and the reality is where we find ourselves in the twenty-first century.

As many have rightly pointed out, the Charter was not prescriptive about the work needed to make the country's systems and institutions compliant. Instead, we've left it to the courts to reference the Charter when striking down the discrimination and inequality inherent in the country's foundational governmental and institutional policies. It's due time for our government to become more proactive rather than reactive and lead the way in bringing about systemic reform that will lead to greater equality. That sort of leadership will set the tone for change at an institutional level.

An article entitled "Understanding How Racism Becomes Systemic," published in August 2020 noted that "despite the institutional appeal of the 'few bad apples' argument, tragic lone acts of racism seldom occur in a vacuum."[6] This makes sense. Think about it. Back in the *Mad Men* era of the 1950s and '60s (and in some cases, still today), women were openly objectified, sexually harassed, and treated as second-class employees in the workplace. Back then, most institutions allowed this behaviour to continue because there was a consensus amongst the white men in the positions of power that it was okay. Women who were threatened by men in the workplace had to suck it up or face the possibility of having their careers extinguished.

I remember going through sexual harassment training in the early 2000s when I worked for a Seattle-based corporation. The program was mandated in part to limit business risk from potential lawsuits brought by the increasing numbers of women standing up for their rights. The unequal treatment of women in the workplace was untenable, but it only became a workplace "issue" when the male-dominated power structures were threatened by societal change. In today's MeToo era, it's clear that much more work remains to achieve gender equity—from equal representation at the executive level and on boards to pay equity, paid parental leave, and the implementation of non-gender-biased performance reviews. According to a 2020 *Forbes* article, "aggregate gender pay gap for all women is 80 [cents] on the dollar."[7] It's even higher for Black women, at 61 cents on the dollar.

Systemic racism can be viewed through a similar lens. In 2020, anyone with an internet connection was privy to video proof of hospital employees harassing an Indigenous patient in a Québec hospital, seemingly unguarded in their despicable behaviour. It's possible they were racist "bad apples" but the

---

6   "Understanding how racism becomes systemic" by Colleen Sheppard, Tamara Thermitus, and Derek J. Jones, *Inclusive Citizenship and Deliberative Democracy*, August 18, 2020. mcgill.ca/humanrights/article/universal-human-rights/understanding-how-racism-becomes-systemic

7   "A Decade of Gender Equity in Ten Trends" by Katica Roy, *Forbes.com*, February 11, 2020. forbes.com/sites/ellevate/2020/02/11/a-decade-of-gender-equity-in-ten-trends/?sh=3d3daa4231ac

fact that they felt comfortable enough to express themselves openly, without fear of risking their jobs, says a lot about their work environment. From my professional experience, I can't imagine any scenario where I could have walked into a business setting and let fly racist or misogynistic comments without the high likelihood I would immediately be shown the door. But obviously, that's still not the case everywhere. Recent studies reveal that "one in five women and one in five racialized Canadians report pervasive harassment in the workplace".[8]

Tackling systemic racism and broader inequality must begin with a collective acknowledgement that it *actually exists* in our public and private institutions. Only then can we begin the process of dissecting the deeply rooted systemic inequalities in our institutions and engage all willing Canadians in reforms that can deliver the necessary and desired change. In later chapters, I share details on how systemic inequality is pervasive in the health-care, education, and criminal justice systems, and how generational discrimination in the workforce and around property and business ownership has created an unsurmountable generational wealth gap that continues to advantage many white citizens and severely disadvantage those from BIPOC communities.

So yes, some progress has been made, but for racialized communities the reckoning is long overdue. And we have quite a journey ahead to achieve true equality. So now we all need to ask ourselves, in a serious and deliberate manner: what role will we play?

---

8   "Harassment widespread in workplaces, finds Statistics Canada," *Workers Health & Safety Centre*, July 4, 2019. whsc.on.ca/What-s-new/News-Archive/Harassment-widespread-in-work-places-finds-Statistics-Canada

Chapter Four
The Ultimate Betrayal

IN EARLY MARCH 1979, MY FAMILY HEADED WEST FROM MONTRÉAL IN OUR 1977 Oldsmobile Toronado, a big white boat of a car. Our giant trunk was packed with suitcases and my heart was filled with apprehension for what lay ahead: five thousand kilometres of open road, and Victoria, British Columbia.

I remember being amazed at how big Ontario was. It took us nearly three eight-hour days to cross it. Highlights included passing the Big Nickel in Sudbury followed by a stop in Wawa. We were welcomed into town by a giant Canada goose monument, which I learned had been erected to lure tourists off the Trans-Canada highway. It was my thirteenth birthday, March 17, 1979—St. Patrick's Day. We checked into a modest motel (the Wawa Motor Inn, I believe) which had a rustic dining room with seats uniformly set with a paper placemat, utensils, a basic water glass, and a brown ceramic coffee cup. We had my birthday dinner there, and I recall blowing out a candle from a slice of cake chosen from the menu. No presents, no cards, not much of a celebration. A foreshadowing of the lacklustre care my parents would demonstrate in my early teenage years.

After a harrowing week of highway whiteouts in the prairies, crossing the majestic Rockies for the first time, passing through the Okanagan (which was having a spring heatwave and looked and felt like California), and lots of angst in the car, we arrived in Victoria. It was a sunny day, and as we crested the last hill of the highway leading to the city, the snow-peaked Olympic Mountains rose high and glimmered in the sunlight. The view was magnificent; it lifted our spirits and gave me hope that things might be okay for all of us.

We checked into a local motel, and the next day our parents gave me and Chris each five bucks and told us to go find a school. I remember we walked toward downtown, eventually ending up at the corner of Yates and Douglas Streets. We asked someone passing by where we could find a high school and were told to head up Fort Street; we would find the school about twenty minutes up the hill. That's how we arrived at Central Jr. High. We walked into the school's office and told the person at the front desk we were looking to enroll, that we had just arrived from Montréal. I remember the look on her face. *Where are their parents,* it asked, *and why did they send them out here alone?*

Next thing, Chris and I were ushered into an office and seated in two empty chairs across from a desk. A man walked in, sat down, and introduced himself:

he was Mr. Keith, the physical education teacher and soccer coach. The soccer detail made Chris and I happy. We didn't know it then, but Mr. Keith would become an important figure in our lives, as our soccer coach, and two of his sons, Adam and Simon, would become buddies of ours.

Mr. Keith had immigrated from England and still retained his Britishness, calling everyone "Master" This or That. To him I was "Master Dorsey." The inflection in his voice when he called your name was a good indication of whether good or bad news was to follow. We always took adolescent pleasure when he'd take attendance and call out our schoolmate Allan Bates's name.

But at this moment, he looked puzzled: why were we in his office without a parent or guardian? He asked all the right questions: our names, where we lived (the Tally Ho Motel), and where our parents were. We lied and said they were both working. He then asked us if we had any transcripts from our old schools. We didn't. But we did have ID. My brother and I each had a passport and social security card (I had secured both when I was twelve). He then dropped a bomb on me: grade seven was not high school in BC. "You have to go back to elementary school," he informed me. *What?* I was gutted. In Montréal, high school began in grade seven and went through to grade eleven. He told me that Sir James Douglas Elementary was just down the hill in the Fairfield neighbourhood and he would call ahead to let them know I was coming. I was upset and a little scared that I was going to be separated from my brother. Not only was I in a new city and a new province, but Chris and I wouldn't be navigating our new school together.

∞

The first house my parents rented was essentially in the countryside, surrounded by farms, with the ocean to the west. We lived on a street called Santa Clara, just off the Pat Bay Highway that led to the ferry terminal. It was a beautiful but isolated place—especially for two teenagers who had grown up spitting distance from a busy metropolis like Montréal and had ridden the subway alone since they were ten years old. It was a fair distance from the schools we had enrolled in, which meant a long commute for us every day. We biked to the nearest bus station and then caught two busses to get to school. It was worth it, though, as we liked our schools and quickly made new friends.

Though I'd been anxious about attending a different school than my brother, the teachers and kids at Sir James Douglas (SJD) were fairly friendly. My skateboard skills (and my high-end board) caught the attention of both the boys and the girls. It was a good icebreaker and made making friends easier. Like my school back east, except for a handful of kids of colour SJD had a nearly all-white student body, but that wasn't something that felt foreign or threatening to me. It was just the way it was. My soon-to-be best friend, Colin, was the only other Black person in the entire school of nearly four hundred.

In addition to getting back to our schooling, my stepfather insisted that my brother and I seek out the Air Cadet squadron in Victoria and re-enroll. Chris had been an air cadet for two years in Montréal and I had snuck in a year early, at age twelve, asking them to make an exception as we were, apparently, inseparable. Chris and I weren't that thrilled at having another reason to be seen as *different* in our new hometown, but we didn't dare go against our stepfather's wishes. He had touted his military service in Belgium (mandatory for every young man in his era) and how it had given him discipline in life. He thought it would be good for us. Looking back now, I think he was playing the long game, hoping a military path for Chris and me would eventually let him off the hook for our care. And he seemed more determined than ever to have his way.

So Chris and I made our way down to the local armoury, home of the 89th Pacific Squadron of the Victoria Air Cadets. Soon enough, we were attending cadet training every Tuesday evening to do drills, shoot rifles in the basement's gun range, and learn about aviation and survival training. Our big annual to-do was marching in the city's namesake parade in early May, which ran down Douglas Street to the provincial Parliament Buildings on the harbour.

For a young teenager, being a cadet sucked. We had to wear ugly green polyester uniforms (someone's bright idea to help modernize the corps) on the city bus, and I remember feeling anxious that someone from our school would see us in our "clown outfits." Even worse, during our time in the 89th, it was clear that my brother and I were treated differently, as the only two boys of colour in the entire squadron.

The cadets are structured very much like the army; you earn promotion and recognition through merit: by displaying your skills in a prescribed manner, achieving high scores on technical tests, and, of course, demonstrating leadership. I remember my brother and I taking the first-aid class three times, and each time having it cancelled partway through. Lots of wasted time, with no explanation as to why we were left hanging. Chris and I were never selected, like most of the other kids were, to demonstrate our leadership abilities, such as taking a turn leading the marching drills. But perhaps most striking, with promotions being central to achievement in any squadron: neither of us was ever promoted from the entry-level rank of Junior Cadet.

Chris and I had long been captains of our various soccer teams back in Montréal because of our skills and competitive natures. The most frustrating aspect of cadets was having to take orders from kids just a few years older who clearly had no respect for us. Their objective seemed to be simply to find new ways to put us down—whether by yelling orders or doing their best to frustrate us during parade and drills—and doing so under the cover of the power and legitimacy bestowed upon them by their rank. Chris and I were often left with a bad taste in our mouths, and we discussed quitting often.

Unfortunately for us, our stepfather insisted we enroll in the six-week cadet summer camp. And because there were no remaining spots at air cadet camp, I had to attend a different camp than my brother. That's how I ended up travelling by myself to Vernon Army Cadet Camp (once a Second World War Canadian Army Basic Infantry training centre) in the Okanagan region of BC. Though this region is known for its lush wine country and fruit orchards, Vernon is dry and dusty in the summer, with temperatures soaring to 40°C. I was the only air cadet and one of only a few people of colour in a camp with 1,300 kids.

I remember being assigned to J Company (J Coy) and being marched off to the barracks—facilities originally built in the 1940s. Boys were separated from girls, and my company was made up of a motley crew from thirteen to sixteen years old. I remember there was one South Asian boy who wore a turban (he was Sikh, I believe), but aside from the two of us, the rest of the kids were white. One kid had a slight developmental disability—not knowing any better, we all simply referred to him as "slow"—and I remember thinking that things would not go well for him at camp.

When you're thrust into such a unique environment, your instincts take over. I grabbed a bunk next to the biggest kid in the barracks hoping to build a relationship, if only due to proximity. There were about twenty-five of us in our group. In a matter of days, the tribal behaviours began—a real-life *Lord of the Flies*. Everyone was testing each other. The older boys were determining which kids they could intimidate, control, bully—even run out of camp. It quickly became clear who was going to lead and who was going to follow.

I kept my head down. I was a tiny little guy—maybe five-foot-six at that time and eighty pounds soaking wet. (People who have only known me since my early twenties find this difficult to imagine. But I didn't get to be six-foot-three until age eighteen, when I grew nearly seven inches in seven months.) Upon our arrival, we had been given new gear and clothes (shirts, pants, shorts, sneakers, and boots)—all of which was too big for me. I had to adapt all my clothing myself: roughly hemming my pants with the thread and needle I had brought to camp with me, stuffing toilet paper into the toes of my boots so they would fit better, and using my army knife to make new holes in my camp-issued belt to keep my pants from sliding down to my feet.

The bullying started soon after I arrived: night raids against unsuspecting kids, including the disabled boy, the boy with the turban, and some white kids who were targeted for seemingly arbitrary reasons. Around midnight, we would start hearing whispers and movement around the barracks as kids prepared to storm their marks. I remember the slow kid, a notoriously deep sleeper, being wrapped to his bunk—which wasn't far from mine—with rolls of toilet paper. Then toothpaste and other substances were squeezed into his sheets. I remember hearing him scream later that morning when he woke up. I never saw him again. The South Asian boy didn't make it through one week, his turban making him an obvious target. Luckily, I was a light sleeper, and I made sure I wasn't on the menu, if you will; I let it be known to the more timid followers that I was not to be messed with. I stood my ground and used the tactics that had worked so far in my life: I either talked my way out of a pinch, had someone bigger step in to tell them to leave me alone (I had found a variety of simple ways to build quick bonds with big kids, such as bribing them), or, when all else failed, I ran away. In short, nobody was going to scare me away. And they didn't.

Eventually I made a couple "buddies"; I was accepted by most of the cadets and tolerated by the others. I found I actually liked army training. The instructors seemed genuinely interested in passing on their skills to us. It felt much different than my Victoria squadron. Of course, I learned nothing about airplanes and flying because they'd sent me to an army camp. My visions of flying gliders all summer remained just that. But I did well in all the classwork. I could also build a fire and a shelter from branches and tarps. I excelled at all sports (I was picked early to be on any team), and I was good at the marching drills. The biggest surprise happened on the range, when I discovered I was a very good sharpshooter. We used FN semi-automatic rifles to shoot targets hundreds of yards away. Though I'm right-handed, I ended up having to shoot with the rifle resting on my left shoulder, because the first time I fired the weapon, I held it incorrectly and the recoil almost broke my right shoulder.

Halfway through camp, disaster struck. Someone managed to open my trunk, steal my wallet with all my money, and even take my belt! All at once, I had three weeks left of camp with no money and no way to hold up my pants. It goes without saying that this wasn't a regular summer camp, where your parents come to visit on the weekends with cupcakes and warm hugs. This was a place where you had to demonstrate your ability to be independent, to take care of yourself. So I didn't report the theft even though I had a pretty good idea the older brother of one of my J Coy buddies was behind it. My wallet was returned to me by a camp administrator the next day with my ID still inside, but all the money gone. Someone had found it in the main camp down the hill. Thankfully I found an old shoelace, which became my best friend: it held my pants up for the rest of my stay.

But I still had one problem: I was broke. I needed to make money so I could buy junk food and go into town on Saturdays to catch a movie and hit the video arcade. Saturday was our day of freedom: the only full day we were allowed to go into downtown Vernon unsupervised. Luckily, it turned out I had a talent for polishing boots; I perfected a system that could turn the toe cap of my boot into a black mirror—you could admire your reflection in it. This was a technique I'd perfected over time, and it took a combination of the right shoe polish, a lighter to heat it up and make it easy to apply, a bit of spit, and a variety of soft cotton cloths. The key to the whole process making tiny circles over and over with the cloth, wrapped tightly around two fingers. This worked the shoe polish into every little crevice in the leather and built up super-smooth layers. Apply polish, spit-shine, and repeat.

We were required to look sharp for the weekly parade, where we'd march up and down the square to be reviewed by officers, so I let it be known to the other kids that I was open for business. My own sparkling boots were the only advertising I needed. I charged one to two dollars per pair, depending on how much work they needed. As the old saying goes, timing is everything. The kids of J Coy were always up to no good. One night, in a fit of teenage angst, we all got into the act of destroying the barrack floors—ripping up the linoleum tiles and using them as frisbees. Complete mayhem. Of course, this resulted in another confinement to our barracks with no privileges. Which was good news for my growing "black market" operation. After my first week, I had already made eighteen dollars.

With my earnings in hand, I convinced an older kid from another barracks to go to the store in town to buy me a case of Coca-Cola and a box of choc-olate bars. I sold them for one dollar each—that's back when a can of Coke cost about thirty-five cents. With a cut to my supplier, I was able to double my money within days. Supply and demand, baby! I put a can of Coke and a chocolate bar under the pillow of the big kid in the bunk next to me to ensure our unspoken "arrangement" remained in place. I was able to afford anything I wanted for the remainder of my stay, and I ended up leaving camp with more money than I'd arrived with. It was only nearing the final week that I pushed my luck too far by ordering pizzas to be delivered to the barracks. They were intercepted by the officers, who enjoyed a feast that night. They never confronted me about my failed scheme, which I found curious.

On the second-last day of camp, I was called before the officers. I thought I was going to get a major dressing-down for my part in all my company's shenanigans and especially for my entrepreneurial activities, but surprisingly I did not. In fact, I had been selected to receive the award for top cadet in our company. Apparently, I had demonstrated resilience and leadership skills. I felt a great sense of pride. As I turned to exit the office, one of my instructors gestured for me to wait a minute and then handed me a new belt, leading me out with a grin on his face.

The next day, all thirteen hundred of us stood at attention on the parade grounds. The Lieutenant-Governor of British Columbia, Henry Bell-Irving, arrived in a big black limousine to preside over our graduation. Half an hour in, I heard my name and, as instructed, I stepped out of the ranks and shouted, "Yes, sir!" I jogged in military style up to the front to receive my award—a beautifully mounted wooden plaque. I still have the photo of me shaking hands with Lt.-Gov. Bell-Irving. As a weird coincidence, he and I would become neighbours just a couple of years later when I moved into a rented house next door to his mansion on Rockland Avenue.

∞

When I returned home to Victoria, I told my family about the award. I'd had a lot of time to think at camp, and the plaque was just the kind of acknowledgement I had never received from my hometown cadets. And so, award in hand, I told my mother and stepfather I was quitting. The commanding officer of Squadron 89 made a personal visit to our house to congratulate me on my achievement and asked that I reconsider, even acknowledging that my brother and I had not been treated fairly. I thanked him for his personal appeal but let him know that it was too late—my mind was made up.

Surprisingly, my stepfather did not intervene in my decision to quit. This was, in part, I believe, because his inability to speak English put him at a disadvantage when the commanding officer came to press his case. But it was also because my award was a tangible symbol of my success and maybe, from his perspective, this had earned me the rare right to make my own decision. More likely, though, given that my stepfather was a coward at his core and had failed in all the ways he defined success—in his career and financially— was that he simply didn't have the fight in him. The right circumstances and timing worked in my favour.

With the award on my shelf, I thought I would be able to enjoy the rest of the summer just like any other kid of thirteen, but that was not to happen. At that point, my brother had returned from air-cadet camp (he *had* gotten to fly gliders) and our stepfather told us to get out of the house and find some work. We ended up going down the hill to Mattick's Farm.

It was owned by old Bill Mattick, a man well known to us because he had lost one arm in an accident and in its place wore an artificial limb capped with an intimidating, two-pronged metal hook. He needed workers and we fit the bill. For about two weeks, from 8 A.M. to 5 P.M., Chris and I knelt in the shit-smelling dirt and picked beans. If you have never done this kind of work, I can tell you it's back-breaking, even for teenage boys. By the time lunch came around each day, the sandwich I had made in the morning was warm and tasted just like I smelled—like shit. After two weeks of this, I remember telling my brother that we needed to study harder at school so we could one day make money using our brains and not our brawn.

∞

That fall, we moved to a new rental house on Shotbolt Road near Gonzales Bay, a beautiful cozy neighbourhood bordering the Strait of Juan de Fuca and the Pacific Ocean, and a short bike ride away from our schools and our friends. I dared to hope this might improve our home life, but the mood in our house just got darker. My stepfather would pace all day, working out various business ideas he was exploring, including setting up a Belgian waffle business. In the meantime, he was burning through his meagre savings and lashing out at all of us. Of course, he only spoke French, so he was relying on my mother, with her limited English, to help him with his various business ideas while Chris and I were at school. I remember him telling my mother one day that she had to go find a job. She hadn't worked outside the home for more than ten years by then, but she went out and got a waitressing job. She was forty-three years old. Even as a young teenager, I was no stranger to working; I'd had paper routes, I was a part-time caretaker at a local motel, and I'd started working in restaurants. I found it interesting that my stepfather never expressed the need to just go and get a job for himself. Instead, his constant entrepreneurial ideation seemed to have become his full-time, unpaid job, and he let the rest of us pick up the slack.

One winter day in early 1980, after we'd been living in BC for a little more than a year, my stepfather sent my sister, Elizabeth, to go play in her room, leaving my brother, mother, and me at the dinner table with him. Out of the blue, he shared the news: things were not working out in BC, and he'd decided to return to Belgium, via a stop in Montréal. My initial reaction was disappointment; I was enjoying living in Victoria. But then I felt a jolt of excitement at the thought of moving to Europe. That brief feeling evaporated with my stepfather's next words.

He thought it would be best for me and Chris to stay in Victoria. He went on to explain how we would not like it in Belgium, and that Black people were not well received in that country for all kinds of reasons—not because Belgians were racist, of course, but because the Black people who had immigrated there had shown themselves to be lazy and unable to properly integrate into a "sophisticated" society. He noted that Africans who had moved to Brussels destroyed their apartments by growing gardens in their living rooms and burning their countertops because of the way they cooked. As a result, there was a lot of violence against people of colour and, my stepfather suggested, it might not be safe for my brother and me to live there. Then he pivoted his sales pitch by telling us how staying in Victoria would be just like going to boarding school. We would be able to finish our studies in a safe and comfortable place. Throughout his speech, my mother stayed silent, a blank look on her face. I kept looking to her for any sign of hope. Were they really going to leave without us?

I thought then of one of my earliest and strongest memories of my step-father. From the time I was about six years old, if ever we complained about something he would tell my brother and me that if we didn't like it, the door was wide open and we could leave. For years, whenever I had tearful moments in my room after being punished, I would envision myself leaving the house with my belongings tucked inside a little red kerchief tied to the end of a stick. I never imagined he and my mother would be the ones to leave. And as much as I was hurt that my brother and I would be left behind, the worst part of it was my mother's silence—especially given the "family unity" promise she had made to us just before we'd pulled up stakes in Montréal a year earlier: *We don't have a big family, but we've got each other, and we'll always stick together.* I felt an overwhelming sense of sadness and betrayal.

I think it was Chris who asked where he and I would live. Our stepfather suggested we speak to friends at school to see if they had room for boarders. Chris and I were only fourteen and fifteen and had just moved to a new city. We had some friends, but the thought that we were now responsible for finding our own place to live made my stomach turn. I remember crying myself to sleep that night. How could they just leave us like this? Would I be separated from Chris, too? He was like my twin; we had been inseparable most of our lives, through the good and the bad.

Days later, Chris came home saying he had spoken to our friend Candice Digeso and that her mom was considering making a room available for him. I realized then and there that I was going to be on my own, living with strangers and separated from my brother. I was terrified. The following week, Candice and her mom, Sharon, came to our house for dinner. My parents put on quite a show. They had cooked a great meal, the wine was flowing, and there was lots of smiling and pretending. Sharon was a divorced mother of three girls: Nina, Gia, and the eldest, Candice, who was my age. She worked an admin-istrative government job and rented a big Victorian house not far from us in the lower-middle class neighbourhood of Fairfield, right next door to Ross Bay Cemetery, one of the oldest cemeteries in Western Canada (and made infamous by the now-discredited book *Michelle Remembers*, which recounts the satanic rituals that apparently took place there and contributed to the "satanic panic" of the 1980s). Sharon didn't speak French, so my mom did most of the talking. She explained that she and my stepfather were going to form a new business with his family in Brussels and, to minimize the disruption to our lives, Chris and I would finish our studies in Victoria. They would send money monthly for room and board—I believe they agreed to seventy-five dollars a week. The entire charade worked. Chris told me after school the next day that Candice had let him know the good news: her mother was open to the arrangement, and happy she could help. That was that. Now the pressure was on me to figure my situation out.

The next day, in one of my classes, I found myself sitting next to Liz Borge, a cool girl who was part of my group of friends at Central. She could tell something was wrong and asked me what was up. I told her the story and that I needed to find a place to live. "We have some room," she said simply. "I'll ask my parents." I was surprised, but suddenly felt a glimmer of hope that things could work out.

I don't recall my parents making any effort to even meet the Borge family; I think they referred Liz's parents to Sharon, whom they thought could explain the situation better without the language barrier. Or they were simply cowards. Either way, next thing I knew, the house on Shotbolt was packed up and everyone went their own way. I have no memory of saying goodbye to my parents and sister, no vivid feelings associated with a formal goodbye. Things happened so quickly that it must have felt like one day simply rolling into the next. They were there, and then they were gone.

∞

Chris moved to Arnold Avenue with Candice and her family and I moved about four kilometres from there, to Belmont Street. The whole thing was a shock to my system. Liz and her family were a tight-knit clan, proud of their Ukrainian heritage. There was nothing fancy about their small home, but what I do remember is that they were very intellectual—everyone was turned on to learning—and there was a lot of love in that house.

Liz's mom, Edith, was a manager at KFC and kept the house in order. I have a vivid memory of her standing in front of a big wood stove in the glassed-in porch making soups, stews, and other delicious concoctions, the smell of her cooking permeating the house. Carl, her husband, was a custodian at City Hall. Quiet and introspective, he could often be found with a pipe in hand, having a drink or two. He liked to do his own thing and kept away from the crowd of teenagers that congregated at his home. But he also had a quirky side; he enjoyed entertaining us with ghost stories that were made even more strange by his slow and deliberate delivery, lanky frame, and wry smile. I never heard the man say a bad word or raise his voice to anyone.

There was a sense of freedom in that home. It was the '80s, and most kids had two working parents so they spent a lot of time on their own. Liz had an older sister, Angela, who was in senior high school, and a kid brother named Charlie who was a few years younger than us. I have a great photo from 1981 that Angela posted on my Facebook page a few years ago of a birthday celebration with the Borge family; in it, everyone is smiling and waiting for me to blow out my candles. It was the first birthday my brother wasn't there to celebrate with me, and I recall trying to hide my sadness from my welcoming host family.

The official "story" my parents had told the host families was that they would send money to Chris and me every month to cover our room and board and extras. But of course, my parents never sent any money, and Chris and I were too embarrassed to share that truth. Instead, we both continued our paper routes, delivering the *Times Colonist* at five o'clock every morning before we went to school, and then worked our restaurant jobs on Thursdays, Fridays, and Saturdays. We were making some tips as busboys to complement our $3.25-an-hour wages, but I honestly can't remember how we paid our way. I imagine our boarders took the money we gave them with the promise of more to come from my parents. I didn't feel good about lying, but we had little choice.

And then suddenly, everything changed again.

About four or five months later, Chris confessed to Sharon that our parents had left us to fend for ourselves, and that everything they'd told her was a lie. She was angry that she had been deceived, but mostly she was shocked that anyone would just leave two children on their own. She did what any responsible person would do: she called Child Protection Services to report the situation. Shit hit the fan.

No more than a week after Sharon's call, Chris and I were assigned social workers. Soon we were standing before a family court judge for a preliminary hearing. The authorities hadn't been able to reach our parents and we were faced with becoming wards of the court. We were asked to confirm the facts of our situation and the judge asked if we understood what might happen. He told us he would see us again in about thirty days, when he would inform us of his decision. I wasn't totally clear on what it all meant, but it seemed serious.

In the interim, Child Protection Services met with Sharon and Edith and set up temporary funding to take care of room and board for me and my brother, and they become our unofficial foster parents. Usually, the Canadian government places children with next of kin or in the home of a family friend or guardian, but we had done the work for them. Chris and I went on with our lives feeling a little more secure for the moment, but unsure as to what lay ahead.

Two weeks later, Chris and I, who by then were both at Central Jr. High, heard our names called over the PA system. *Chris and Stephen Dorsey, please report to the office immediately.* They said it twice for effect. When we entered the school office, there were a bunch of teachers and administrators there, all busy working away but definitely out of sorts; I remember all of them turning to look at my brother and me as we entered the room. The secretary said, "Your parents are on the phone and want to talk to you." I'd received nothing but a letter or two in the months since my mother and stepfather had left us—and never a phone call. Chris grabbed the receiver and held it between us so we could both hear, and he spoke: "Allo?"

It was our mother on the line, but we could hear our stepfather in the background dictating, word for word, what she should say. She told us that if the government made Chris and I wards of the state, it would ruin any chances we might have of a successful future. She said we would be disqualified from attending university, from becoming lawyers or doctors, or from joining the army to become pilots (an aspiration I had voiced as a young boy); we would be marked as losers for the rest of our lives. We were then instructed to leave Victoria as soon as possible, and to not tell anyone—not even the families who had taken us in. We were to grab what we could carry in our backpacks, get on a Greyhound bus, and travel to Montréal, where they were still finalizing their trip to Belgium.

I remember Chris and I both crying on the phone, fully immersed in the moment, unaware of all the adults in the office likely wondering what the hell was going on. We were crushed that we would have to part with our close friends and lose the stability we had created for ourselves against all odds. We were also afraid of going back to live with the very people who had so callously left us behind. What else could be waiting for us on the other side of the country? And most of all, we were conflicted over the idea of deceiving those who had shown us such love and care.

We composed ourselves in the hallway outside the office, resigned to the fact that we had to do what our parents had ordered. After school that day, we huddled with our close friends and told them our secret. We all cried. We walked down the hill to the bus station to find out the schedule and to buy tickets. There was a bus departing eastward at six o'clock the next morning. Chris paid for our tickets and he and I made plans to meet at the depot at 5 A.M. We then headed to our respective homes to pack.

I couldn't keep it a secret. I told Edith and Liz what had happened, and that I had to leave. They were upset for me and Edith told me I was always welcome back. Her words gave me some level of comfort. I got up at 4 the next morning to find Edith waiting with a cup of hot coffee for me, just as she had done every morning when I got back from my paper route. We sat together quietly until it was time for me to say goodbye. Liz had gotten up by then and offered to walk me to the bus stop down the street. I arrived just in time. It was a fifteen-minute ride downtown to the bus depot, and when we got there, Chris was waiting along with Candice and our close friends Sarah and Colin. We sat silently on the bench outside, as no one was sure what to say. The heavy sadness of the moment was overwhelming.

Finally, we heard the "All aboard" call. There were hugs, tears, and promises to keep in touch. Sarah took off a beautiful necklace she had around her neck and placed it in the palm of my hand, telling me she hoped it would bring me comfort. Sadly, I lost the necklace years later, but this loving memory has stayed with me. Chris and I grabbed our packsacks and the pillows we had also brought along and hopped on. We grabbed the two seats near the driver and as we pulled out, we waved goodbye to our friends.

∞

After a stressful six-day cross-country bus ride—in and out of dirty, scary bus terminals, keeping an eye on sketchy fellow passengers, and trying to find ways to sleep on a bus—Chris and I arrived in Montréal filled with anxiety. I felt a sense of relief when I saw our mother and our sister, Elizabeth, waiting for us. We all hugged and then headed to the car where my stepfather was waiting. Barely a minute later, our sister, now an exuberant ten-year-old, announced that Chris and I were not in fact going to be living with them but would be boarding with an aunt. For the first few days, though, we would be camped out at my parents' three-bedroom apartment. Located in a giant high-rise next to the Longueuil Métro station, it was only a few kilometres from the home where we had grown up. It was strange to be back in such familiar surroundings when everything felt so different.

I remember my stepfather talking more nonsense at the breakfast table the next morning, trying his best to rationalize his decision to have us come back to Montréal, explaining why we couldn't stay with them, and detailing their plans to go ahead with the move to Belgium—without us. It was still unclear how this was all going to shake out for Chris and me, and I found it profoundly disturbing that neither my stepfather nor my mother expressed any regret for their neglectful actions. There were no apologies.

In the days that followed, Chris and I re-registered at our former school, LeMoyne D'Iberville. We reconnected with a few buddies, but things were already so different. Life here was serious, and everyone seemed more mature than our Victoria crowd; kids were already experimenting with drugs, sex, and pushing the boundaries of rebellious teenage behaviour. Our life in Victoria suddenly seemed innocent, and I missed it.

On my first day back at LeMoyne, I bumped into Renée, a good friend—and my first crush—from Royal Charles Elementary in Saint-Hubert. Like me, she was a francophone who went to English school and this identity formed part of our bond. When she first saw me, she gave me a big hug and commented on my large afro (my parents had always kept our hair short), which, with my diminutive stature and boyish features, made me look about ten years old. It was a nice welcome, but it was one of the last times we'd really talk, as she was already running with an older crowd. Girls would need to wait anyway; unlike most kids my age, I was in survival mode.

Chris and I did find some joy in rejoining our soccer club, Vasco da Gamma. Willie Cognee, our long-time soccer coach, was happy to help us re-integrate. We had played on his team for eight years before leaving Québec. It was the indoor season and I just happened to excel in that format as my small stature, speed, and foot skills were an asset in a gym setting. It was a great outlet for me to release pent-up anger, which I used to fuel my competitive fire. I was a scoring machine, and I didn't stop for anything or anyone—going through or around much bigger kids and picking myself up if I was pushed down, determined to not be a loser on this field of play. Perhaps because I felt defeated in so many other parts of my life, soccer was where I felt some semblance of control.

After staying with our parents for a few days, Chris and I were driven about a kilometre away to our Aunt Yvette's place. Though we'd grown up in Montréal, we had never met her. We soon discovered she was not our real aunt but a distant cousin of our mother's. She was in her late fifties, and had a son in his early twenties who lived with her. They welcomed us warmly and showed us to our room. The house was within walking distance of our school, which was a bonus.

My parents left shortly after dropping us off and another chapter began. The weeks that followed were mostly spent either at school, hanging with our friends, or playing soccer, with practices during the week and weekend matches downtown. We'd usually see my parents on weekends when we'd spend time with our sister. But as usual, for Chris and me, our sense of normalcy was in the time we spent together. We were each other's only constant.

Yvette and her son were Jehovah's Witnesses, and it was clear they had an agenda to bring us gently into the fold. They were nice enough people, and in fairness to them, we had knocked on *their* door. But they did and said certain little things to pass on teachable moments—God's truths, from their unique perspective. Having never been indoctrinated into any religion, Chris and I respected the commitment they had to their faith, but we also knew deep down that this living situation was not going to work long-term.

Looking back at it now, there was a great irony in my stepfather sending us to stay with Aunt Yvette. A decade earlier, he had made it clear to my mother that most of her relatives, who had embraced the Jehovah's Witness faith, were not welcome in his house. Unbeknownst to my siblings and me, this was one of the reasons we rarely saw our uncles and cousins when we lived on Pelletier Street.[1] I wasn't aware of this at the time, but my stepfather had clearly been desperate to get rid of me and my brother.

---

[1]   In fact, it would be decades before I would forge my own friendships with my long-lost Québec-based cousins, Nancy and Luik, who are like a brother and sister to me today. Through them and their great friends, I'd truly reconnect with my French-Canadian roots.

Chris and I had recently turned fifteen and sixteen respectively, and on a blizzardy Sunday in March, our parents invited us for brunch at their place—the one small tradition we'd maintained in our dysfunctional life. We were enjoying our meal when my stepfather announced that Chris would now be responsible for taking care of himself. I looked to my brother for a reaction and listened as my stepfather went on to tell him that now that he was sixteen, he would have to quit school and get a job.

My brother was naturally taken aback. "What kind of job would I get?" he asked with anger in his voice. "You could drive a taxi," our stepfather responded. Perhaps we shouldn't have been surprised. He had done the same to my brother Peter years before when he had been just fifteen.[2]

Chris was incredulous and told our stepfather this was not going to happen. Our stepfather was shocked that Chris would talk back and told him he was out of line to question his authority. With that, Chris looked at me and told me we were out of there. Our mother said nothing. We grabbed our winter coats and boots and made the one-kilometre walk back to Aunt Yvette's home in a major blizzard, the snow and wind whipping the tears from our faces as we walked silently shoulder to shoulder, just the two of us against the elements.

It would be years before my brother and I gained a clearer understanding of the real reason behind our secret escape from Victoria. When the government stepped in, they began looking for trustworthy guardians to take responsibility for our care, and to buck up and pay our living expenses. It was against the law in British Columbia to leave minors to their own devices, as our parents had done. BC social services had even contacted our biological father, whom Chris and I had never even met or spoken to—and wouldn't, until we were in our early twenties. So, fearing that the authorities could gain rights to his assets or income—and maybe even garnish his wages—my stepfather decided that controlling the situation would be best for *him*. Self-interest and self-preservation were the only reasons he'd had us repatriated to Montréal.

As I've said before, at his core, my stepfather was a coward. When it became evident that he was losing control of the situation, he always found a way to unload us. But this time it was different. Although we rarely spoke back to him, our stepfather could tell by and the way we now looked at him that we didn't agree with him. It infuriated him that his word was no longer accepted as law. Chris and I were sponges for knowledge and it had become obvious to us that our stepfather had a skewed world view. Even back then, we knew that Black people were not inferior, and that they could accomplish great

---

[2] At the time, we still had very little contact with Peter. We would connect again in the early '80s, when his and his beautiful girlfriend Signe's home in North Vancouver became a de facto home base for Chris and me until well into our forties.

things. There were plenty of examples of respected, successful Black people who, through their work and advocacy, made it clear that Black people were second to no one.

Over the years, my stepfather had often lamented that things weren't going his way. "The French Canadians don't like me because I'm an immigrant," he would say—even though he was a white, French-speaking immigrant—or boast that "the Jews get along with me." Though I expect the Jewish people he did business with recognized him for the shyster he was. He was an equal-opportunity racist with views about every ethnic and cultural group. His conversation was a regular diatribe of stereotypical prejudice, the core purpose of which was to make others feel inferior while putting himself on a pedestal. He believed his European heritage granted him the right to spew his outdated and offensive colonial perspectives and attitudes.

The next day, Chris called Sharon in Victoria to ask if he could come back to her house. She agreed. Chris had money saved, and that very day he went to a travel agency and bought his ticket. Suddenly, he was gone. He hadn't told me of his plans; I found out when he announced it to everyone. I can't remember if I had discussed the possibility of going back to BC with my brother, but it was clear he'd been left with no choice but to fend for himself. Still, his departure created a huge void and left me confused and sad. I'd never felt more alone or uncertain of my own future.

I remember leaving my aunt's place just a few days after Chris and moving back into my parents' apartment. My stepfather had weighed his discomfort with having me under his roof with the room and board he had to pay my aunt and decided he'd prefer to save the money. There was no great reconciliation.

I had nightmares about what my future would look like if I stayed in Montréal—if I was forced to leave school to drive a taxi, how would I reach the gas pedal or see over the dashboard? Would delivering pizzas be the pinnacle of my career, as it had for my uncle Michael? The atmosphere in the apartment was tense. No one spoke of Chris's departure or what would happen next. As far as I knew, my parents still had plans to migrate to Belgium, and I expect my presence was only complicating matters. I remember weeks passing where I immersed myself in school and soccer. I had practice twice a week and a match every weekend. With zero support from my parents, I would catch the subway and buses to get to practices and matches on my own. I also took that opportunity to spend more time with my sister, Elizabeth, which was nice, and I took her to her gymnastic classes at the local community centre.

One morning weeks later, I woke up knowing exactly what I had to do. I was confused about a lot of things, but I knew one thing for sure. I needed to be with my brother. I'd reached out to Edith, who had already told me I was welcome to come back and stay with her. I asked my mother for the three hundred dollars to buy a one-way plane ticket to Victoria, but my stepfather told her not to give it to me. I don't know what tipped the scale, but days later, my mother gave me the money and I quickly bought myself a ticket. The following week, my parents and my sister drove me to Dorval Airport, and we said our goodbyes at the gate. I didn't know it then, but I wouldn't see my mother again for eight years.

When the plane touched down in Victoria six hours later, a sense of relief washed over me. Even though we didn't live in the same house, it was great to be reunited with my brother, with my friends, and to get back to Central. We checked in with the Child Protection Services office and, after a gentle scolding, were given a court date. A few weeks later, we found ourselves in front of the same family court judge, and he made it clear that our "escape to Montréal" was not to be repeated. We assured him that we understood and had no desire to do so. With a thump of the gavel, Chris and I became wards of the court. Until the age of nineteen—three years for me, and two for Chris—our basic needs would be taken care of.

Our social workers advocated for my brother and me to remain in the homes we'd chosen for ourselves and shuffled the necessary paperwork to make the Digesos and Borges our official foster families. Everything went well for Chris at the Digesos, but despite the loving atmosphere, I found it difficult to make enough space for myself in the Borges' busy home. After about six months, I followed my intuition and made the decision to leave. After bouncing around from one foster home to another over a period of a few months, I finally landed with the Viponds. Paul Vipond, a friend from school, had lobbied his parents, Ralph and Marion, and his two sisters, Maureen and Cynthia, to welcome me and provide the support I needed.

Up until that point, I had spent most weekends hanging out and sleeping over at Paul's place. His house was just up the hill from where Chris lived, and we were all friends. Saturday mornings, I would pop upstairs—Paul had a great basement room—and make myself at home. I'd help myself to a section of Ralph's newspaper (I was already a news and politics junkie), grab a cup of coffee, and sit on the sofa next to him in the living room, both of us quietly reading. We'd usually end up engaging in a conversation about some major news or political topic, a bond that would remain central to our decades-long friendship.

Ralph and Marion worked full-time just to make ends meet, and us kids mostly took care of ourselves, got our chores done, and managed to get ourselves to school every day. Family dinners were always a special occasion, when we came together to share the stories of our day. It was a time and place filled with laughter, and I cherish those loving memories to this day. In November 1981, four months short of my sixteenth birthday, the Viponds became my official foster family.

Thirty years later, in 2011, Ralph Vipond and I would sit alone in his sunlit hospital room looking at the snow-capped North Shore mountains having what would be our final conversation. It was sad, but we laughed, remembering the good times and the winding road we had travelled together. He went quiet suddenly and I could see tears welling in his eyes. He asked me why I had chosen him and his family all those years ago. I smiled through my tears. *I had chosen them.* Ralph had understood and accepted me exactly as I was. The only true father, it turns out, I ever had. I told him that I could feel the love within the home and family he had created.

I knew I would be safe with them.

Chapter Five

It's Complicated

WHEN I WAS TWENTY-ONE AND ATTENDING COLLEGE IN VANCOUVER, I received a call from my foster father, Ralph, asking if I could meet him for lunch. He said he had something important to share, and I knew from his tone it was a serious matter. That weekend, I met him at a local restaurant in his west-end neighbourhood. We grabbed a table on the patio overlooking beautiful English Bay. We had just ordered drinks and were perusing the menu when he asked me if I had any idea why he'd asked to meet. I had no clue. He asked me to guess. I asked him if he was sick or dying. He said no. Relieved, I took a breath before blurting out, "Are you a homosexual?" He looked at me and said, "Yes, actually I am."

I was surprised but not shocked. Subconsciously, I must have known. Subtle clues I had dismissed in the past instantly revealed themselves. He asked me what I thought. I told him that I loved him and this didn't change anything for me. If living his life as a gay man made him happy, that was good enough for me. What saddened me was what he said next: "You're the last one of the kids I shared the news with; I was scared to tell you." I asked him why. He admitted he'd worried about how I'd react, given some of the pronouncements I had made as a teenager around the dinner table back on Rockland Avenue.

He noted that I had often blurted out things like "that's so gay" or "he's such a stupid fag" when referring to other kids at my high school. In my mind at that time, these words had no connection to sexual preference; they were just common adolescent putdowns intended to mean *uncool*—at least that's the way I had used them. And I wasn't alone. In his book *A Promised Land*, former President of the United States Barrack Obama details a similar experience using derogatory terms as a youth, noting, "like many teenage boys in those years, my friends and I sometimes threw around words like 'fag' or 'gay' at each other as casual put-downs—callow attempts to fortify our masculinity and hide our insecurities." I also remember using the word "fuck" a lot back then, thinking it made me more mature and edgy.

I realized in that moment, sitting across from Ralph, how insensitive I had been and how much it must have hurt him to hear those words come out of my mouth—especially given that he had welcomed me into his home with open arms and unconditional love. I teared up and apologized. I had no anti-gay sentiment in my heart, but my words had been hurtful nonetheless. Ralph was reassured that his fears had been misplaced. Our relationship as adults grew in strength from that moment on, and I learned much from him over the years, gaining a better understanding of the issues and challenges faced by the LGBTQIA+ community, who want to be able to love whomever they choose to love and to do so openly, proudly, and with equal rights protected in law.

Over the decades I've reflected often on the impact of my words and the lesson I learned that day when Ralph came out to me. It caused me to turn inward and revisit other transgressions in my past that, upon reflection, left me with a deep sense of shame.

∞

Growing up in Ralph's home was stimulating and fun. I remember fondly how we'd all come together at the dinner table each night, sharing the happenings of our day, discussing world events, and telling funny stories and jokes. The latter included taking loving jabs at each other, making fun of the quirks and personalities unique to each of us. Ralph was one of our favourite targets; we all found ways to point out his less-than-stellar physique: he was allergic to exercise, but he loved his wine, cigarettes, and food. My foster sister Cynthia, Ralph's youngest, whom he affectionately called "peanut," had a routine called *The Chubby Family*. She would stand behind Ralph with her arms acting as his, pinching and moving his chubby cheeks as she spoke for him in a funny voice. "Hello, my name is Chubby. My face is chubby, my body is chubby, my whole family is chubby." It was very funny, and Ralph always laughed the hardest.

Of course, my being Black offered up a trove of material for my foster family. Back then, I had a very large gap—à la David Letterman—between my front teeth. I remember Ralph asking me at dinner whether that made it easier for me to spit out watermelon seeds. It was funny because it played to the idiotic stereotype that had begun in early emancipation America of African Americans' "excessive fondness"[1] for watermelon, but it was even funnier because they all knew I didn't like melon of any kind.

During those years, I'd lean into my "Blackness" often to make others laugh. On occasions when chicken was on the menu, I would put on a Black southern accent and mimick a famous TV ad of the day, exclaiming, "I have two words for this chicken: Mmmmm, Mmmmm." We'd all laugh. My foster mother, Marion, tried to hold in her laughter and would allow herself only a restrained giggle. Religion was central to Marion's life; she attended church regularly and her life was guided by her faith. That didn't stop us from taking

---

[1] "How Watermelons Became a Racist Trope" by William R. Black, *The Atlantic*, December 8, 2014. https://www.theatlantic.com/national/archive/2014/12/how-watermelons-became-a-racist-trope/383529/

our best shots at her. My foster brother Paul used to do a spot-on imitation of Dana Carvey's Church Lady, an iconic recurring character on *Saturday Night Live* at that time. Channelling the Church Lady, he would interrogate her: "So, Marion, what were you doing earlier tonight, hanging out downstairs with your little friend...SATAN!?" It was hilarious, and Marion couldn't help but burst out laughing in those moments.

These dinner-table shenanigans were an important touchpoint that reinforced the bond of love we had for each other. I expect this is an experience many readers can relate to. Out of context, of course, it's clear that our back-and-forth would have been viewed by outsiders as insensitive, hurtful, and even racist. But for our family, the dinner table, with its wide-ranging conversation, was a safe place to express ourselves devoid of hateful intent.

My relationship with racially based humour also extended to my close group of high-school friends. This included my brother, Chris, my best friend, Colin Richards (who is still a friend forty years later), and Mohamed Elewonibi—all of us Black. Most of our friends were white. Some were of Irish, Scottish, and British heritage and others were Greek, Portuguese, and Italian—children of immigrants who, not long ago, had been regarded by the white majority as lower-caste whites and discriminated against as a result. Our close-knit friend group included Candice Digeso (my brother's foster sister), Lloyd, Sarah, Tracey, Hilda, Maureen and Paul (my foster sister and brother), Taki, and Tom Bendsten (my brother's best friend). It also extended to a few Indigenous friends, including long-time family friend Steve Hunt (son of Tony Hunt, a renowned west coast artist), and a handful of Asian and South Asian buddies, including Annie Chan and Harvey Chow.

Because my friends and I were left to mostly fend for ourselves—this time, in a good way—our social group became a natural extension of our families; we spent a lot of time together at school, after school, and on weekends. We looked out for each other, we counted on each other, and we trusted each other. The bond we shared also gave us an unspoken green light to take loving jabs at each other—a way of engaging that helped us shape our personalities as we transitioned into young adults. "Taking the micky" out of friends was just part of how we had fun together. We never consciously thought about why we did it, but in the process we learned to stand up for ourselves and give as good as we got.

Victoria had a very small Black population. In 1981 there were fewer then 600 Black people living in Victoria proper, out of a total population of 65,000. These numbers have changed very little over the years. (The 2016 census notes 1,130 Black citizens out of a total population of over 85,000—which puts the Black population in Victoria at a staggeringly low 1.3 percent.) But in the summer season, there would always be an influx of Black American tourists.

I remember whenever I'd walk down the street with my non-Black friends, they'd point to these Black tourists and ask if they were my "brother" or "sister." As in *soul brother* or *soul sister*. It was stupid, but funny.

When we were just hanging out, a flow of Black jokes was often part of our repertoire. I remember one particular joke being very funny and smart, and I still recall to this day. It went like this:

> On a city bus full of Black and white passengers, a shouting match ensues regarding who can sit where. The argument escalates to the point where the bus driver pulls to a stop, stands up, and shouts at the passengers: "That's it! I have had enough of all this fighting and shouting. From now on, there are no more Black or white people on this bus. You're all green. Now, all you dark green people, to the back of the bus!"

I can't remember all the Black jokes, but there were many more, some funnier than others. My friend Colin and I were on the phone recently, chatting about this period in our lives, and we had a good laugh recalling some of the more stupidly funny ones. Of course, I had my own racialized jokes at the ready whenever I felt the need to "defend" and "attack"—all targeted at friends I loved; there was never malice behind them.

I know this might be difficult for some people growing up in the current social climate to understand, but it's the way it was. In recent decades, for example, Black people have reclaimed the word *nigger* and used variations of the word as a term of endearment when speaking to or about their Black brothers and sisters. Black comedians like Chris Rock, Richard Pryor, and Dave Chappelle come to mind. But of course, using that word is not the same if it's coming from a non-Black person. The word is a derogatory racial slur that whites used to degrade free and enslaved Africans over four centuries—a word still used today by racists as a verbal weapon, often in conjunction with real violence targeting Black people. There is debate amongst the Black diaspora that perhaps the word and versions thereof should not be used, but for many Black people, reclaiming the word is, in part, a form of power and self-determination. For this reason, it's become a term of endearment among the descendants of the very people who once had to face its original, hateful intent. Among many young Black people today, the word essentially means friend, as in "He's my nigger," or its more casual variation, "nigga."

My race-based repertoire of jokes highlighted the kinds of racial stereotypes I had become familiar with, while those targeted at my white friends exploited traits I knew they were sensitive about—if they were overweight, had bad teeth or a big nose, or wore glasses. Others, like Polish or Newfie jokes, focused on non-sensical cultural stereotypes or the person's hometown or neighbourhood. Low-hanging fruit. My jokes reflected my own very narrow perspective, limited by my experiences in that small Victoria community—a very insular town without much racial or cultural diversity. My perspective, I'm now ashamed to say, included my view of some Indigenous peoples at the time.

At that point in my young life, I'd observed Indigenous people primarily downtown in various states of intoxication or passed out on the sidewalk. While this wasn't at all reflective of the varied lived experiences of Indigenous peoples on Vancouver Island and across Canada, it was a stereotype conveniently amplified by my own limited contact with anyone who identified as Indigenous up to that point. As my friend Lisa, an Indigenous person disenfranchised due to adoption, recently shared with me, there were probably many, many more drunk white people living on Rockland Avenue (the well-heeled street where I lived), only they had the privilege of stumbling about indoors, out of sight.

I also had an Indigenous high-school buddy, Paul, whose brother John could often be found sniffing glue on the steps of the public library at Yates and Blanshard, slowly killing himself. It was troubling and sad to witness, but I remember it became almost normal to see him there. Of course, I had no awareness of the intergenerational trauma negatively impacting him or Indigenous communities on a much grander scale, or the centuries-old systemic legislation that had created the very problems I was witnessing. Looking back, my own experience feels representative of the broader societal view: the problem was in plain sight, but easy for me to ignore for much too long.

My jokes were never really targeted at a specific Indigenous friend or person, but just generally made fun by leaning into a negative perception of an entire community. I had no prejudice in my mind or heart that motivated my jokes. I was playing for laughs at the expense of the other. One of my more insensitive jokes involved an Indigenous couple driving down the road. The passenger makes what seems like a loving comment: "Hey, you're passionate." The driver responds, "What?" "I said, 'you're passin' it.' You're passing the liquor store." Juvenile, certainly, but also incredibly racist. I had not intended to be racist, I simply knew it would always get a laugh. And it did, for the many years I told it. I was oblivious to the reality that this "joke" played on the false and harmful stereotypes that sexualize Indigenous women and girls and suggest Indigenous men are drunks.

I made these kinds of jokes openly; we all did. Like most teenagers, it didn't even occur to me at that time to dig deeper. And of course, I had my own problems to deal with. I was a kid who didn't have all the information, trying to make sense and navigate the world around me without anyone really pushing back on what I said and did. No one to tell me it was wrong.

Having taken much time to reflect over the years, I believe my friends and I also allowed ourselves to laugh at racial jokes—including the Black jokes made about us—as a form of protection against the *real* racists, which many of us faced on a regular basis in our small community. Perhaps it numbed the pain of those attacks and the hurt they caused. In a 1990 CBC interview, former National Chief of the Assembly of First Nations Phil Fontaine described meeting with other survivors of residential schools whom he knew personally over the years to share their recollections. "We end up joking and laughing about what we experienced....[I]t's essentially a way of avoiding a sense of embarrassment and shame one feels—face-saving and really a form of protection."[2]

Humans are complicated. Most of us have heard the old saying "laughter is the best medicine" and in fact, science reveals that the endorphins released through laughter improve our well-being, and help to relieve stress and anxiety.[3] Humour, and particularly self-deprecation or self-directed humour, actually "leads to increased optimism, which in turn, boosts our resiliency and enables us to thrive when we're faced with adversity."[4] As such, writes journalist Cindy Lamothe, referencing a 2018 Spanish study[5], "many of us are happiest when we can laugh at our past misfortunes." However, as much as humour can be a balm, a protective shield, and even a form of medicine, when it's misdirected it can be hurtful and perpetuate negative stereotypes, fuelling systemic racism. And unfortunately, I was no stranger to both ends of this kind of humour.

Looking back, it's clear that my ignorance of the challenges faced by Indigenous peoples over centuries was no accident. The education system when I was a student, in the 1970s and '80s, provided a very narrow perspective of Indigenous history in Canada. Much of what we were taught was stripped of the cultural and societal richness of the various First Nations who call this land home. For the most part, we were indoctrinated in the "discovery" narrative: that Christopher Columbus *discovered* America in 1492—even though Indigenous peoples had lived on this land since time immemorial. Columbus and other explorers such as John Cabot were, in fact, granted rights to discover and possess any territories under the "Doctrine of Discovery" issued by

---

2   "Phil Fontaine's shocking testimony of sexual abuse," CBC archives. Original broadcast October 30, 1990. cbc.ca/archives/entry/phil-fontaines-shocking-testimony-of-sexual-abuse

3   "Laughter is the Best Medicine" *HelpGuide*, July 2021. helpguide.org/articles/mental-health/laughter-is-the-best-medicine.htm

4   "The Benefits of Laughing at Yourself, According to Science" by Cindy Lamothe, *Shondaland*, June 22, 2018. shondaland.com/live/a21755063/benefits-laughing-at-yourself-self-deprecation-science-psychology/

5   "Is the use of humor associated with anger management? The assessment of individual differences in humor styles in Spain" by Jorge Torres-Marin, Ginés Navarro-Carillo, and Hugo Caretto-Dios, *Personality and Individual Differences*, Vol. 120, January 1, 2018, pp. 192–201. sciencedirect.com/science/article/abs/pii/S0191886917305457

Pope Nicholas V in 1455.[6] This international law gave license to explorers to claim vacant land (called *terra nullius*) in the name of their sovereign. Vacant land was defined as land that was not populated by Christians. If the lands were not so occupied they could be "discovered" by Christians, and sovereignty, dominion, title, and jurisdiction claimed. An estimated two hundred thousand Indigenous peoples were living in the country now known as Canada when Europeans first came to settle on this land.

Our history lessons left out much of the proud cultural heritage of Indigenous peoples, the unique societal characteristics that differentiated the many First Nations—distinct sovereign nations that thrived in this land before colonization—or the many wrongs that have been committed against Indigenous peoples for centuries: broken treaties, discriminatory government policies, and even attempted genocide. It would be decades before I would gain a fuller understanding of the systemic racism perpetrated against Indigenous peoples in this country, by this country. To do that, I had to take responsibility for my own unconscious biases and my own unlearning.

My Unlearning

The key to my unlearning was *wanting* to do this work. I engaged directly with Indigenous people, made an effort to know them, to learn from them, but not to rely on them to teach me. I've always loved history, so I sought out Indigenous histories that were being published by new historians and academics who had actually done the work of excavating the truth and debunking much of the propaganda we had all been spoon-fed in school.

Most importantly, I read information published by various First Nations outlets whose writers shared their own truths—many of the facts left out of the Canadian historical narrative. I also made a conscious effort to dig deeper myself, to understand the challenges still faced by First Nations communities in this country—issues yet to be fully resolved, most notably including the reclamation of culture (including language) and lands, and particularly the fallout from policies enacted in the 1876 Indian Act, which enforced government control over every aspect of Indigenous lives—from health to status to resources—and the creation of which was an attempt at mass assimilation. A desire to better understand the lived experiences of others, combined with purposeful action, has allowed me to contribute in small ways to championing change for the benefit of Indigenous peoples in Canada. This has fuelled a

---

6   "The Doctrine of Discovery: The International Law of Colonialism" by Professor Robert J. Miller, Sandra Day O'Connor College of Law, Arizona State Univ. Chief Justice, Grand Ronde Tribe Court of Appeals. doctrineofdiscovery.org/assets/pdfs/DiscoveryElementsOnondaga2014.pdf

desire to see Canada deliver the promised equity measures (many detailed in the ninety-four Calls to Action in Canada's Truth and Reconciliation Commission report) intended to deliver the long-overdue recognition that Indigenous peoples in Canada have rightly demanded for centuries.

I made time to dig deeper to better understand the Indigenous histories of this land—all of the information that had been omitted from the history books of my youth—including the dark chapters of residential schools and the Sixties Scoop. I was searching for a broader perspective on the *why*s and the *how*s so I could engage more effectively in conversations and debates with friends, neighbours, elected officials, and Indigenous leaders—youth and elders I met along the way.

My civic engagement also provided me a tangible way to make a positive impact. For more than fifteen years, I've been engaged in political activities with the Liberal Party of Canada, highlighted by my participation as a delegate in the Party's biennial conventions, and engagement in the Indigenous Peoples Commission (IPC) in 2006, 2009, 2016, and 2021. The IPC is an important organization that represents and promotes the interests of Indigenous peoples in Canada within the Party. It's where policies focused on uplifting Indigenous peoples are developed and debated by Party delegates, with some eventually adopted and put into practice when the Liberals form government.

At the 2016 convention held in Winnipeg, Manitoba, I had the opportunity to directly share a discussion paper I wrote with newly elected federal ministers, including the Minister of Crown-Indigenous Relations, The Honourable Carolyn Bennett, and then Minister of Innovation, Science and Industry, the Honourable Navdeep Bains. My paper, "Winning in the New Economy: Seven Steps Toward a Canadian Digital Innovation Strategy," proposed bringing high-speed broadband infrastructure to Indigenous and Northern communities by leveraging Canadian knowhow, offering direct access to the global, online economy, and unlocking and unleashing the creative and business talents of Indigenous peoples. I noted that the Canadian government should allocate "a significant portion of its proposed infrastructure investment" in these high-impact digital infrastructure opportunities, and that it should do so by leveraging current and future government satellite infrastructure.

Just a few years after I shared that paper, in 2019, I was pleased to see the Liberal-led Canadian government announce a new investment, to be allocated over a decade, of between $5 billion and $6 billion to bring high-speed internet to 100 percent of Canadians. This included $100 million targeted specifically at satellite-based technology known as Low Earth Orbit (LEO) satellites, collaborating with Canada's Telesat to address the needs of rural communities, including 190 Indigenous communities. As of July 2020, 599 communities out of a planned 975 had been connected, positively impacting

158,000 rural and northern households. In June 2021, the Canadian government announced an additional \$9.5 million dollars in federal funding to bring high-speed internet to underserved households, including three thousand Indigenous households.[7]

Providing high-speed internet to Indigenous communities has many positive impacts, including improving access to health services and facilitating health service delivery, enabling augmented education by providing classroom access to online resources, facilitating commercial and business development by plugging business leaders and entrepreneurs into global opportunities and services, and enabling video conferencing. It even offers protectionary measures for Traditional Knowledge from Indigenous communities, "allowing elders for example to communicate their culture and language to audiences near and far—helping preserve and revitalize Indigenous languages."[8]

I had carved my own path for my allyship journey, and I was finally beginning to understand the unique ways in which I could personally help make meaningful change.

Homelessness

Homelessness is another area in which bias and prejudice have had real and harmful implications on our society and which has spurred much debate among friends and neighbours. From debating whether we should give our spare change to those begging outside the grocery store to bigger issues like the lack of affordable housing, each of us holds personal views shaped by conscious and unconscious biases.

Considering that I spent part of my childhood without secure and stable housing, it might seem hard to believe that the issue of homelessness was not something I spent much time thinking about. But like many young people, I thought mostly about myself. Later, as I began my career, I spent much of my energy striving to be a top professional in my field and achieving business successes. It wasn't until 2006, when I moved back to Canada from the US, that I started engaging more purposefully with social causes, policy issues, and community initiatives that interested me.

---

[7]   "Government of Canada Invests Over \$9.5 Million to Bring High-speed Internet to 6,124 Homes in Rural and Indigenous Communities in Ontario." Press Release by Science and Economic Development Canada, June 23, 2021. newswire.ca/news-releases/government-of-canada-invests-over-9-5-million-to-bring-high-speed-internet-to-6-124-homes-in-rural-and-indigenous-communities-in-ontario-832948908.html

[8]   "The Impact of Internet Access in Indigenous Communities in Canada and the United States" by Dr. Heather E. Hudson, *Internet Society*, Reston, VA, internetsociety.org/wp-content/uploads/2020/07/Impact-Indigenous_Communities-EN.pdf

In 2015, I became involved with a local non-profit called Haven Toronto, a drop-in centre providing support to homeless and marginally housed men over fifty. I was introduced to the agency by my friend Fred Gaysek (who sadly passed away suddenly from a COVID-related illness in 2020), who had reached out to ask for help with a grant application. This volunteer engagement led to Haven hiring me a year later to help them develop the first strategic plan in their eighty-year history. This included rebranding the agency and developing content to support their fundraising efforts. As I learned more about the services they provide and the men they support, I was compelled to look inward and ask myself: how did I feel about homelessness? These insights, I knew, would enable me to develop more authentic stories that could resonate broadly with intended donor audiences. But I had no idea how deeply they would affect me personally.

I had a very impactful experience when I interviewed four Haven clients for a video I was writing, directing, and producing. The men, who ranged in age from fifty to sixty-two, came to trust me with their personal stories, detailing how they went from living fairly "normal" lives to descending into homelessness and despair. Some had dealt with deep loss that led to depression, while others detailed struggles with addiction and mental health and a downward spiral that had ultimately led to a life on the streets.

What struck me most in their emotional testimonials was this: they were no different than the rest of us; these were fathers, grandfathers, brothers, and sons, who, through unfortunate circumstances, found themselves alone, isolated, and with few options. This experience made me reflect on my own biases around homelessness. As a teenager, I'd held the view that all homeless people were bums—why else would these adults be begging for money on the street when they could be working or looking for a job? I had been working and making my own money from an early age, so I could not understand how a grown person could not do the same.

In my twenties I became less judgmental as I gained a broader understanding of homelessness as a major problem with complicated societal and political drivers. I was a voracious consumer of news, and I gravitated to stories about the human condition. Many focused on the factors contributing to homelessness, and the discourse of the day focused on how the shuttering of mental health institutions in the midst of the opioid epidemic had aggravated homelessness in Vancouver's downtown. More and more, I read about how you couldn't go anywhere in the downtown core without homeless people begging you for spare change.

I was still young and naïve when, in 1986, at the age of twenty, I moved to Vancouver to work at the World Expo—and I confronted homelessness for real. Walking the city streets, I sometimes found myself compelled to give all the change I had in my pocket, and other times I felt conflicted and kept walking, ignoring their pleas. I ventured into the Downtown Eastside—ground zero for Vancouver's homelessness and drug epidemic—to have a look for myself at what I'd heard was a rough part of town. I went to the notorious Balmoral Hotel for a drink with a buddy from France who was eager to experience the city's underbelly. We only stayed for a quick one, as it was clear that danger was all around us. Back then, the homeless population occupied several city blocks, with some people openly shooting up in doorways and alleys.

Vancouver's Downtown Eastside had the worst concentration of homelessness I'd ever witnessed anywhere in the world. But it still felt, somehow, like it was manageable because the problem was confined (or so it seemed) to a few city blocks in one neighbourhood. I imagined the number of homeless people must be quite small in terms of the overall population. I was sure that it would only be a matter of time before municipal leaders came up with a solution that would alleviate, if not eliminate, the problem.

Turns out I wasn't the only one who didn't see a major problem. Thirty years later, when I was visiting family in Vancouver, my older brother Peter took me on a drive through East Hastings. We drove for blocks, travelling what seemed like two kilometres east past Main Street, which bisects East Hastings in the now affluent Gastown area. I was shocked by the exponential growth of the homeless problem since my first visit. The Balmoral and other buildings had been deemed unsafe and were now boarded up (apparently squatters still lived there in hazardous conditions), while thousands of marginalized citizens were essentially living on the sidewalks. It looked like a bombed-out city inhabited by zombies. It was a sad and disturbing scene.

Prior to this, in the early 2000s, I had lived and worked in Seattle for six years. Like many North American cities, including New York, Los Angeles, Vancouver, and Toronto, Seattle finds itself in the unenviable position of possessing both enormous wealth and staggering levels of poverty and homelessness. Although I'd observed some homelessness in Seattle's downtown, it seemed to me that the issue was under control: low-income housing and local support services were mixed in with higher-end condos and businesses. This socio-economic diversity model—an approach to urban planning with supports for marginalized people—was, at the time, considered a viable model for addressing the growing problem of homelessness, a model to combat economic segregation.

My understanding was that community activists had pushed the city to give socio-economic diversity a try in the downtown core. In my desirable Belltown neighbourhood, just a few blocks from the iconic Pike Market (home to the first-ever Starbucks), I'd walk out of my luxury condo and pass by neighbours living in a nearby shelter on their way to get a meal at the mission.

There was even a designated spot (albeit, on a street corner) where Latin American labourers could congregate and vie to be selected for daywork on construction sites. Each morning, the lucky ones would pile into the back of a pickup truck and be spirited away to the many developments sprouting up all over town, where they would make a good day's wage. This socio-economic mix seemed promising from my limited vantage point.

In 2019, I returned to Seattle for a visit. I met a friend for coffee downtown in the historic Pioneer Square neighbourhood, near the Central bar where Nirvana played their first gig, and what I saw made my jaw drop. For blocks on end, neglected human beings lived outdoors, with tents strewn amongst garbage and drug paraphernalia. It seemed the city's homeless had been completely left to fend for themselves. It was hard to imagine that leaders in such an affluent city could have allowed things to deteriorate so badly.

My work with Haven, and my direct interactions with homeless men, provided me with the insights, personal relationships, and emotional understanding that fundamentally changed how I perceived this challenging societal reality. I realized that when I was younger, I hadn't seen the homelessness problem because I couldn't see homeless folks as individual people, with diverse and compelling backgrounds and stories. I was struck by how lives could be upended by unforeseen challenges, and how easily this could lead to negative outcomes—including homelessness.

There are millions of Canadians who live paycheck-to-paycheck with little in savings to fall back upon. Take for example the 66 percent of working Canadians who make less than $46,000 a year. It wouldn't take much for any of these people to find themselves in a perilous housing situation—the loss of a job and the inability to find new work; a sudden, unforeseen financial calamity; a tragic death of a child that led to a mental breakdown; an addiction that spiralled out of control. We live in a country with a safety net of sorts, but unfortunately some people fall through the cracks. It's estimated that there are more than ten thousand homeless people in Toronto alone.

Through my own journey of discovery, which has included many conversations with thought leaders and experts working to alleviate homelessness, it has become evident that making affordable and safe housing widely available to our communities' most vulnerable is central to stabilizing their lives. Housing can make it possible to provide the managed care many people require (counselling, therapy, and health supports) to live more meaningful and productive lives within a healthier community. My relationship with Haven has propelled me to personally engage at an even deeper level, inspiring me to develop a documentary project, *Homeless Not Hopeless*, which is intended to shine a spotlight on the homeless and the housing crisis plaguing our nation.

My young kids now have an annual tradition of collecting clothing and putting together care kits for donation to Haven clients ahead of the holidays. I have taken what I have learned and turned it into an opportunity to teach. My children will grow up knowing the importance of empathy and of helping others.

Making Change Now

Broadly speaking, I expect that many readers can relate to my youthful transgressions and the journey of self-discovery and awareness I embarked upon in the decades following. But who we once were does not have to dictate who we are now, or who we could be. We all hold within us the ability to unlearn our biases. It does take effort to step outside of our comfort zones, to become more aware and to gain a deeper understanding of the realities lived by others, but this deliberate action can lead to personal growth and contribute to bringing about positive change.

Along the way, I was able to synthesize these views to form a more nuanced understanding for myself, and to make the changes necessary to become an ally—an effort that continues to this day. We are all on our own unique journeys to better understanding the world around us. Ultimately, if you have a desire and an innate drive to walk through life in a state of greater awareness, you are sure to stumble upon some personal revelations that will help shape your behaviour. But I urge you to seek these lessons out, rather than waiting for them to come to you. Yes, it will be challenging, but you need to get comfortable with uncertainty. Humble yourself. Do the work. Reach out to allies who can help you make sense of what is unfamiliar to you, and seek out others' experiences and ways of understanding the world. Ask questions and listen. Listen.

Like most Canadians, I'm still learning and adapting my understanding of the complex world around me and adjusting my thinking and behaviours accordingly. It all comes down to one simple thing: a genuine desire to do better, to be better, and to live better. As a Black Canadian seeking long-overdue equity and equality for racialized Canadians, it's imperative that I also stand up and demand equal rights for those who are not Black. My deliberate engagement to better understand the challenges facing Indigenous peoples, for example, has been part of that effort.

How can we hope to achieve the societal cohesiveness that will enable Canada to reach new heights of opportunity and growth if we don't have equality for all? It's simply not possible. Canada's democracy must deliver on this singular promise through tangible action as soon as possible. This means that we *all* have work to do. Each of us needs to work on letting go of long-held, often subconsciously biased beliefs, and instead embrace an approach of openness and understanding toward those who are different than we are. That can be easier said than done, and it can be somewhat destabilizing to realize you have so much work to do.

I get it. But the time has come for us to get comfortable with being uncomfortable.

Chapter Six

Systemic Inequality: Law and Dis-order

PART 1. POLICING

IF THERE WAS ONE ASPECT OF THE BLACK LIVES MATTER MOVEMENT THAT seemed to fully ignite and unite Black people everywhere, it was a general discontent with law enforcement. The anger and frustration were palpable, the chorus "defund the police" echoing across North America. The heavily armed police, especially in the United States, had become a visible symbol of the oppression Black people had faced for more than four centuries.

In the late twentieth century, police across America targeted, harassed, arrested, and incarcerated a disproportionately high level of Black people, filling for-profit penal institutions with generations of young Black men. The 1950s and '60s were synonymous with the brutal beatings of Black civil rights activists pushing back against Jim Crow–era oppression, largely through peaceful protest, such as the famous marches to Selma and beyond. And further back still, over four centuries of legalized slavery, Black people feared the "slave patrols"—organized groups of armed slave catchers with the legal authority to chase down those brave enough to attempt escape.[1]

Academics have identified these slave patrols as foundational to today's modern policing institutions in the US. As Gary Potter, a crime historian at Eastern Kentucky University, explains:

> The first publicly funded, organized police force with officers on duty full-time was created in Boston in 1838 to replace a private system created by businesses who had been hiring people to protect their property and safeguard the transport of goods from the port of Boston. They used their power and political influence to shift the cost of this protection to the public.[2]

[1] "The racist roots of American policing: From slave patrols to traffic stops" by Connie Hassett-Walker, *The Conversation*, June 2, 2020. theconversation.com/the-racist-roots-of-american-policing-from-slave-patrols-to-traffic-stops-112816

[2] "How the U.S. Got Its Police Force" by Olivia B. Waxman, *Time.com*, May 18, 2017. time.com/4779112/police-history-origins

In the South, the creation of police forces (beginning with slave patrols in Carolina in 1704) was centred on the preservation of the slavery system—specifically "chasing down runaways and preventing slave revolts." Later, during Reconstruction, many of the slave patrols were overtaken by local sheriffs, who were, responsible for "enforcing segregation and the disenfranchisement of freed slaves."[3] By the late nineteenth century, and for a period of more than eighty years, an era known as Jim Crow mandated laws that systematically discriminated against Black people. Notable among these laws was segregation, which relegated Black people to separate and lesser public spaces—from schools to water fountains.

Enforcing segregation was the job of police, and Black citizens who seemingly violated the laws often endured police brutality. White people also often took "justice" into their own hands, reprising slave-era practices such as lynching Black people.[4] These perpetrators often went unpunished, their crimes ignored by a judicial system that failed to hold the public or the police accountable.[5]

Today there are nearly 700,000 full-time law enforcement officers in the US policing 330 million Americans. Although the US federal government has "forbidden the use of racist regulations at the state and local level"[6] for the past fifty years, people of colour remain more likely than whites to be killed by police.

Canada's police institutions have different foundational beginnings, but they were similarly created in order to control and punish racialized, immigrant, and Indigenous communities within their jurisdictions. First came the North-West Mounted Police (NWMP) in 1873, which would evolve into the RCMP in 1920, a paramilitary organization largely modelled after the French and British policing systems, established to enact federal law on the newly created Northwest Territories, formerly held by the Hudson's Bay Company.

According to the RCMP Heritage Centre, the NWMP was formed to "establish friendly relations with the First Nations, enforce Canadian authority, pave the way for settlers, and maintain law and order on the western frontier."[7] Back in Ottawa, Prime Minister Sir John A. Macdonald looked to use this paramilitary force as a way to "secure Canadian sovereignty and prepare the way for

---

3   *Ibid.*

4   "American Experience: Lynching in America," PBS. pbs.org/wgbh/americanexperience/features/emmett-lynching-america

5   "The racist roots of American policing: From slave patrols to traffic stops" by Connie Hassett-Walker, June 2, 2020. theconversation.com/the-racist-roots-of-american-policing-from-slave-patrols-to-traffic-stops-112816

6   "Reconciling Results on Racial Differences in Police Shootings" by Roland G Fryer J., *American Economic Review* (forthcoming). scholar.harvard.edu/fryer/publications/reconciling-results-racial-differences-police-shootings

7   "Exhibitions: Creating a Mounted Police," RCMP Heritage Centre. rcmphc.com/en/creating-a-mounted-police. thecanadianencyclopedia.ca/en/article/north-west-mounted-police

[white] settlement."[8] The presence and power of the NWMP in the Northwest Territories allowed the force to make diplomatic connections with a number of Indigenous bands who had lived on the land for millennia, convincing them to sign treaties that were not always to their benefit.

As Pam Palmater, a Mi'kmaw woman and an attorney from Eel River Bar First Nation in New Brunswick, explains, this included:

> ...trapping First Nations people on reserves, not allowing them to hunt and fish, making them live on rations, sexually exploiting and abusing First Nations girls on reserves, making sure settlement could continue, and railways and mining, and everything the settler or colonial government wanted to do.[9]

After a few decades of performing everything from mail delivery to surgery to maintaining peace between white and Indigenous communities—largely by keeping them separate—the NWMP expanded north to the Arctic in 1903. After the First World War, the NWMP merged with the Dominion Police (Parliamentary guards in Ottawa) to form the Royal Canadian Mounted Police (RCMP).[10] Though there are other regional police forces across Canada, this institution, known for its iconic image of officers in red serge riding on horseback, is Canada's national police force.

As Robyn Maynard says in her bestselling book, *Policing Black Lives*,

> Few who do not study Black Canadian history are aware that dominant narratives linking crime and Blackness date back at least to the era of the transatlantic slave trade, and that Black persons were disproportionately subject to arrest throughout Canada as early as the nineteenth and early twentieth centuries.[11]

The result is a systemic lack of trust and fear of the police within BIPOC communities. As OmiSoore Dryden, the James R. Johnston chair in Black Canadian studies at Dalhousie University, explains, "For many, that [police] uniform is a symbol of harm and abuse and fear. It is not a symbol for care and kindness and support."[12]

---

8   "North-West Mounted Police" by Edward Butts, *The Canadian Encyclopedia*, February 6, 2006. thecanadianencyclopedia.ca/en/article/north-west-mounted-police

9   "Relation between Indigenous and RCMP founded on oppression, as strained as ever: activist," *CityNews*, May 19, 2021. toronto.citynews.ca/2021/05/19/relation-between-indigenous-and-rcmp-founded-on-oppression-as-strained-as-ever-activist/

10 "North-West Mounted Police" by Edward Butts, *The Canadian Encyclopedia*, thecanadianencyclopedia.ca/en/article/north-west-mounted-police

11 *Policing Black Lives: State Violence in Canada from Slavery to the Present* by Robyn Maynard, Fernwood Publishing, Halifax, 2019 (4).

12 "Canada's policing failures show systemic need for better mental health crisis response" by Cassandra Szklarski, *Global News*, June 15, 2020. globalnews.ca/news/7068392/canada-policing-mental-health/

Recently, the Ontario Human Rights Commission published a timely report[13] of its inquiry into racial profiling and racial discrimination of Black persons by the Toronto Police Service, detailing in part how "Black people in Toronto, while only 8.8 percent of population, represented almost 32 percent of people charged with a crime, and were twenty times more likely to die from an encounter with police."[14] Think about that.

This threat weighs heavily on Black people across North America. Every day of our lives we are instructed, even if only subconsciously, to stay away from the police at all costs. In contrast, white advantage means not having to burden oneself with this daily, potentially deadly reality. For this reason, white and white-passing individuals mainly regard the police more favourably than Black people do; they tend to see policing as an institution doing what it was intended to do: keep law and order and protect citizens from harm.

In June 2015 Gallup revealed the results of its American "confidence in institutions poll," which revealed that 50 percent of whites have "a great deal of confidence" in the police's ability to gain the trust of the public compared with only 22 percent of Black people. White people are much more likely than Black or Latinx people to say their experience with the police has been "mostly good." But who is really being protected, and who is being targeted?

Black parents carry the extra burden of worry that their children will be targeted every time they leave the house. Black youth are often racially profiled—stopped by police simply because of the colour of their skin. Their being targeted can be amplified based on what type of clothes they are wearing, and whether they happen to be walking in a "high-crime neighbourhood."[15] "The assumption...that Black people are likely to be criminals results in more Black people being watched, charged and incarcerated," Maynard explains. "It is Black people who will be made into criminals by the very policing strategies that target them."[16]

---

13 *A Disparate Impact: Second interim report on the inquiry into racial profiling and racial discrimination of Black people by the Toronto Police Service*, Ontario Human Rights Commission, August 2020. ohrc.on.ca/sites/default/files/A%20Disparate%20Impact%20Second%20interim%20report%20on%20the%20TPS%20inquiry%20executive%20summary.pdf#overlay-context=en/disparate-impact-second-interim-report-inquiry-racial-profiling-and-racial-discrimination-black

14 "Black people face 'disproportionately' high charge, arrest rates from Toronto police: report" by Adam Carter, *CBC News*, August 10, 2020.cbc.ca/news/canada/toronto/black-people-human-right-commission-police-1.5680460

15 *Review of the RCMP's Policies and Procedures regarding Street Checks Report*, Government of Canada: Civilian Review and Complaints Commission for the RCMP, Royal Canadian Mounted Police Act Subsection 45.34(1). crcc-ccetp.gc.ca/en/review-rcmps-policies-and-procedures-regarding-street-checks-report

16 *Policing Black Lives: State Violence in Canada from Slavery to the Present* by Robyn Maynard, Fernwood Publishing, Halifax, 2019 (87).

Desmond Cole, a Toronto-based journalist, activist, broadcaster, and author, is one of the people credited with bringing to light the abuses of the controversial, long-standing practice of "carding" in his home city. In his many articles, essays, and his recent book, *The Skin We're In*, he describes the practice, commonly referred to as "street checks," which involves the arbitrary stopping, questioning, and documenting of individuals when no particular offence is alleged to have taken place. He claims to have personally been carded at least fifty times in Ontario alone. As he wrote for *Toronto Life* in 2015,

> By now, I expect it could happen in any neighbourhood, day or night, whether I am alone or with friends. These interactions don't scare me anymore. They make me angry. Because of that unwanted scrutiny, that discriminatory surveillance, I'm a prisoner in my own city.[17]

Carding began in Canada in 1957 when Toronto police were given actual cards, called "Suspect Cards," "to document and forward information about persons of interest to detectives."[18] The card subsequently evolved into a "form" and later a "report." In the US, specifically in New York City, this practice was called "stop and frisk," a process that involves "detaining, questioning and at times searching civilians on the street for weapons and other contraband"[19] on the sole basis of "reasonable suspicion"—the stated objective being to reduce crime. At its peak, this discriminatory practice saw nearly 686,000 stops, with 53 percent of those stopped being Black, 34 percent Latinx, and only 9 percent white. Over half (51 percent) were between the ages of fourteen and twenty-four and most (88 percent) were found to be innocent of any crime.[20]

In a 2013 court ruling, the NYPD's tactics were found to have violated the US Constitution's 4th Amendment, which protects citizens from unreasonable search and seizure. A 2020 analysis of crime patterns initiated by the *Washington Post* found that "major felonies declined during NYC Mayor Bloomberg's three terms from 2002 through 2013, but the reduction did not correspond to the increase in stops by police."[21] By 2016, only 12,404 stops were recorded,

---

[17] "The Skin I'm In: I've been interrogated by police more than 50 times—all because I'm black" by Desmond Cole, *Toronto Life*, April 21, 2015. torontolife.com/life/skin-im-ive-interrogated-police-50-times-im-black

[18] "Here's What You Need to Know About Carding," *CBC Firsthand: The Skin We're In*, CBC TV (n.d.). cbc.ca/firsthand/m_features/heres-what-you-need-to-know-about-carding

[19] *Ibid.*

[20] "Annual Stop-and-Frisk Numbers," NYCLU (n.d.) nyclu.org/en/stop-and-frisk-data

[21] "Bloomberg said 'stop and frisk' decreased crime. Data suggests it wasn't a major factor in cutting felonies." by Dan Keating and Harry Stevens, *The Washington Post*, February 27, 2020. washingtonpost.com/nation/2020/02/27/bloomberg-said-stop-frisk-decreased-crime-data-suggests-it-wasnt-major-factor-cutting-felonies/

with Black and Latinx citizens accounting for 83 percent of those stopped; white people accounted for 10 percent.

In Canada, the *Review of the RCMP's Policies and Procedures regarding Street Checks* report, released in February 2021, states, "Street checks have the potential, in certain narrow situations, to be a valuable tool to the police to support investigations or to provide criminal intelligence. However, they also threaten the basic constitutional rights of Canadians."[22] Between the years 2009 and 2011, 1.1 million names were entered into Toronto's carding database—that's approximately one for every three Toronto residents—and the data clearly shows that Black and Indigenous people were disproportionally targeted. As reported in the *Toronto Star* in the summer of 2014, due to a change in procedure in July 2013 which mandated the issuance of a receipt to those who had been carded, there was a 75 percent drop in overall carding, but a rise in the carding of Black people, from 23.3 percent to 27.4 percent—a number that was 3.4 times the proportion of Toronto's Black population.[23]

Though the Province of Ontario banned carding in 2016, accommodations were made in favour of police; street checks were reframed as "regulated interactions," allowing police to continue to stop citizens and ask for information so long as the officer was in the process of investigating a crime. Traffic stops were also excluded from the ban, to the disappointment of many—including Black Lives Matter Toronto, which advocated for an outright ban on all unauthorized carding.[24]

A year into the change, it was reported that many officers and police chiefs blamed the ban for a rise in violent crime, including gun violence, in Toronto. In a 2018 interview with the *Globe and Mail*, Peel Regional Police Chief Jennifer Evans claimed a direct correlation between violent crime and the ban, stating, "[street-check legislation] has empowered criminals, who think officers won't stop them, they now are more confident that they will get away with carrying guns and knives."[25] Matt Skoff, president of the Ottawa Police Association, called the new legislation "crippling," saying, "You are seeing a correlation between our lack of interacting with the public and an increase—a

[22] *Review of the RCMP's Policies and Procedures regarding Street Checks Report*, Government of Canada: Civilian Review and Complaints Commission for the RCMP, Royal Canadian Mounted Police Act Subsection 45.34(1). crcc-ccetp.gc.ca/en/review-rcmps-policies-and-procedures-regarding-street-checks-report

[23] "Carding drops but proportion of blacks stopped by Toronto police rises" by Jim Rankin et al., *Toronto Star*, July 28, 2016. thestar.com/news/insight/2014/07/26/carding_drops_but_proportion_of_blacks_stopped_by_toronto_police_rises.html

[24] "New Ontario rule banning carding by police takes effect" by Muriel Draaisma, *CBC News*, January 1, 2017. cbc.ca/news/canada/toronto/carding-ontario-police-government-ban-1.3918134

[25] "Toronto area police chief faults new Ontario restrictions on carding for rise in violent crime" by Molly Hayes and Jeff Gray, *The Globe and Mail*, June 28, 2018. theglobeandmail.com/canada/article-toronto-area-police-chief-faults-new-ontario-restrictions-on-carding/

sharp, dramatic increase—in the number of shootings." Mr. Skoff provided no evidence for this correlation.[26]

A 2019 article by Rosie DiManno called the correlation "dubious," and an independent 2018 review ordered by the Ontario provincial government[27] and conducted by The Honourable Justice Michael H. Tulloch, which asked two fundamental questions—*Do random street checks actually work?* and *Should random street checks ever be allowed?*—recommended that "no police officer should arbitrarily or randomly stop individuals to request their identifying information."[28] Mr. Tulloch found no evidence to substantiate any correlation in the reduction of carding with an increase in shootings but noted that "there is also evidence that a substantial number of young people who are experiencing or perpetrating youth violence are being regularly subjected to police stops."[29] The entire misdirection approach by Mr. Skoff and others was an example of a deliberate attempt by police leadership to seed disinformation.

Interestingly, in April 2021, as Ontario was gripped by the third wave of the COVID-19 pandemic, Ontario's Ford government passed emergency legislation that gave the police enhanced powers to stop and request identifying information of citizens—both pedestrians and those in vehicles—to determine their reason for leaving their homes, and to fine and arrest anyone found to be non-compliant with the stay-at-home order.[30] It was carding by a different name. The uproar by civil liberties advocates was instantaneous and powerful and, in a twist, police services across the province—including the Guelph, London, and Ottawa Police—publicly denounced the enhanced powers.[31] Within twenty-four hours, Premier Doug Ford pulled the order.

Deadly Force

On February 26, 2012, Trayvon Martin, a seventeen-year-old African American teenager, was chased down and shot to death by a neighbourhood watchman near a gated community in Florida. Martin, who was walking home after buy-

26   *Ibid.*

27   *Report of the Independent Street Checks Review* by The Honourable Michael H. Tulloch, Ministry of the Solicitor General, Government of Ontario, Queen's Printer for Ontario, 2018. mcscs.jus. gov.on.ca/english/Policing/StreetChecks/ReportIndependentStreetChecksReview2018.html

28   *Ibid.*

29   *Ibid.*

30   "Ontario gives police authority to stop people, vehicles, ask purpose of travel" by Bryann Aguilar, *CTV News*, April 16, 2021. toronto.ctvnews.ca/ontario-gives-police-authority-to-stop-people-ve-hicles-ask-purpose-of-travel-1.5390805

31   "Many Ontario police forces won't use new COVID-19 powers to conduct random stops" by Colin Perkel, *Global News*, April 27, 2021. globalnews.ca/news/7765907/ontario-police-forces-new-covid-19-powers

ing a pack of Skittles at a convenience store, was profiled by the watchman, who decided this Black teenager looked like "a real suspicious guy...up to no good."[32] The fact that he was wearing a hoodie—a garment long associated with "Black hoodlums" in the media[33]—was later noted as one reason for his supposed guilt. The security guard claimed he was scared for his life. Martin, who was unarmed, fought to escape his assailant but was shot dead on the spot. The security guard remained uncharged for weeks afterward, and only after the governor of Florida appointed a special prosecutor to the case was the watchman charged with second-degree murder. He was found not guilty at his trial in June 2013, and set free.[34] Trayvon Martin had committed no crime; he was killed simply because he was Black.

The police killing of twenty-six-year-old Breonna Taylor on March 13, 2020, in Louisville, Kentucky, was another example of fatal error on the part of white police officers causing the death of an innocent Black person. The raid, which had been ordered by a warrant but concerned a drug crime taking place in a location far from Taylor's home, was deemed by a *New York Times* investigation to have been "compromised by poor planning and reckless execution."[35]

While the United States is on the world's radar for violence against Black people, Canada should be, too. Over the past four decades, I've lived in several of Canada's largest cities, including Montréal, Toronto, and Vancouver—places where police have been responsible for the killing of Black citizens, people of colour, and Indigenous peoples at a rate disproportionate to that of white citizens and the overall population. In Toronto, Canada's most populous and diverse city, stories abound of Black men cut down by police under dubious circumstances. A 2018 *CBC News* article detailed that out of 461 fatal encounters over eighteen years, only two officers were convicted, and more than one-third of victims in Toronto were Black.[36] Though Black people made up only 8.3 percent of the population at the time of the study, they represented 37 percent of the victims.

In the summer of 2020, just a couple months before the George Floyd killing, D'Andre Campbell, a resident of the Toronto suburb of Brampton, called

32 "Shooting of Trayvon Martin" by André Munro, *Brittanica.com*, February 26, 2012. britannica.com/event/shooting-of-Trayvon-Martin

33 "Nine years after Trayvon Martin's killing, hoodies still spark debate" by Priya Elan, *The Guardian*, February 27, 2021. theguardian.com/fashion/2021/feb/27/trayvon-martin-hoodies-black-young-people

34 "Shooting of Trayvon Martin" by André Munro, *Brittanica.com*, February 26, 2012. britannica.com/event/shooting-of-Trayvon-Martin

35 "What to Know About Breonna Taylor's Death" by Richard J. Oppel Jr., Derrick Bryson Taylor, and Nicholas Bogel-Burroughs, *The New York Times*, April 26, 2021. nytimes.com/article/breonna-taylor-police.html

36 "Deadly Force: Fatal Encouters with Police in Canada: 2000–2017" by Jacques Marcoux and Katie Nicholson, *CBC News* (n.d.). newsinteractives.cbc.ca/longform-custom/deadly-force

911 seeking help with a mental health crisis. Within two minutes on the scene, officers had shot Campbell in his home, killing him and traumatizing several family members who witnessed the shooting. A subsequent investigation exonerated the officers of criminal responsibility.[37] This is just one example of many. And Toronto is not the only culprit.

On August 9, 2008, two Montréal police officers approached an unarmed eighteen-year-old Honduran man named Fredy Villanueva and his friends who were playing dice in a parking lot of Henri-Bourassa Park in the poor neighbourhood of Montréal North. An officer identified two of the youth, including Villaneuva's brother, Dany, as gang members, and wanted to issue them tickets for gambling. The arresting officer wrestled the young man on the ground. Later claiming he was afraid for his life "as the group of young people advanced toward him,"[38] the officer shot and killed Fredy Villanueva and wounded two others.

On November 30, 2021, videos surfaced showing Québec City police officers "punching and kicking snow in the face"[39] of an eighteen-year-old Black man named Pacifique Niyokwizera while he was lying on the ground outside a nightclub. A man whom they had neither put under arrest or charged with any crime. Another video at the same scene shows police "dragging a young Black woman through the snow." Five officers were suspended pending an investigation. Another in a long series of assaults on Black people by police that probably would have gone unreported but for the video evidence.

These cases are just the tip of the iceberg. In 2020, thirty-four people were killed by police officers in Canada, with 67 percent of the victims identifying as BIPOC (48 percent Indigenous and 19 percent Black).[40] While police violence against Black people continues across North America, some people prefer not to acknowledge it. In fact, some argue that members of the Black community point to extreme examples to make their case against the police, preferring to believe that police are just doing their job. The lack of lived experience with police harassment or intimidation can, like all aspects of white advantage, lead people to believe it's not happening. But a tree that falls in the forest *does* make a sound even if you are not there to hear it. Believe me.

---

[37] "D'Andre Campbell fatally shot by police in Brampton home after calling for help, family says" by Farah Nasser, *Global News*, June 12, 2020. globalnews.ca/news/7058201/dandre-campbell-family-peel-regional-police-shooting/

[38] "A decade after Fredy Villanueva's death in Montreal North, what has changed?" by Lex Perreaux, *The Globe and Mail*, August 5, 2018. theglobeandmail.com/canada/article-a-decade-after-fredy-villanuevas-death-in-montreal-north-what-has

[39] "5 Quebec City police officers suspended after video shows violent treatment of Black youth," *CBC News*, November 30, 2021. cbc.ca/news/canada/montreal/quebec-city-police-officers-suspended-1.6268340

[40] "En 2020, 34 personnes sont mortes sous les balles de policiers au Canada," Liam Casey et. al, *Le Devoir*, December 21, 2020. ledevoir.com/societe/592110/en-2020-34-personnes-sont-mortes-sous-les-balles-de-policiers

The reality is that white people in Canada are advantaged because it is less likely that they will experience incessant harassment and targeting by law enforcement. It's spelled out in black and white. *A Disparate Impact*, the second interim report in the Ontario Human Rights Commission's inquiry into racial profiling and racial discrimination of Black persons by the Toronto Police Service (TPS), published in August 2020, confirms that Black people are more likely than people of other races to be arrested, charged, over-charged, struck, shot, or killed by Toronto police.[41] Although they represent only 8.8 percent of Toronto's population, Black people represented almost one-third (32 percent) of charges.

My Personal Experience

My personal experience with the police in Canada has been negligible, and I recognize that's outside the norm. But I think I understand why. As a teenager, I lived in Victoria, a small city of nearly three hundred thousand with a very small Black population. I felt like I actually knew most of the Black people who lived there, including my brother, Chris, and my friends Colin, Mohamed, and their siblings and parents. More often than not, I was the only Black person present at a gathering, in my classrooms, at a restaurant, a cinema, or walking down the street. As I had during my foundational years growing up in Montréal, I lived with a white family in a white neighbourhood and I went to a mostly white school. There was no Black community to speak of. We were anomalies, really; invisible in plain sight. Consciously and subconsciously, I expect, I leaned into my whiteness. I had no other cultural or social references. No Black family. I felt in fact, like a white kid in a Black body. Black culture was something I saw on American TV, and it felt foreign to me rather than a reflection of who I was. I had not been born in, nor had I ever lived in, a Black neighbourhood. The 'hood wasn't a reality for me.

In 1980s Victoria, I experienced my fair share of blatantly racist taunts and intimidation from white kids and adults alike, and I also had to deal with many instances of "polite" racism (some purposeful; others rooted in ignorance)—verbal musings by white people that today we'd characterize as microaggressions. But the visible, systemic racism was predominantly targeted toward Indigenous peoples; even as a kid, I could tell they were widely seen as second-class citizens and treated as such. The harassment and discrimina-

---

[41] *A Disparate Impact: Second interim report on the inquiry into racial profiling and racial discrimination of Black persons by the Toronto Police Service*, Ontario Human Rights Commission, August 10, 2020. ohrc.on.ca/en/disparate-impact-second-interim-report-inquiry-racial-profiling-and-racial-discrimination-black

tion, combined with centuries of oppression and mistreatment suffered at the hands of colonial forces and their descendants, further fuelled the negative societal impacts on the First Nations of the region. I saw how those same citizens who mistreated Indigenous peoples supported the police forces that did their bidding and kept them safe.

My personal experience with systemic racism and law enforcement in Canada came later in my life, when I began travelling the world for work and pleasure. I stopped counting the number of times I was profiled by Canadian customs officers for looking "suspiciously" Black. In the '90s and early 2000s, I made many trips to Jamaica to visit friends. The island had become a sort of second home to me even though I had no family connection there. If, like me, you've ever returned to Canada from a Jamaican vacation, you may have noticed a number of customs officers waiting just outside the gate as you deplane. If you're white—even with a great tan—you may not have noticed that these officers are profiling passengers as they exit. Over a twenty-year period during which I travelled to Jamaica at least a dozen times, I never saw a white traveller pulled aside to be interrogated. It happened to me almost every time.

On one occasion, I felt eyes on me and knew I would be pulled from the crowd. I was asked repeatedly what I had been doing in Jamaica and if I was travelling alone. The officer asked me at least five different ways where the rest of my family was and whether they would be coming off the plane with more bags. The first time they asked, I told them I was travelling alone. The second time, the officer noticed my rising annoyance, and the final time, I pushed back, letting him know he had asked me the same question several times already. That was it. He grabbed my passport and sent me to the secondary-inspection room where I spent thirty minutes answering questions while my bags were searched. After finding nothing incriminating, they told me, without apology, to pack my bags and get on my way. Welcome home.

Some people may suggest that these are just security measures to stop criminals at the border, but when its mostly Black people being pulled aside, it's clear something else is at play. A 2018 *CTV News* investigation uncovered troubling, if unsurprising, data to suggest that airline passengers travelling "from the Middle East and countries where most people are black are more likely to face luggage searches or additional questioning by Canada Border Services agents than other travellers."[42] People flying into Canada from African and Caribbean countries in 2017 were flagged nearly four times more often than citizens from European Union countries for secondary inspection, with a

---

[42] "Air travellers from Middle East, Africa, Caribbean more likely to face secondary inspection: CBSA data" by Glen McGregor, *CTV News*, May 30, 2018. ctvnews.ca/politics/air-travellers-from-middle-east-africa-caribbean-more-likely-to-face-secondary-inspection-cbsa-data-1.3952908

total of 11 percent of passengers with passports from Middle Eastern countries and 11 percent of African or Caribbean travellers "pulled aside for customs issues," compared with 2.7 percent of EU citizens.[43]

When I was living and working in Seattle in the early 2000s, I often drove home to Vancouver to visit family and friends—a three-hour drive made more enjoyable behind the wheel of my Audi TT convertible. One morning on my way back to Seattle at five in the morning (to make it to my desk by 8 A.M.), the American customs officer shouted at me to turn off my car and hand over my passport. Every other time, I had been told *not* to turn off my engine. But I complied.

He asked me where I was going. I explained I was returning home to Seattle and directly to my workplace. I told him that my work visa was in my passport. He disregarded what I'd said and began interrogating me—how I could get a job at this company over a US citizen? I answered politely, not wanting to create friction, and explained that my professional credentials had led to me being hired. Was this my car? It was. How could I afford a car like this? I told him it was leased and that I was well compensated for my work. He tried to bait me with other insulting and demeaning questions, but I kept my cool. I knew that he knew he held all the power—including the right to strip me of my work visa on the spot. He handed me back my passport, tugged at his belt, adjusted his gun holster, and dismissed me with a look of scorn.

If you've never had to experience this or other forms of harassment by law enforcement simply because of the colour of your skin, that's an advantage you have, even if you are not aware of it.

To Serve and Protect: Double Standards

At the height of North America's 2020 reckoning on race, the RCMP took weeks to reverse its initial public position that systemic racism did not exist amongst its ranks. Only after public pressure mounted did RCMP Commissioner Brenda Lucki publicly concede that the RCMP had "not always treated racialized and Indigenous people fairly."[44] Acknowledgement and a commitment to change are good first steps, but changing the reality is another.

Just a few months after this announcement, in the fall of 2020, Mi'kmaw lobster fishers of the Sipekne'katik band in southwestern Nova Scotia were verbally and physically assaulted by a mob of non-Indigenous fishers. The non-Indigenous fishers were protesting the band's harvesting outside of the

43 *Ibid.*

44 "Statement by Commissioner Brenda Lucki," Royal Canadian Mounted Police, June 12, 2020. rcmp-grc.gc.ca/en/news/2020/statement-commissioner-brenda-lucki

regulated season, though they were doing so under their treaty right to fish for a "moderate livelihood." The protest culminated in the setting ablaze of a lobster pound where Indigenous catch was being stored for processing. This all occurred in front of a large contingent of RCMP officers who stood idly by and did little to intervene—all of which was captured by local and national media at the scene.

The backlash was immediate. Mark Miller, then Canada's federal Indigenous Services Minister noted,

> We must also recognize that once again as evidenced by the scenes of violence, Indigenous people have been let down by the police, those who are sworn to protect them....The protection of people on both sides has to prevail, and clearly that has not been the case up until now.[45]

Then–Assembly of First Nations National Chief Perry Bellegarde called for the commissioner to resign, stating, "Given months of civil unrest and multiple issues relating to the safety of First Nations people across the country, I will be writing to Prime Minister Trudeau to express that we have lost confidence in Royal Canadian Mounted Police Commissioner, Brenda Lucki."[46]

Several RCMP officers initially made excuses for the force's inaction. When public pressure grew, Commissioner Lucki finally expressed concern and made a commitment to investigate and bring those responsible to justice. Watching the news footage made my blood boil, as it was yet another tangible example of the double standard that racialized and Indigenous communities have experienced in this country at the hands of the law. If white fishers had been the ones attacked and their property set on fire by Indigenous fishers, there is little doubt in my mind that the RCMP would have come down hard on those responsible. It took several months for suspects to even be identified and charged for the various crimes. Over a year later, Mi'kmaw dock lines are still being cut, their boats set adrift. In May 2021, a United Nations committee on the elimination of racial discrimination called on Ottawa "to respond to claims it didn't properly intervene in or investigate racist violence against Mi'kmaw fishers in Nova Scotia."[47]

---

[45] "Federal minister criticizes RCMP response in lobster fishery dispute as more officers dispatched to intervene" by Ryan Tumilty, *The National Post*, October 19, 2020. nationalpost.com/news/politics/federal-minister-criticizes-rcmp-response-in-lobster-fishery-dispute-as-more-officers-dispatched-to-intervene

[46] "AFN chief calls for resignation of RCMP commissioner as N.S. fishery dispute continues" by Ryan Patrick Jones, *CBC News*, October 23, 2020. cbc.ca/news/politics/afn-chief-rcmp-commissioner-resign-1.5774499

[47] UN committee calls on Canada to respond to claims of racist violence against Mi'kmaw fishers" by Taryn Grant, *CBC News*, May 10, 2021. cbc.ca/news/canada/nova-scotia/united-nations-committee-mi-kmaw-moderate-livelihood-lobster-fishery-1.6020492

Perhaps the most blatant recent example of this double standard was observed during the United States Capitol attack of January 6, 2021. The mob of Trump supporters, Qanon, and other white supremacist groups were handled with such kid gloves by law enforcement they were able to overtake security, break into the Capitol building, and storm the chambers of Congress. This almost hands-off approach to protesters was in sharp contrast to the intense police brutality with which many peaceful Black Lives Matter protesters were met during the summer of 2020.

Defunding & Reforming

Progressive-minded white Canadians must find a way to embrace that systemic racism is at the core of the issues facing policing in Canada. What can we hope to achieve in terms of tangible systemic change? The call for "defunding the police" has put many white people on edge. The prospect of fewer police, for a group that largely sees police as doing good, brings with it a fear of increased crime and the belief by some that their communities could be put at greater risk. In 2020, we heard many progressive voices call for the police to be stripped of budgets, and in some cases, of their military-like resources—tools they contend be used to oppress Black people.

But like the term "white privilege," I believe the call to "defund the police" has muddied the waters from a communications standpoint. Kent Roach, a legal scholar at the University of Toronto says it best:

> I fear that it's [a] divisive and ultimately unsuccessful political slogan for what I think is a very important idea. And that is...an increasing recognition both among activists and by researchers that we need to place the public money that we spend on safety, security, [and] well-being, into a broader institutional context that includes other public agencies and community groups, as well as the police.[48]

As Toronto city councillor Kristyn Wong-Tam explains, "defund" doesn't mean "abolish," but it does mean "reform." "[It] is an acknowledgment that law enforcement has ballooned to encompass far-ranging responsibilities it's incapable of addressing."[49] What we should really be talking about is the need for *serious systemic reform* of police institutions. What many have advocated

[48]   "The Modern Policing File," *Toronto Star* (n.d.). thestar.com/thefile/the-modern-policing-file/index.html

[49]   "Canada's policing failures show systemic need for better mental health crisis response" by Cassandra Szklarski, *Global News*, June 15, 2020. globalnews.ca/news/7068392/canada-policing-mental-health

for is a long list of reforms, including bans on chokeholds and no-knock warrants, the reprioritizing of police tasks, and the removal of legal protection for police officers deemed to have violated the rights of the citizens they're paid to protect.

In Canada, many reforms have been advocated for by members of the public, activist organizations, and government officials. Black Lives Matter Toronto, under the banner of "defunding the police," called for the "demilitarizing, disarming and dismantling"[50] of police, arguing that the more than $40 million a day spent on policing in this country should be re-allocated to community support and crime-prevention strategies, among other things. They contend this would put an end to the continual constraint of movements, and the harm and killing of Black and Indigenous people and people of colour across Canada.

In 2020, Ontario premier Doug Ford and Québec premier François Legault were quick to push back on any discussion regarding the "defunding of police," instead insisting that the police needed to remain "strong," but conceding that more should and could be done regarding mental health. Ford stated simply, "I don't believe in that for a second,"[51] while Legault remarked, "I don't see why we have to decrease the funding of police."[52]

Mental Health

No matter how you look at the "defund the police" movement, it is clear that we have an historical opportunity to re-imagine our police institutions and, where possible, look to alternatives to the services they provide. For example, it's become evident that having police officers show up to manage mental health crises is a recipe for a negative outcome—especially for members of racialized and Indigenous communities.

Two recent examples illustrate the disconnect between the need to police crime and the need to respond to mental health crisis situations. In August 2020, Ontario's Special Investigations Unit cleared five Toronto police officers of wrongdoing in the May 2020 death of twenty-nine-year-old Regis Korchinski-Paquet, an Indigenous Ukrainian Black Canadian woman who fell to her death from her twenty-fourth-floor apartment balcony while police burst into her home.

---

50   "Defund the Police," *Black Lives Matter* (n.d.). blacklivesmatter.ca/defund-the-police

51   "'I don't believe in that for a second': Ontario Premier Doug Ford dismisses call to defund police," *CBC News*, June 9, 2020. cbc.ca/news/canada/toronto/doug-ford-defund-police-1.5604747

52   "Police defunding movement gains steam in Montreal as Mayor Plante weighs in" by Rob Lurie and Selena Ross, *CTV News*, June 8, 2020. montreal.ctvnews.ca/police-defunding-movement-gains-steam-in-montreal-as-mayor-plante-weighs-in-1.4975609

Though they claimed the police had been negligent in their "duty of care" when it came to their handling of Korchinski-Paquet's "mental health crisis," the family continues to pursue justice.[53]

Not even one year later, in June 2021, the federal government's Public Prosecution Service announced that no criminal charges would be filed against the New Brunswick police officer who fatally shot Chantel Moore, a twenty-six-year-old Indigenous woman from the Tla-o-qui-aht First Nation in British Columbia. She had been shot by a member of the Edmundston Police Force during a wellness check in the early hours of June 4, 2020. An ex-boyfriend of Ms. Moore's called police to request the wellness check after becoming concerned about messages she had posted on social media. Investigators claimed the shooting occurred after the young woman approached the officer holding a knife.[54] Witnesses commented that Ms. Moore had been intoxicated earlier in the evening—a detail later confirmed by autopsy, and used in the police force's defense.[55] Grand Chief Stewart Phillip of the Tla-o-qui-aht First Nation stated that "justice remains elusive" for all of Moore's family, and for all Indigenous peoples across the country, "who experience, year after year, the devastating impacts of racialized policing, colonial violence, and institutionalized racism."[56]

What these tragic cases illustrate is how the majority of police officers are neither trained nor equipped to deal with people experiencing mental health crises. Because of this, they fall back on their police training, using force that too often leads to deadly outcomes. It seems sensible to me that we need reform on how police deal with mental health calls—and whether they should deal with them at all. The Canadian Mental Health Association (CMHA) puts it plainly: "most people would agree that a person with mental illness should be treated rather than punished." The CMHA suggests that police receive better training in order to "recognize symptoms of mental illness and have the capacity to immediately refer to mental health services instead of the criminal justice system."[57]

One solution would be to match officers with mental health experts in the field, professionals who could take the lead to assess and attempt to diffuse

---

[53] "SIU clears police officers in the death of Regis Korchinski-Paquet" by Rachel Ward, *CBC News*, August 26, 2020. cbc.ca/news/canada/toronto/fifth-estate-regis-korchinski-paquet-siu-1.5699999

[54] "No charges against N.B. police officer in shooting of Indigenous woman Chantel Moore" by Kevin Bissett, *CTV News*, June 7, 2021. atlantic.ctvnews.ca/no-charges-against-n-b-police-officer-in-shooting-of-indigenous-woman-chantel-moore-1.5459930

[55] *Ibid.*

[56] "New Brunswick police officer who fatally shot Chantel Moore won't be charged" by Shane Magee, *CBC News*, June 7, 2021. cbc.ca/news/canada/new-brunswick/chantel-moore-no-charges-officer-shooting-police-1.6056025

[57] "Police and Mental Illness: Increased Interactions," Canadian Mental Health Association: BC Division, March 2005. cmha.bc.ca/wp-content/uploads/2016/07/policesheets_all.pdf

volatile situations before they escalate, limiting or eliminating the need to use force. This would require reforming the police system to accommodate the integration of mental health personnel, to redefine citizen-engagement protocols, and perhaps even requalify some officers—training and certifying front line police and providing them with the skills to engage effectively and collaboratively, with de-escalation being their primary objective.

Whatever the way forward, it's clear that mental health crises are not being handled appropriately by our policing institutions, and people of colour are amongst those paying the ultimate price.

Community Policing

For decades now we've heard about community policing, with many forces employing this approach in the BLM era. Traditionally, this has been characterized as a shift from traditional crime-control methods to the building of relationships and trust between individual police officers and the citizens living in the communities they serve. Over the past decade, the cities of Newark and Camden, New Jersey, have been held up as shining examples of both successful community policing and structural police force reform. Their efforts have included a combination of firing and rebuilding their police force in an effort to eliminate systemic racism and reduce crime.

In 2013, Camden disbanded its police force, cancelled the police union contract, and hired new officers. The new police department paired up with New York University's Policing Project, which consulted on an overhaul of the department's policies. Those new officers were then trained in community policing and anti-bias programs, which included detailed policies and accountability guidelines following those enshrined by the American Civil Liberties Union of New Jersey. As reported in the *Guardian* in 2020, the crime rate that year was 42 percent lower than in 2012.[58] It currently sits at a fifty-year low, and excessive-force complaints have dropped from sixty-four to three. They attributed this success in part to a combination of new leadership, crime-prevention tactics, working with residents, using technology effectively, and exercising best practices. There has been some pushback, especially as police in both communities have continued to use surveillance tactics that appear to heavily target Black community members—much like the street checks that caused such controversy in Toronto—but it's a start.

---

[58] "These New Jersey cities reformed their police – what happened next?" by Ankita Rao, *The Guardian*, June 25, 2020. theguardian.com/us-news/2020/jun/25/camden-newark-new-jersey-police-reform

In Toronto, community policing is not a core practice but a small program, where only 156 (out of more than 4,800) uniformed officers are embedded throughout the city. As "ambassadors" of the police force, they are meant to engage productively with citizens but have little power to make systemic impacts. For a city like Toronto, this is a drop in the bucket, and quite frankly, not a serious attempt at putting community policing at the forefront of citizen engagement. Canadian cities, big and small, should look to successful models from around the world, including the US, where steps towards progress have been made.

∞

As we've seen over and over, police have pushed back hard on any talk of reform, and most are not willing to give up any ground without a fight. As activists and other vocal critics of the police point out, law enforcement institutions proactively invest resources to protect their officers from the legal consequences of the use of deadly, unlawful force. This is because many police organizations have oversight on their internal investigative processes. The police are essentially policing themselves.

In June 2020, the Canadian Press found that the majority of independent investigators delving into alleged police misconduct in Canada are white, male, and former police officers. Of the seven provincial independent investigation units reviewing incidents involving police, 111 of the 167 members were former officers or had previous working relationships with police, and 118 were men.[59] How is anyone who doesn't fit this profile supposed to expect a fair and unbiased investigation? How do we move forward?

Local, provincial, and territorial police institutions and the RCMP should be stripped of their internal oversight powers and a combination of civilian and justice department oversight should be put in place, accountable to the public. This would bring a greater degree of transparency to a historically opaque process, while meeting a core demand for fairness and equity for members of racialized and Indigenous communities. Police unions also bear some responsibility for being more focused on protecting their ranks—digging in, if you will, rather than ensuring their membership is truly accountable. As the *New York Times* put it, police unions are "one of the most significant roadblocks to change."[60] In recent years, police unions on both sides of the

---

[59] "Most independent investigators probing alleged police misconduct in Canada are white, former officers" by Kelly Geraldine Malone, *The Toronto Star*, June 19, 2020. thestar.com/news/canada/2020/06/19/most-independent-investigators-probing-alleged-police-misconduct-in-canada-are-white-former-officers.html

[60] "How Police Unions Became Such Powerful Opponents to Reform Efforts" by Noam Scheiber, Farah Stockman, and J. David Goodman, *The New York Times*, June 6, 2020. nytimes.com/2020/06/06/us/police-unions-minneapolis-kroll.html

border have aggressively fought to protect officers accused of misconduct, often keeping investigative proceedings behind closed doors, and lobbying politicians or supporting them financially to block reform and soften legislation that would lead to more openness and transparency.[61] In June 2020 the *Times* reported that a single New York police union had spent over $1 million on state and local political races since 2014.

Back in 2002, in response to mostly unfavourable reporting on carding, the Toronto Police Association launched a $2.7 billion class action libel suit against *The Star* newspaper. The suit was later dropped.[62] Time, of course, would reveal carding to be what it always was. Unjust, predatory and discriminatory. Some police service organizations and their unions are willing to go to great lengths in order to protect their traditional systems—even in the face of evidence that those systems are biased and unjust.

Reforming the police unions can only happen from within, but the local police services boards in most Canadian cities can have real impact. Made up of civilians and elected officials appointed by the province and the city (Toronto mayor John Tory sits on the board in his city), the boards have the power to push for reforms, hire police chiefs who support and champion reform, and seek concessions from police unions at the collective bargaining table. And this is where the "system" needs to be re-imagined. The policies championed by board members are key, so electing officials with a gusto for real police reform is where change can begin to take root. Voting in municipal and provincial elections does matter. For white progressives asking themselves what they can do to support change, voting for those who support reform is a good start.

Technology & Weapons

There's also ongoing debate about the effectiveness of using technology, such as body-worn cameras (BWCs), to reduce police violence. The belief is that videos released publicly can help hold officers to account and thereby curb the systemic targeting of BIPOC. Organizations like BLM Toronto cite the recommendations from the African Canadian Legal Clinic, among which is the demand that all police officers are required to wear BWCs.[63] A March

---

61 *Ibid.*

62 "Racial profiling still has no place here" by John Sewell, *The Toronto Star*, February 11, 2020. thestar.com/opinion/2010/02/11/racial_profiling_still_has_no_place_here.html

63 "Amid pushback to body cameras, PM Trudeau says they are 'one measure amongst many'" by Rachel Gilmore, *CTV News*, June 9, 2020. ctvnews.ca/politics/amid-pushback-to-body-cameras-pm-trudeau-says-they-are-one-measure-amongst-many-1.4976429

2021 study found use of these cameras correlated with a 10 percent drop in use of force in both fatal and non-fatal encounters, along with a 17 percent drop in complaints against police.[64]

Personally, I'm an advocate for the wide implementation and use of BWCs for front-line police officers. In the social media age and the era of "alternative facts," our society—particularly those living in the bubble of white advantage—needs to see to believe. Combined with strict rules and guidelines—including heavy penalties for officers found tampering with their cameras—and additional reforms suggested by BLM Toronto (such as disarming police, as in the UK, and decriminalizing drug use[65]), BWCs would be useful in capturing the evidence of a truth that will otherwise continue to be disputed. I believe the reckoning we are experiencing today around systemic racism would not have happened if not for the nearly nine-minute video of George Floyd's murder by police that was shared with millions around the world.

Demilitarizing the police is another absolutely necessary part of reform. Beginning in 1997, following the wars in Iraq and Afghanistan, the US military transferred more than $7 billion in excess military equipment (grenade launchers, armoured vehicles, body armour, and weapons) to more than eight thousand law enforcement agencies across the country. Through generous subsidy programs from the government, police departments made additional purchases, resulting in billions of dollars flowing to defense contractors. As a result, over the past few decades, we've seen street protests turn into war zones with highly weaponized police forces being brutally deployed against citizens.

The 2010 G20 summit held in Toronto remains a stain on the Toronto police; its use of excessive force and questionable control tactics led to the detention of more than one thousand citizens. While a "small band"[66] of protestors had incited violence, the majority were peacefully protesting globalization, poverty, and environmental concerns. The result was the largest mass arrest in Canadian history.[67]

It's due time for the institution of policing to remove its military-style body armour, rid itself of its military-grade equipment, and get back to its original

64   "Study: Body-Worn Camera Research Shows Drop In Police Use Of Force" by Cheryl Corley, *NPR*, April 26, 2021. npr.org/2021/04/26/982391187/study-body-worn-camera-research-shows-drop-in-police-use-of-force

65   "[Landing Page]," *Black Lives Matter* (n.d.). blacklivesmatter.ca/#BelowIntro

66   "Toronto police pay $16.5m to protesters wrongfully held at 2010 G20 summit" by Tracey Lindeman, *The Guardian*, August 18, 2020. theguardian.com/world/2020/aug/18/g20-protesters-toronto-police-canada

67   "G20-related mass arrests unique in Canadian history" by Jill Mahoney, *The Globe and Mail*, June 28, 2010. theglobeandmail.com/news/world/g20-related-mass-arrests-unique-in-canadian-history/article4323163/

mandate of serving and protecting communities. Otherwise, police will continue to be viewed by peaceful, law-abiding citizens as a source for violence, and a force to be feared. There is a mountain to climb to reform policing in Canada, but we need to start now. It's going to take firm commitment, followed by tangible action from those in positions of power, to ensure that all people are treated equally and justly. Only then will police ever have a chance of becoming part of the solution instead of remaining part of the problem.

What's Happening Now

Thankfully, there does appear to be some progress south of the border. Since the killing of George Floyd, more than 140 police oversight bills aimed at increasing accountability and overhauling rules on the use of force in various American States have been passed. Illinois recently enacted a Statewide Use of Force Standardization Act, which rewrote many of the state's policing guidelines, including making body cameras mandatory. In March 2021, the city of New York moved to make it easier for citizens to sue officers. The Maryland legislature, which decades ago became the first to adopt a Law Enforcement Officers' Bill of Rights, became the first to eliminate it. And many jurisdictions are looking to bring about new legislation that would remove certain officer immunity against prosecution.[68] These efforts show that making systemic change *is* possible.

Canada is also showing some signs of progress. In July 2020, Toronto City Council adopted thirty-six decisions related to police reform, including public safety, crisis response, and police accountability.[69] A month later, the Toronto Police Services Board approved eighty-one recommendations on police reform, which it claims will lead to "concrete action" in everything from community safety–response models to various steps to address systemic racism and improve trust within communities. A Police Reform Implementation Dashboard was created to provide transparency as to the progress achieved regarding the implementation of the 81 recommendations,[70] addressing a long-standing concern that police data and information was kept behind

---

[68] "As New Police Reform Laws Sweep Across the U.S., Some Ask: Are They Enough?" by Victor J. Blue, *The New York Times*, April 18, 2021.nytimes.com/2021/04/18/us/police-reform-bills. html?referringSource=articleShare

[69] "Policing Reform," City of Toronto (n.d.). toronto.ca/community-people/get-involved/community/ policing-reform to provide transparency around the progress achieved in relation to implementation of the 81 recommendations

[70] "Police Reform Implementation Dashboard" by The Analytics & Innovation Unit, Toronto Police Service. storymaps.arcgis.com/stories/98dd64b7376345bd83663fbc0069c083

closed doors. As of November 2021, forty-nine of the recommendations had been completed and 32 percent were in progress.[71]

∞

I have friends who are police officers. My impression is that they are proud of and serious about the work they do, and that they are honest, truthful, passionate, fair, and generous of spirit. The people I know are not racists. They've expressed to me the difficulties of their jobs, the work they are expected to do, the risks they take, and how they sometimes struggle to manage citizens' expectations. They place a high importance on keeping people safe while having the backs of their brothers and sisters in uniform. It's not an easy job. I get it. Not all police officers are racists; the real issue is the systemic racism inherent in the police institution itself. That is where our primary focus for change needs to be. But I believe that every police officer still owes it to the citizens they are hired to protect to take a look at their own unconscious biases, many of which have likely been ingrained as a part of their police training. Like all of us, they have some unlearning to do.

PART 2. SENTENCING & CORRECTIONS

UNFORTUNATELY, POLICING IS ONLY ONE ASPECT OF THE CANADIAN CRIMINAL justice system that needs serious reform. The racial biases within the judicial and corrections systems have also exacerbated the inequality faced by Black and Indigenous people. The data continues to show that, compared to whites, Black and Indigenous peoples in North America are disproportionally arrested, given harsher prison sentences, and experience disadvantages once incarcerated as a result of bias and discriminatory laws. In order to understand the harmful generational impacts of this reality in Canada, it's helpful to take a continent-wide view. The first question we should ask ourselves is a simple one with a complex answer: How did we get here?

A big part of the problem is the American-led War on Drugs. In June 1971, Richard Nixon, the thirty-seventh president of the United States, who would go on to be disgraced due to the Watergate scandal, declared drug abuse "public enemy number one." He formally declared a "War on Drugs" that would be directed toward "eradication, interdiction, and incarceration." Since Nixon's initial pronouncement, it is estimated that the US has spent more than $1 trillion on the War on Drugs—with $3.3 billion spent annually to incarcerate citizens for drug-related offences alone.

---

[71]   *Ibid.*

My own view of the war on drugs came into focus when Ronald Reagan became president in 1981, and his wife, Nancy Reagan, championed an anti-drug campaign. At every opportunity, the First Lady asked children to "just say no."[72] For my friends and me, that just meant it was harder to get our hands on a stash of sinsemilla. Reagan greatly expanded the reach of the drug war, and his focus on criminal punishment over treatment led to a massive increase in incarcerations for non-violent drug offenses, from fifty thousand inmates in 1980 to four hundred thousand in 1997. Specifically, the Anti-Drug Abuse Act of 1986[73] allocated $1.7 billion to the War on Drugs and established a series of mandatory minimum prison sentences for various drug-related offenses. It was "the first federal criminal law to differentiate crack from other forms of cocaine."[74] Another notable feature was the massive differentiation between the amount of crack versus powder cocaine possession that resulted in the same five-year-minimum sentence: five grams of crack versus five *hundred* grams of powder cocaine.

A National Household Survey on Drug Abuse (NSDHA) study,[75] which followed drug-related crime in America from 1979 to 1998, estimated that 72 percent of all drug users were white, while only 15 percent were Black. However, it also found that "the comparison of racial proportions of drug users and drug arrests...reveals a markedly higher arrest rate of black drug offenders compared to both whites and to the black proportion of the drug using population." With each passing year of the study, the number of drug-related arrests for Black folks was double that of whites. The study points out that these "racial disparities in drug arrests did not reflect racial differences in violations of drug laws prohibiting possession and sale of illicit drugs."[76]

Not only were police targeting low-income, majority Black neighbourhoods, but Black people were already more likely to be arrested than whites. Add to this that crack is the cheaper form of cocaine, more likely to be procured in those over-policed neighbourhoods, and you have a perfect scenario for an

---

72 "Black people 5 times more likely to be arrested than whites, according to new analysis" by Anagha Srikanth, *The Hill: Changing America*, June 11, 2020. thehill.com/changing-america/respect/equality/502277-black-people-5-times-more-likely-to-be-arrested-than-whites

73 "The History of The War on Drugs: Reagan Era and Beyond," Landmark Recovery, February 13, 2019. landmarkrecovery.com/history-of-the-war-on-drugs-reagan-beyond

74 *[Abstract] Powder Cocaine and Crack Use in the United States: An Examination of Risk for Arrest and Socioeconomic Disparities in Use* by Joseph J. Palamar et al., Drug and Alcohol Dependence, Vol. 149, 2015 (108-116). ncbi.nlm.nih.gov/pmc/articles/PMC4533860/

75 "Punishment and Prejudice: Racial Disparities in the War on Drugs: VII. Racially Disproportionate Drug Arrests," Human Rights Watch, Vol 12., No. 2, May 2000. hrw.org/reports/2000/usa/Rcedrg00-05.htm#P366_83787

76 *Ibid.*

overpopulation of Black people in the criminal justice system. It should be no surprise then, that mandatory minimums led to increased incarceration rates for non-violent Black drug offenders, as well as claims that the War on Drugs was truly a war on Black people.

In 1994 President Bill Clinton passed the controversial Violent Crime Control and Law Enforcement Act. With a $30 billion price tag, it was the largest crime-control bill in American history.[77] As fate would have it, then-Senator—now President—Joe Biden, was a major architect and promoter of the bill. Nearly thirty years later, he's now working to undo much of its damage. Looking at it through a purely political lens, the bill wasn't just about crime, but public perception.

As a 2020 *Vox* article explains, "Biden and other Democratic authors of the law were clear about their intentions: supporting a more punitive criminal justice system to rebuke criticisms that they were 'soft on crime.'" The law imposed tougher prison sentences at the federal level and encouraged states to do the same. It provided funding for states to build more prisons and backed grant programs encouraging police officers to carry out more drug-related arrests. One of the most negative aspects of the bill was the "three strikes" law, which meant that anyone convicted of a third felony would automatically receive a sentence of twenty years to life, with no eligibility for parole until twenty years served.

Lauren-Brooke Eisen, director of the Justice Program at the Brennan Center for Justice, a New York–based non-partisan law and policy think tank, says one of the most significant and long-lasting impacts of the legislation was that "the federal money incentivized the prison construction boom and the funding encouraged states and cities to increase arrests, prosecutions, and incarceration, playing a tremendously powerful part in growing the size and scope of our correctional system."[78] This concept is often referred to as the "prison–industrial complex," a term derivative of President Dwight D. Eisenhower's concern over the threat of the military–industrial complex to American democracy back in the 1950s. As Eisenhower famously stated in his 1961 Farewell Address, "The potential for the disastrous rise of misplaced power exists and will persist."[79] In this case, the "misplaced power" is the prison system itself.

---

[77] "Violent Crime Control and Law Enforcement Act of 1994: Fact Sheet," US Department of Justice, October 24, 1994. ncjrs.gov/txtfiles/billfs.txt

[78] "Fact check: 1994 crime bill did not bring mass incarceration of Black Americans" by Doug Stanglin, *USA Today*, July 3, 2020. usatoday.com/story/news/factcheck/2020/07/03/fact-check-1994-crime-bill-didnt-bring-mass-incarceration-black-people/3250210001/

[79] "President Dwight D. Eisenhowers Farewell Address (1961)," U.S. National Archives & Records Administration (n.d.). ourdocuments.gov/print_friendly.php?flash=false&page=&doc=90&title=President+Dwight+D.+Eisenhowers+Farewell+Address+%281961%2

In 1980, there were twenty-five thousand people in federal and state prisons for drug violations. Today that number is estimated at over three hundred thousand, with 45 percent of those incarcerated in federal prisons for drug offences. That growth has disproportionally affected African Americans, Native Americans, and Latinx people. More than two-thirds of people serving federal life or virtual life sentences have been convicted of non-violent crimes, including 30 percent for a drug crime.[80] According to the ACLU, one out of every three Black boys born today can expect to go to prison in his lifetime, as can one of every six Latino boys—compared to one of every seventeen white boys.[81]

In the summer of 2021, I reconnected with my friend Brian O'Dea, who was in Toronto awaiting his papers to return home to California. Brian is an infamous former international drug smuggler I met nearly ten years ago through a mutual friend. His story is right out of a Hollywood movie. In fact, he published a book in 2006, *High: Confessions of an International Drug Smuggler*, that formed the basis for several TV documentary programs. A white Newfoundlander, Brian went from a petty neighbourhood drug dealer in the 1970s to operating a $100-million-a-year, 120-person drug-smuggling business in the 1980s, overseeing shipments of cocaine from Columbia through Jamaica and into Florida. He also developed what he calls "a terrifying addiction"[82] to cocaine. He turned his life around in 1986—quitting the habit cold turkey and volunteering to help other recovering addicts. Unfortunately in 1991, he committed to one last big smuggling job—importing $300 million of marijuana into Washington state from Asia—before retiring for good. When a former colleague of his made a deal with the authorities to avoid a harsher sentence on an unrelated crime, Brian was arrested by the DEA and sentenced to ten years at the Terminal Island federal penitentiary in Los Angeles.

During his time behind bars, Brian learned intimately about the disadvantages the criminal justice system imposed on Black men. He made Black friends in prison, many of whom were serving harsher sentences for drug offences than white inmates who had committed similar or worse crimes. "Pure racism," as Brian calls it. Recently, Brian shared an insightful story with me about "movie night" at FCI Terminal Island. The facility held about thirteen hundred inmates, but the room where movies were shown only accommodated about three hundred people. You had to get in line early after dinner to score a seat. His first time lining up, Brian watched as a Black prison guard let three

---

80   *Still Life: America's Increasing Use of Life and Long-Term Sentences*, The Sentencing Project, Washington, 2017 (13). Sentencingproject.org.

81   "Mass Incarceration," American Civil Liberties Association (n.d.). aclu.org/issues/smart-justice/mass-incarceration

82   *High: Confessions of an International Drug Smuggler* by Brian O'Dea, Other Press, 2009.

Black men in ahead of the lineup. Brian lamented to his white and Latinx buddies that that was "bullshit." His white friend set him straight. "If this is as bad as it gets for you, this is as good as it gets for them. You did a way worse crime and you got way less time than them. Do you want to take that from them? It's one of the privileges the guard can extend to them, knowing they will be rotting in jail for a long time because of the unfair system. You will learn to be okay with that."

"And that was that," Brian added.

In addition to the benefits of his whiteness, because of his status in the community Brian had the benefit of public support. Before he was sent to prison, more than one hundred people in Santa Barbara, California, wrote letters of support and sent them to the DA, the president of the United States, and many other officials, noting how Brian had turned his life around and was now contributing positively to the community, helping others recover from addiction. This advocacy effort had an impact on the district attorney, who came to believe that, while he could not help Brian with a shorter jail sentence (because Brian refused to implicate his criminal associates), he could recommend a transfer to Canada.

Just over a year into serving his sentence in LA, Brian was transferred to Canada, where he spent two more years in prison before being released on parole. It is not lost on Brian that had he been denied a transfer back to Canada—an option unavailable to his fellow inmates, as Americans—he would have remained in the California penal system, where, by law, he would serve a mandatory 85 percent of his sentence (8.5 years), minimum.

Not much has changed in the years since. Data shows that Black and Indigenous men are given much longer sentences with fewer opportunities for early release or parole; this is the reality faced by many for non-violent drug offences.[83] The length of the sentence seems to have no real link to rehabilitation objectives or successful reintegration into society. In fact, research demonstrates that long prison sentences aren't successful for several reasons. A 2016 study published by the US-based National Institute of Justice found that "increasing the severity of punishment does little to deter crime" and "prisons may exacerbate recidivism." [84] Rather than severity, the study found that certainty, referring to "the likelihood of being caught and punished for the commission of a crime," plays a much more significant role. In fact, the study suggests, the more time a person spends in prison, the more effective a criminal they become, learning "more effective crime

[83] "Bias behind bars: A Globe investigation finds a prison system stacked against Black and Indigenous inmates" by Tom Cardaso, *The Globe and Mail*, November 11, 2020. theglobeandmail.com/canada/article-investigation-racial-bias-in-canadian-prison-risk-assessments

[84] *Five Things About Deterrence*, US Department of Justice, National Institute of Justice, May 2016. ojp.gov/pdffiles1/nij/247350.pdf

strategies" from other inmates. Desensitization to future imprisonment may also occur, the more time an individual spends behind bars.

Even post-release, parole conditions for BIPOC can lead to issues securing employment and housing, as well as potential disqualification from government benefits. For example, most US states ban those individuals convicted of drug-related felonies from being eligible for federal public assistance and food stamps.[85]

Brian's son-in-law, who is Black, was sentenced to seven years for a DUI—a single-vehicle accident not involving others—and after an early release several years into his sentence, he was sent back to prison from a halfway house where had been residing for months, his parole officers informing him that he had been released too soon. He ended up spending another year in prison as a result of the apparent mix-up. And his situation is not an isolated one.

A study by researchers at Florida State University, the University of Connecticut, and the University of Iowa,[86] reviewing 2000 and 2001 data for more than twenty-one-thousand people released from North Carolina state prisons, showed recidivism in more than 58 percent of Black men within the eight-year follow-up period, compared to fewer than 50 percent of the white men. Researchers in another study, highlighting the intersectionality of race and gender on reincarceration, attributed "the regularity of negative interaction with police coupled with the systemic racism Black men navigate as a major factor in these slanted recidivism rates."[87] In short, systemic racism is contributing not only to the increased imprisonment of Black people, but to increased rates of reimprisonment.

Since his own release from prison more than three decades ago, Brian has reinvented himself several times. Like many reformed successful marijuana peddlers, he has become an in-demand consultant to the cannabis industry in North America. Ironically, many governments, after legalizing cannabis, are now embracing revenues for the very product they once spent billions criminalizing, and which led to generations of overincarceration. Brian continues to be a passionate advocate for the decriminalization of all drugs, for the reform of the criminal justice system in Canada and the US, and for, in his words, "putting an end to the war on Black and Indigenous people."

∞

[85] "From prisons to communities: Confronting re-entry challenges and social inequality" by Melissa Li, *The SES Indicator*, American Psychological Association, March 2018.

[86] "Black men have higher rates of recidivism despite lower risk factors: study" by Crime and Justice Research Alliance, *Phys.org*. phys.org/news/2018-10-black-men-higher-recidivism-factors.html

[87] "A New Approach to Combat High Recidivism Rates Amongst Black Men" by Taneasha White, *Verywellmind.com*, February 27, 2021. verywellmind.com/combatting-high-recidivism-in-black-men-5114164

Beginning in the 1980s, Canada's war on drugs closely mirrored the US practice of convicting and incarcerating those caught with illegal drugs[88]—with possession punishable by up to five years in prison, or more if the accused was a repeat offender—and this had a similarly devastating impact on BIPOC communities across the country. According to a 2019 report by the John Howard Society of Canada, nearly thirty-nine thousand adults were held in custody on an average day in 2017–18.[89] Of those, about fourteen thousand had been sentenced to over two years and were in federal penitentiaries, and twenty-five thousand were in provincial jails. Ten thousand of them were sentenced to fewer than two years, and about fifteen thousand were awaiting plea or trial.[90]

In 2012, Stephen Harper's Conservative government introduced Bill C-10, the Safe Streets and Communities Act, a keystone in its fear-based "law-and-order" mandate, which pushed an ideology that Canada needed to be tough on crime to protect our communities. (Sound familiar?) The problem with their misguided policy was that the police-reported crime rate was at its lowest point since 1969 and both the crime rate and crime-severity index had been steadily dropping since 1994.[91]

As a complement to the government's 2007 National Anti-Drug Strategy, the bill "intensified legal consequences for minor drug offences and further criminalized non-habitual drug use,"[92] introducing a mandatory one-year sentence for those who commit an additional offence within a ten-year period.[93] The government made its stance clear: drug crime was a law-and-order issue, not a health issue. As a result, more than $500 million over five years was allocated to anti-drug enforcement while major cuts (more than $40 million over the same five-year period) were made to Health Canada's Drug Treatment Funding Program, which had a devastating impact on groups running street-level rehabilitation programs for addicts.[94]

---

[88] "Harper's anti-drug strategy gets a little less compassionate" by John Geddes, *Macleans*, July 25, 2012. macleans.ca/news/canada/drug-money/

[89] "Latest data show too many people in jails and prisons," The John Howard Society of Canada, July 11, 2019. johnhoward.ca/blog/latest-data-shows-too-many-people-in-custodyproblems-in-jails-and-prisons

[90] *Ibid.*

[91] "Canada's crime rate: Two decades of decline," Statistics Canada (n.d.). www150.statcan.gc.ca/n1/pub/11-630-x/11-630-x2015001-eng.htm

[92] "The Canadian war on drugs: Structural violence and unequal treatment of Black Canadians" by Akwatu Khenti, *International Journal of Drug Policy*, Vol. 25, 2014 (190–195). health.gradstudies.yorku.ca/files/2016/09/The-Canadian-war-on-drugs-Structural-violence-and-unequal-treatment-of-Blacks.pdf

[93] "Mandatory minimum sentencing for drug offences unconstitutional say rights advocates," *CBC News*, January 13, 2016. cbc.ca/news/canada/british-columbia/mandatory-minimum-sentencing-for-drug-offences-unconstitutional-say-rights-advocates-1.3402252

[94] "Harper's anti-drug strategy gets a little less compassionate" by John Geddes, *Macleans*, July 25, 2012. macleans.ca/news/canada/drug-money

We're still dealing with the fallout from the Harper government's law-and-order approach. In 2017–18, Black people made up 7.3 percent of Canada's federal prison population, despite accounting for only 3.5 percent of the country's overall population.[95] The situation is even more dire for Indigenous peoples across this country, who accounted for more than 30 percent of Canada's prison population, yet only 4.5 percent of its total population, according to 2018/19 data from the federal government.[96] In Manitoba, data suggests that Indigenous peoples are incarcerated at seven to eight times the rate of non-Indigenous peoples.[97] Canada's Minister of Justice and Attorney General David Lametti called this racial disparity "shameful," suggesting it is "due in good part to current sentencing laws, which focus on punishment."[98]

Assessing Risk

Before researching this book, I had little idea that, once convicted and sent to prison, bias and discrimination continue to negatively impact Black and Indigenous peoples. And then I came across a *Globe and Mail* article published in October 2020, which details the use of "risk assessments" in federal prisons:

> Risk assessments are the high prophets of the prison system, used to divine an inmate's true nature through a mix of numerical scores on standardized tests and parole officers' raw judgments. They're steeped in decades of research—and they are also fundamentally, powerfully biased against Indigenous and Black inmates, placing them in higher security classifications and assigning them worse odds of successfully re-entering society. Simply put, Indigenous and Black inmates aren't at the same starting line as everyone else.... In 2018, the Supreme Court of Canada agreed, ruling that the CSC had failed to ensure psychological risk assessments were not culturally biased. The following year, a Senate report noted the security clas-

---

95 "Canada's prison service trying to better understand the needs of Black offenders" by Jim Bronskill, *The Toronto Star*, January 21, 2020. thestar.com/news/canada/2020/01/21/canadas-prison-service-trying-to-better-understand-the-needs-of-black-offenders.html

96 "Adult and youth correctional statistics in Canada, 2018/2019," Statistics Canada, December 21, 2020. www150.statcan.gc.ca/n1/pub/85-002-x/2020001/article/00016-eng.htm

97 *A Case Study of Diversity in Corrections: The Black Inmate Experience in Federal Penitentiaries Final Report*, Office of the Correctional Investigator, Government of Canada, February 28, 2014. oci-bec.gc.ca/cnt/rpt/oth-aut/oth-aut20131126-eng.aspx

98 "Canada attempts to address 'shameful' racial disparity in criminal justice system" by Anna Mehler Paperny, *Reuters*, February 18, 2021. reuters.com/article/uk-canada-politics-sentencing-idUKKB-N2AI2YB

sification tools may be resulting in harsher incarceration terms for racialized people.[99]

This extensive *Globe* investigation reviewed thousands of records from the Correctional Services of Canada (CSC), focused primarily on the offender security level and reintegration scores, and found that "Black men were almost 24 per cent more likely to end up with the worst security classification score compared with white men, and Indigenous men were close to 30 per cent more likely than white men to receive the worst reintegration potential score. Interestingly, the data showed that both groups were less likely than white men to reoffend given their current scores."[100]

Why are these risk-assessment scores so important? As the article explains, these scores have "wide-ranging consequences," in that they are a major factor in determining "where [a prisoner] will serve their sentence and under which conditions (restrictions vs. privileges), the kinds of treatments and services they can access, and their likelihood of being paroled."[101] And of course, as in the US, it is evidently more difficult for Black and Indigenous inmates to be paroled than their white counterparts, in part due to the risk-assessment scores.

Acknowledging Negative Realities

Let's review: Black and Indigenous citizens are over-policed, over-sentenced, over-incarcerated, and further disadvantaged post-release. It's a vicious cycle. As you can see, the data clearly indicates that Black and Indigenous peoples face discrimination within the criminal justice system as a result of both individual bias and systemic racism. "White advantage" is heavily at play here, as white people—whether being approached on the street, charged with a crime, or serving time—are treated more favourably by the police, by the judiciary, and by the corrections service. Conversely, the BIPOC community has had to live with hundreds of years of state-mandated discrimination, with severely damaging multigenerational impacts. If we are truly intent on realizing our "ideals" as a liberal democracy with equality for all as a central tenet, then Canadians must come together to demand serious change in our criminal justice system.

To begin, we need broad acknowledgement by Canadians that systemic inequality in our criminal justice system is real and therefore needs serious attention. As with all challenges to systemic racism, facing the truth is the first step.

---

[99] "Bias behind bars: A Globe investigation finds a prison system stacked against Black and Indigenous inmates" by Tom Cardaso, *The Globe and Mail*, November 11, 2020. theglobeandmail.com/canada/article-investigation-racial-bias-in-canadian-prison-risk-assessments

[100] *Ibid.*

[101] *Ibid.*

We need buy-in at the front end. We can't be distracted by fear—it's so often stoked by those advantaged by the status quo. I've heard some people say we should only look to the future and stop bringing up the past. But I know from experience that we have to fix the problem and address the hurt it has caused before we can get to a better place, together.

No one is calling for going soft on violent criminals; we need to protect our communities. But we have to realize that we're not truly protecting our communities if whole segments of the population are being sacrificed for the majority to feel "safe." In order to prevent systemic discrimination toward non-violent racialized offenders, we need to fix the biased sentencing process and the prejudicial rules that impact re-integration. We then need to follow through with a thorough public and independent analysis of the criminal justice system—a deep dive into the available data to uncover all the biases and disadvantages—but one that includes, as part of its core mandate, an inclusive debate with diverse views on solutions for reform and modernizing our criminal justice institutions. This has to be followed by a broad sharing of the findings so that we can arrive at a wide acknowledgement of the truths. Only then can we begin thinking about how to fix what is broken.

Time for Change

The good news is that we're already seeing some real energy being directed toward reform. In December 2018, the US congress, responding in part to pressures from prison-reform activists, civil rights groups, the BLM movement, and strong support from elected officials (including Senator Cory Booker and, surprisingly, President Donald Trump) passed a bipartisan criminal justice bill. The First Step Act (FSA)[102] has been widely lauded as a "historic criminal justice reform bill in America."[103] Among a number of key objectives, the FSA worked to decrease the federal inmate population and make the federal justice system fairer, with an added focus on rehabilitation.

Included were important provisions that allowed judges the discretion to impose a lesser sentence than the mandatory minimum, and it abolished the five-year mandatory minimum sentence for simple possession of crack cocaine. It also made those serving time in federal prison for pre-2010 crack cocaine offenses eligible to apply for resentencing. The latter had an immediate effect, with nearly five thousand federal inmates granted reduced sentences.

---

[102] "The First Step Act of 2018: An Overview," Congressional Research Service, March 4, 2019. sgp.fas.org/crs/misc/R45558.pdf

[103] "How the FIRST STEP Act Became Law—and What Happens Next" by Ames Grawert and Tim Lau, *BrennanCentre.org*, January 4, 2019. brennancenter.org/our-work/analysis-opinion/how-first-step-act-became-law-and-what-happens-next

One year after the FSA was signed, the federal prison population had dropped by about five thousand.[104] Much more work needs to be done, but it appears that the broader support from a more aware citizenry, is having a positive effect on elected officials with the power to make reforms happen.

In Canada, after years of talk, it appears that we could finally be seeing some tangible, meaningful action. In 2020, the Correctional Service of Canada announced it would work with the Parole Board of Canada to examine the issue of systemic racism. In July 2020, the agency established a joint committee with the Parole Board for this purpose, with the goal of developing a national approach to working with ethnocultural offenders.[105]

In February 2021, Justice Minister David Lametti introduced Bill C-22, which would amend the criminal code by repealing mandatory minimum penalties for certain drug offences—penalties that disproportionately harm Indigenous and Black offenders as well as those experiencing addiction. The bill would make changes to both the Criminal Code and the Controlled Drugs and Substances Act with the objectives of making the system both more effective and fair, while ensuring public safety is maintained. If passed, it would repeal more than a dozen mandatory minimum penalties on the books—including penalties for all drug-related offences in the Controlled Drugs and Substances Act. Most importantly, this bill would allow judges to consider sanctions other than imprisonment in drug-possession cases—an important shift from a focus on incarceration toward a policy of treatment that would see individuals diverted to drug-treatment courts, a model already used in Toronto and Vancouver.

In May 2021, ahead of expected Fall 2021 elections, Minister Lametti proposed additional reforms, "pledging $216.4 million over five years, and $43.3 million each year after that, to divert Black and Indigenous youth and young people of colour from the courts."[106] Just one month later, the Trudeau government tabled legislation for a simpler and more cost-effective method of allowing "lesser offenders" to apply for pardons, which ultimately would improve opportunities to integrate non-violent offenders into society. Speaking on the proposed legislation, Public Safety Minister Bill Blair noted that "some 10 per cent of Canadians have a criminal record and no pardon, also known as a 'record suspension.' Nearly three quarters of that 10 per cent have never served jail time and yet they carry the heavy burden of a criminal

---

104 *Ibid.*

105 "Anti-racism framework and actions," Correctional Services Canada, July 2021. csc-scc.gc.ca/publications/092/005007-0006-en.pdf

106 "Proposed federal justice reforms could reduce number of Indigenous, Black people in system, say advocates" by Olivia Stefanovich, *CBC News*, May 10, 2021. cbc.ca/news/politics/legal-advocates-welcome-ottawa-budget-bipoc-justice-1.6018034

record throughout their entire lives."[107] Taken together, the proposed federal government reforms could have a tangible effect in alleviating the discrimination and disadvantages faced by BIPOC offenders at the hand of Canada's criminal justice system. With government plans always subject to electoral cycles, it will be interesting to see if the proposed reforms actually happen.

And still, much more can be done. Like the US, Canada should seek to pass legislation to release many of the incarcerated Canadians (disproportionality BIPOC) who are serving longer sentences than they should, given the proposed amendments for possession. There has also been a long-standing debate that would see the broadening of drug decriminalization in order to lower the number of possession-related arrests. Justice Minister Lametti was asked about this in February 2021, and he said he would "not rule out the possibility of decriminalization," adding that "what I'm focusing on today is the sentencing element."[108]

We know decriminalization of drugs can work based on Portugal's example. The country decriminalized the possession of drugs for personal use in 2001 and downgraded the charges to an administrative offence punishable by fine and without either imprisonment or criminal record. The results speak for themselves.

In May 2021, a briefing by Bristol, England's Transform Drug Policy Foundation marked the twentieth anniversary of Portugal's drug reforms.[109] It noted that decriminalization of personal possession is only one part of broader health-centred drug policy reforms that focuses on treatment and harm reduction. The facts contradict the fearmongering that decriminalization would lead to increased use of drugs by minors, an increase in crime overall, and community decay. The briefing noted that Portugal averages about 6 overdose-related deaths per 1 million citizens (fewer than 76 total deaths) annually, while the EU averages 23.7 deaths per 1 million. In comparison, Canada has approximately 105 overdose-related deaths per 1 million, averaging nearly 4,000 per year (4,618 in 2018). In the US, that number was 47,590 in 2018. And Portugal has some of the lowest usage rates in Europe among those between the ages of fifteen and thirty-four. Decriminalization in Portugal also contributed to a dramatic decline in HIV and AIDS in drug users, a reduction in crime, and a reduction in addicts in the prison system. This has clearly been an extremely successful policy.

---

[107] "Liberals table bill to make criminal pardons quicker, cheaper" by Christopher Reynolds, *CTV News*, June 10, 2021. ctvnews.ca/politics/liberals-table-bill-to-make-criminal-pardons-quicker-cheaper-1.5464656

[108] "Liberals introduce new bill to relax penalties for drug offences" by Catharine Tunney, Christian Noel, *CBC News*, February 18, 2021.

[109] "Drug Decriminalisation in Portugal: Setting the Record Straight," Transform Drug Policy Foundation, May 13, 2021. transformdrugs.org/blog/drug-decriminalisation-in-portugal-setting-the-record-straight

The legalization of marijuana in Canada and across many US states did not lead to the societal carnage envisioned by opponents of legalization. What *has* had a tragic impact on North American communities over the past decade has been the exponential increase in the use of prescription opioids, such as Fentanyl. Where the current crisis differs from the crack epidemic of decades past is that it is disproportionately devastating white communities. Could this be one of the reasons a broader swath of politicians is suddenly more open to criminal-justice reform for drug-related offences? Whatever the case, the momentum for reform is a positive development. And there's no time to waste.

Tackling systemic inequality in the criminal justice system is a heavy lift, but it's a challenge that must be taken up with purposeful action. Before we can change the system, we need to acknowledge the problems, examine the facts, and come together to devise effective solutions. Recent progress is encouraging, but much more needs to be done. If you are white and unconsciously advantaged by these complex realities, becoming more aware and acknowledging the facts is a good start.

Chapter Seven

Systemic Inequality: Health Care, Education, and Barriers to Opportunity

HEALTH AND ILLNESS

IN 2020, THE COVID-19 PANDEMIC EXPOSED THE SYSTEMIC INEQUALITY IN the health-care system—the virus having disproportionate negative impacts on BIPOC communities and individuals. The intersectionality of race and socio-economic inequality was at the root of some citizens facing higher rates of negative outcomes than white, socio-economically advantaged citizens.[1]

There were many long-standing contributing factors, including the social determinants of health—the non-medical factors in our lives that influence health outcomes.[2] These include things like income and education inequality, and systemic bias and prejudice in the health-care system. Numerous studies suggest that these determinants are responsible for 30 to 55 percent of health outcomes. That makes them of higher influence than health care or lifestyle.[3] There are many perspectives and just as many proposed solutions for ways to overcome these complex issues. Hopefully I can provide a basis for better understanding and a jumping-off point for further reflection.

Research confirms that racialized populations have much higher rates of pre-existing conditions such as diabetes, obesity, high blood pressure, and anxiety.[4] The reasons are two-fold: as a society, we have not taken care of these

---

1   "More Exposed and Less Protected," Canada: Systemic Racism And COVID-19, Western Centre for Research & Education Against Women & Children (n.d.) vawlearningnetwork.ca/our-work/backgrounders/more_exposed_and_less_protected_in_canada_systemic_racism_and_covid19
2   "Social determinants of health," World Health Organization (n.d.). who.int/health-topics/social-determinants-of-health#tab=tab_1
3   *Ibid.*
4   "Health Equity Considerations and Racial and Ethnic Minority Groups," Centers for Disease Control and Prevention, November 30, 2021. cdc.gov/coronavirus/2019-ncov/community/health-equity/race-ethnicity.html

populations adequately or equally from a preventative health-and-wellness perspective; and we have failed to bring forward effective policies to address the inequalities that influence the social determinants of health. The American Centers for Disease Control and Prevention (the CDC) defines health equity as a "basic principle of public health...that all people have a right to health," noting that differences between groups are commonly referred to as "health disparities."[5]

Who is affected by these disparities? Mostly groups marginalized based on race, ethnicity, socio-economic status, and other identifiers, including gender and geographic location—and of course, for many it's a combination of factors.[6] Health outcomes within marginalized groups are also determined by factors such as access to healthy food and safe and healthy housing—homes free of moulds and other toxins.

All of Canada's nearly 38 million citizens—including permanent residents—have access to free, publicly funded health care ("universal health care," as many call it) that provides them with medically necessary hospital and physician services. These services are administered and delivered via thirteen provincial and territorial tax-funded public insurance plans.[7] If you get sick in Canada, you can access a doctor and be treated for your medical issues at no personal cost. For those Canadians belonging to marginalized, racialized groups, access to free health care should be at least one less barrier than their US counterparts have to navigate.

According to 2020 data, the US is now in its "most severe public health crisis in a century," with reports that 13 percent of Americans under sixty-five (that's more than 35 million people) are without health insurance.[8] That's almost the total population of Canada. Imagine having no access to health care during COVID. And imagine that even with access to health care, your health is still at higher risk because you are Black, Indigenous, or a person of colour. That is the reality for millions in the US and Canada.

In her 2020 report, *From Risk to Resilience: An Equity Approach to COVID-19,* Dr. Theresa Tam, Canada's Chief Public Health Officer, makes the case that the health impacts of the pandemic "have been worse for seniors, essential workers, racialized populations, people living with disabilities and women...

5   Promoting Health Equity: A Resource to Help Communities Address Social Determinants of Health by Laura K. Brennan Ramirez et. al, Atlanta: U.S. Department of Health and Human Services, Centers for Disease Control and Prevention, 2008. cdc.gov/nccdphp/dch/programs/healthycommunitiesprogram/tools/pdf/sdoh-workbook.pd

6   *Ibid.*

7   "International Health Care Systems Profiles: Canada" by Sara Allin, Greg Marchildon, and Allie Peckham, North American Observatory on Health Systems and Policies, University of Toronto, June 5, 2020. commonwealthfund.org/international-health-policy-center/countries/Canada

8   "The number of Americans without health insurance has been trending up. Let's turn it down again" by Sara R. Collins, *Statnews.com*, January 25, 2021. statnews.com/2021/01/25/health-insurance-needed-by-more-americans

populations that have historically experienced health and social inequities."[9] She emphasizes that health inequality was a reality for these groups prior to COVID due to the social determinants of health, which "drive health inequities because they shape the ways that power, money, and resources are distributed in society which provide individuals with greater or lesser ability to have control over their health."[10]

Dr. Tam also notes that generational trauma aggravated by ongoing inequality is one aspect that contributes to poor health outcomes in BIPOC communities. Indigenous peoples in Canada "continue to live with the legacy of forced displacement from traditional territories, residential school experiences of abuse and neglect and the disruption of traditional culture and practices," while Black Canadians experience trauma due to "Canada's history of colonialization and slavery and the resulting racism and discrimination."[11]

Dr. Tam's report should be required reading for decision makers at all levels of government, but if we are honest with ourselves, her assessment only validates what many Canadians already suspected.

Black Canadians, people of colour, Indigenous people, new immigrants, and the poor are the ones who have been doing the bulk of the essential jobs during the COVID-19 pandemic—working in grocery stores and factories, cleaning schools, hospitals, and nursing homes, driving taxis. Those essential workers have little choice but to put themselves at risk, their paycheques critical to the daily survival of their families. Unlike those of us who have the luxury of safely working remotely from home and having our food delivered from our grocery stores and restaurants by those very essential workers.

Many of these racialized, economically disadvantaged Canadians are more likely to have pre-existing chronic health issues stemming from the socio-=economic realities of their lives. Their higher likelihood of diabetes, obesity, and high blood pressure, and their overall higher levels of stress and anxiety, can elevate the severity of the impacts of the COVID-19 virus if they become infected.[12] The virus is, in effect, much deadlier for BIPOC communities because we have not taken care of them adequality or equally.

Let's take a look at some of the social determinants of health that disproportionately impact BIPOC communities.

---

9   *From risk to resilience: An equity approach to COVID-19: Chief Public Health Officer of Canada's Report on the State of Public Health in Canada 2020*, Public Health Agency of Canada, October 2020. canada.ca/en/public-health/corporate/publications/chief-public-health-officer-reports-state-public-health-canada/from-risk-resilience-equity-approach-covid-19.html

10 *Ibid.*

11 *Ibid.* [Footnote 149]

12 "11 common health conditions that may increase risk of death from the coronavirus, including diabetes and heart disease" by Andrea Medaris Miller et. al, BusinessInsider.com, November 10, 2020. businessinsider.com/hypertension-diabetes-conditions-that-make-coronavirus-more-deadly-2020-3

Access to Affordable Healthy Foods

As academic Paula Braveman describes in her paper "Monitoring Equality in Health and Healthcare," health inequities are "disparities in health or its social determinants that favour the social groups that were already more advantaged."[13] These determinants all have to do with an individual's position in society, and their commonality is that they are "strongly associated with different levels of social advantage or privilege as characterized by wealth, power, and/or prestige."

One of these social positions is access to affordable, healthy foods. In many of North America's cities, there are areas referred to as "food deserts"[14]; these are typically lower-income areas—which we know are more likely to be populated by racialized people—where there are no nearby supermarkets. Take the city of Toronto, where I live. Although the city itself boasts an abundance of supermarkets, a 2015 Toronto Public Health food strategy paper says "there are almost 31,000 households in the city's lowest income areas that are more than 1 km walking distance to a supermarket."[15] These neighbourhoods have an over-abundance of stores and restaurants offering less-healthy foods at a more affordable price. And of course, some people do not have a means of transportation to access healthier foods—if they could even afford those foods in the first place.

Organizations like Foodshare in Toronto and Urban Growth Collective in Chicago are working to combat food deserts and "food injustice," which is the result of "sweeping cuts to programs and initiatives that are intended to lift people out of poverty and food insecurity."[16] These and many other organizations across North America are working to address the specific inequalities and the systemic racism within the food system. Although these organizations may have differing missions, at the core they are all working to mitigate food insecurity and to increase access to high-quality, affordable, and nutritious foods for racialized and socio-economically disadvantaged communities. As an example, research continues to suggest that urban agriculture can produce a range of social, health, and economic benefits for communities," so some groups are "support[ing] communities in developing systems of their own where food is grown, prepared, and distributed within the community itself."

---

[13]   "Monitoring Equity in Health and Healthcare: A Conceptual Framework" by Paula A. Braveman, Center on Social Disparities in Health, Department of Family and Community Medicine, School of Medicine University of California, San Francisco, 2003. citeseerx.ist.psu.edu/viewdoc/download?doi=10.1.1.461.6961&rep=rep1&type=pdf

[14]   "[Media Release] New Fact Sheets Show Growing Racial Disparities in Canada," Ontario Council of Agencies Serving Immigrants March 21, 2019. ocasi.org/new-fact-sheets-show-growing-racial-disparities-canada

[15]   *Ibid.*

[16]   [Foodshare homepage] Foodshare (n.d.). foodshare.net/take-action-food-justice

In 2018, I formed a venture called Northern Roots, a state-of-the-art indoor farming enterprise with a mission to work with communities in Canada's North to develop a sustainable source of fresh, healthy, and affordable leafy greens. The goal was to help address regional challenges in the areas of food insecurity, health and wellness, employment, economic development, and health equity. Northern Roots was a spinoff of a fully operational commercial indoor-farm enterprise located in Toronto that was singularly focused on providing leafy greens to premium restaurants in the downtown core—indoor farm-to-table, if you will—just a few kilometres from the city's top kitchens. Unfortunately, organizational challenges and the pandemic have put the final development and launch of Northern Roots on ice—for now.

With food-security further exposed by the pandemic since 2020, I think local, indoor hydroponic farming, at the scale envisioned, could play a small part within a system-wide effort to improve health outcomes for BIPOC communities. The Northern Roots operational model focused on deploying prefabricated 4,000-square-foot commercial indoor farms (producing 3,500 units of leafy greens per week) in regional hub cities and towns, including Indigenous communities. The farms would not only deliver fresh produce locally, 365 days a year (especially in areas where the growing season is 60-days a year or less), but do so efficiently and economically.

Currently, the Canadian government subsidizes delivery of food (by plane or ship) to Northern communities through its Nutrition North program. In 2019 it spent nearly $80 million subsidizing delivery—$25 million for fresh produce alone.[17] Aside from the major carbon footprint generated by transporting food such long distances, the produce delivered remains very expensive and is often of poor quality by the time it reaches consumers. And of course, transportation issues due to inclement weather add another level of food insecurity for residents in Northern regions.

"Feeding My Family," a popular Facebook page with over twenty thousand followers, details consumer grocery experiences in Nunavut, including many examples of obscene prices for fresh produce. In 2016, the CBC reported that it cost $28.58 for a 1-kilogram bag of grapes that would cost about $8 in Toronto—and that's after the Nutrition North subsidy is factored in.

In addition to providing year-round access to fresh, nutritious produce, commercial indoor grow facilities can create sustainable, local employment, contributing to economic development. In recent years, some organizations have deployed local growth systems in the North, including a company called Growcer, which builds small-scale, turnkey systems using refur-

---

[17] *2018-2019: Full Fiscal Year*, Nutrition North Canada, April 23, 2020. nutritionnorthcanada.gc.ca/eng/1583247671449/1583247805997

bished shipping containers. Others are testing greenhouse systems with thermal heat energy sources to grow in cold-weather regions year-round—all-important innovations that are looking to solve real local challenges.

In researching organizations like Foodshare and the Urban Growth Collective, it struck me that indoor grow facilities could also be deployed effectively in urban centres to achieve similar objectives. State-of-the-art modular farms could be integrated into community centres, co-located in newly built affordable-housing complexes, or built as stand-alone facilities on city-owned or -donated land in identified food-desert communities. The produce could be made available to the public at affordable prices, given the efficiency of growth techniques and the elimination of most transportation costs.

Access to fresh, healthy food, combined with preventive wellness and nutrition programs, would go a long way toward addressing some of the determinants of health that affect racialized and socio-economically disadvantaged communities in urban, rural, and Northern and Indigenous communities. Addressing this basic human right would contribute to alleviating high blood pressure, obesity, and diabetes. It would save lives, create stronger communities, and work to right the historical imbalance of disadvantage experienced in BIPOC and lower-income communities.

Getting the Basics Right: Safe Water and Safe, Affordable Housing

Water

Issues of food insecurity, food deserts, and poor health outcomes related to inadequate nutrition are real—even if these things don't affect you. Turning on the tap and pouring a cold glass of water is something most Canadians take for granted. It's hard to believe that Canada has still not completed efforts to ensure that all Indigenous communities across the country have safe, fresh drinking water—a crisis that has persisted for decades.

Beginning in 2015, the federal government finally took action to lift 109 long-term boil-water advisories. As of fall 2021, forty-two advisories remain in thirty Indigenous communities.[18] Can you imagine if people living in Toronto or New York were forced to boil water every day to ensure it was

---

[18] "Achieving clean drinking water in First Nations communities," Government of Canada, November 11, 2021. sac-isc.gc.ca/eng/1614385724108/1614385746844

safe for drinking, cooking, or bathing—and having to do so for twenty or thirty years?

In 2014, Flint, Michigan, made national headlines when a cost-saving decision to switch the city's water supply from Detroit's water system to the highly toxic Flint River resulted in lead-contaminated water being supplied to homes for more than eighteen months.[19] It just so happens that more than 60 percent of Flint's population is made up of Black people and people of colour. The results were devastating. The contaminated water caused at least twelve deaths and more than eighty people to become infected with legionnaires' disease.

Former local and state officials are now charged with a range of crimes, from willful neglect of duty to manslaughter. The then-mayor of Flint, Karen Weaver, summed it up well: "An official report came out and said this was about race.... Class [also] played a role in this; if this community had been made up differently it would have been addressed much quicker."[20]

The long-term effects of elevated lead in water on the health of residents—especially children (an estimated six thousand to twelve thousand of whom were affected)—is still being felt today, nearly five years since the government, prompted in part by court-ordered legal remedies, finally addressed the problem. According to the CDC, exposure to lead can seriously harm a child's health, causing everything from brain- and nervous-system damage to slowed growth and development, learning and behaviour problems, hearing and speech problems, lower IQ, decreased ability to pay attention, and underperformance in school.[21]

As is most often the case with systemic racism, intersectionality comes into play. In Flint, the disproportionate negative impact on Black people is compounded by systemic socio-economic inequality. At least 40 percent of Flint's population lives below the US poverty line, with an individual annual income of less than $12,760.

19   "Flint Water Crisis: Everything You Need to Know," *NRDG.org*, November 8, 2018. nrdc.org/stories/flint-water-crisis-everything-you-need-know

20   "Flint water crisis: Race 'was factor' in authorities' slow and misleading response, says city's black mayor" by Andrew Buncombe, *The Independent*, May 28, 2018. independent.co.uk/news/world/americas/flint-water-crisis-michigan-racism-city-mayor-karen-weaver-police-a8369981.html

21   "Flint children exposed to lead suffer from dental problems, learning disabilities, other issues" by Isis Simpson-Mersha, *MLive.com*, September 28, 2021. mlive.com/news/flint/2020/10/flint-children-exposed-to-lead-suffer-from-dental-problems-learning-disabilities-other-issues.html

Housing

For many in the BIPOC community, the lack of safe, affordable housing has magnified the systemic challenges related to health and wellness. Toronto's community housing, for example, is crumbling from decades of neglect and in need of billions of dollars in renovations.

In 2019, the federal government pledged $1.3 billion to Toronto Community Housing (TCH) to help them address a $1.6-billion backlog. That backlog affected 110,000 residents living in 58,000 units in buildings across Toronto—units with cracked and leaking windows and roofs and boilers that failed to provide adequate heat in winter. These sub-par housing conditions can lead to dangerous moulds which can create health problems, including respiratory conditions like asthma, and are yet another negative health determinant for racialized, low-income people.[22]

The Canadian government announced additional funding in spring 2021 for the Affordable Housing Innovation Fund, part of a COVID-recovery plan which would see the creation of up to 12,700 affordable housing units, bringing the national total to over 300,000.[23] But thousands of people continue to live in inadequate private rental spaces managed by slumlords and foreign corporations with little interest in the community or its citizens.

During elections, I canvassed some of these buildings in my riding, not far from my own comfortable home, and was shocked to see how deplorable the conditions were—broken elevators, dodgy electrical systems, and, most difficult to witness, children playing in dirty hallways and stairways strewn with litter. Often, landlords make cosmetic repairs to these buildings and units to justify rent increases and attract more affluent tenants, leaving those with less money even fewer options.

In fall 2021, Berlin citizens held a referendum calling for the expropriation of private rental units from companies with 3,000 or more rental units—a move to address the growing crisis caused by the city's ever-shrinking inventory of affordable housing. The grassroots initiative wants to see these corporate rental properties made public. With a vote of 56 percent for and 39 against, the group who called for the referendum has claimed victory, with the city's senate called upon to pass a new law that would "expropriate and socialize

---

[22] "Ottawa's $1.3B investment is 'critically urgent' to fix Toronto's affordable housing, TCH head says" by Amara McLaughlin, *CBC News*, April 8, 2019. cbc.ca/news/canada/toronto/ottawa-s-1-3b-investment-is-critically-urgent-to-fix-toronto-s-affordable-housing-tch-head-says-1.5088626

[23] "Government of Canada to Create 30 000 Affordable Housing Units Through Innovation Fund," Canadian Mortgage and Housing Corporation, Newswire.ca, April 26, 2021. newswire.ca/news-releases/government-of-canada-to-create-30-000-affordable-housing-units-through-innovation-fund-865770074.html

large housing groups."[24] The citizen activists are hopeful the city will take control of 240,000 apartments, but the vote is not legally binding and huge legal and political barriers remain. But it makes the point that safe, healthy, and affordable housing is needed everywhere.

A good example of what can be achieved with proper funding, and in collaboration with community leaders and developers, is the Regent Park revitalization program in Toronto. An initiative begun in 2005 by the City of Toronto, it is focused on rebuilding the neighbourhood of 12,500 residents over a fifteen-to-twenty-year period, providing affordable housing for the working poor and the homeless.[25]

Government leadership, through deliberate policies and actions, should be working to at least get the basics right for all citizens. Prioritizing policies that bring equity to racialized and socio-economically disadvantaged citizens would be transformative for our society. Lest we forget, housing should not be a luxury. As the Ontario Human Rights Commission states, "the right to shelter, to have one's own bed to sleep in, a roof over one's head, [and] a place where one's person and possessions are safe is a human right."[26]

Health Care

Across the country, BIPOC communities frequently encounter inequitable treatment when they turn to the very institutions that are supposed to help them. Systemic racism in the health-care system is at the core of the social reckoning on race we are currently experiencing—a flood of published reports and studies have detailed how bias and prejudice play a part in negative health outcomes for racialized people. A 2004 essay by lawyer Sana Halwani, published by the Ontario Human Rights Commission, outlines how socio-economic factors, the underrepresentation of racialized groups in the medical profession, barriers to health screening, and unconscious bias contribute to a lower level of care for racialized people.[27]

24 "Berliners vote to expropriate large landlords in non-binding referendum" by Riham Alkousaa and Matthias Inverardi, *Reuters.com*, September 27, 2021. reuters.com/world/europe/berliners-vote-expropriate-large-landlords-non-binding-referendum-2021-09-27

25 "Regent Park Revitalization Plan," *Wikipedia*, August 18, 2021. en.wikipedia.org/wiki/Regent_Park_Revitalization_Plan#:~:text=The%20Regent%20Park%20Revitalization%20Plan,%2D%20to%2020%2Dyear%20period

26 "Housing as a human right," Ontario Human Rights Commission (n.d.). ohrc.on.ca/en/right-home-report-consultation-human-rights-and-rental-housing-ontario/housing-human-right

27 "Racial inequality in access to health care services," Ontario Human Rights Commission (n.d.). ohrc.on.ca/en/race-policy-dialogue-papers/racial-inequality-access-health-care-services

A December 2020 report entitled *In Plain Sight: Addressing Indigenous-specific Racism and Discrimination in B.C. Health Care* confirms the existence of systemic inequality in BC's health-care system and offers solutions. It makes it clear that in order to address Indigenous-specific racism, the "roots of the problem" must be attacked. "There must be changes in systems, behaviours, and beliefs."[28] As the report details, the *systems* are "the structures, processes and contexts we operate through and within"; *behaviours* are "the norms and actions that are taken, and how they reflect an anti-racist skillset and are respectful of Indigenous human rights, health, and well-being"; and *beliefs* are "attitudes and understandings that individuals or groups hold, which reflect, enable or reinforce anti-Indigenous racism." Yes, it's multifaceted and complex, which is why it requires serious attention, analysis, and solutions.

In 2019, the Viens Commission report was tabled in Québec.[29] The commission had been set up by the provincial government to investigate the well-publicized controversy that stemmed from the experiences of dozens of Indigenous women who had been subjected to violence and intimidation, sexual harassment, and sexual assault from provincial police (Sûreté du Quebec) officers in Val d'Or, Québec. The commission was to review what happened in Val d'Or, but was also given a broader mandate to investigate discrimination and racism within public services throughout the province, including in health care.

In his report, Justice Jacques Viens stated that Indigenous people in Québec are victims of systemic discrimination when it comes to receiving public services. He issued 142 calls to action to address the government's shortfalls.[30] The Commission highlighted discriminatory practices within hospitals and health-care services in the province. It noted that misconceptions of Indigenous people—that they are "disorganized, unable to care for their families and children, uninformed, violent, dependent, neglectful of their health and property, [and] privileged due to their exemption from paying taxes"—persist, leading to "judgement by non-Indigenous people." The report found that it was clear that "prejudice toward Indigenous peoples remains widespread in the interaction between caregivers and patients."[31]

28 *In Plain Sight: Addressing Indigenous-specific Racism and Discrimination in B.C. Health Care*, Hon. Dr. M.E. Turpel-Lafond (Aki-Kwe), December 2020. engage.gov.bc.ca/app/uploads/sites/613/2021/02/In-Plain-Sight-Data-Report_Dec2020.pdf1_.pdf

29 *Public Inquiry Commission on relations between Indigenous Peoples and certain public services in Québec: listening, reconciliation and progress: Final Report*, Gouvernement du Québec, 2019. cerp.gouv.qc.ca/fileadmin/Fichiers_clients/Rapport/Final_report.pdf

30 "Calls for 'Justice for Joyce' after Indigenous woman's death in Quebec hospital" by Julia Page, *CBC News*, September 20, 2020. cbc.ca/news/canada/montreal/joyce-dominique-one-year-after-publication-viens-report-1.5743501

31 *In Plain Sight: Addressing Indigenous-specific Racism and Discrimination in B.C. Health Care*, Hon. Dr. M.E. Turpel-Lafond (Aki-Kwe), December 2020. engage.gov.bc.ca/app/uploads/sites/613/2021/02/In-Plain-Sight-Data-Report_Dec2020.pdf1_.pdf

Almost a year to the day after the Viens report was made public, we learned of the tragic death of Joyce Echaquan, an Indigenous woman, who died as a result of a lack of proper medical care in a Québec hospital. Systemic racism was acknowledged as a factor in her death. She was wrongly assumed to have been experiencing an overdose, an ugly stereotype that cost Echaquan her life. This once again heightened public awareness of the persisting systemic issues at play. (More about this story in Chapter Ten.)

∞

In 1993, at the age of twenty-seven, I joined an indoor recreation soccer league with my brother and friends—getting back to playing a team sport I loved after nearly a decade away. I was out of shape, my skills were rusty, but my competitive spirit was still alive and well. We played at night, and on the third match of the season, I ripped my right knee to shreds, my foot catching on the artificial turf as I tried to challenge an opponent for the ball. I remember hearing a loud crack like a two-by-four breaking, followed by the sound of me screaming at the top of my lungs as I writhed uncontrollably on the field. Everyone rushed toward me and one of our teammates—a doctor, stepped in to take a closer look. It was bad news.

My brother drove me downtown to Toronto Western Hospital, near where I lived. We arrived around midnight. I was checked in and waited until the attending physician came to speak with me. He sized me up (I was wearing my sweats and a hoodie), took a quick look at my knee, and asked a few questions as to what happened. He then asked me if I had insurance. Like all Canadians, I was covered by my government-funded health insurance; I even had additional coverage via my employer. I wondered to myself why that mattered, given that I was injured and needed emergency care. I wasn't there for discretionary plastic surgery. I knew that under the Canada Health Act, I was entitled to "medically necessary" care.[32]

The doctor left and a nurse administrator came to see me. She asked me some basic medical questions—and then she also asked me if I had insurance. I gave her the same answer. I had now been sitting in the hospital bed for nearly an hour. Another member of the medical staff stopped by. She asked me who I worked for—and whether I had insurance. She checked off something on her clipboard and walked away. I realized then that having—or not having—private insurance was going to have an impact on the level of care I would receive. I also had the feeling that being a Black man was somehow affecting how I was being managed by the hospital staff. My status as "worthy of the best care" appeared to be in question, simply because of my Blackness

---

[32] "Canada's Health Care System," Government of Canada, September 17, 2019. canada.ca/en/health-canada/services/health-care-system/reports-publications/health-care-system/canada.html

and the correlation they seemed to be making with my socio-economic status. I would realize later that my instincts were right.

I continued to sit in my hospital bed, anger growing by the minute, though the pain in my knee was still manageable—the adrenalin coursing through my body from shock was still doing its job. No one had yet asked me my pain level or offered me any medication. Finally, I'd had enough. I yelled out to no one and everyone: "I have insurance and I want someone to come take care of my fucking knee right now." That seemed to do the trick.

The doctor returned and told me I had probably torn ligaments and they were going to do an MRI and take X-rays to confirm the diagnosis. I would need to come back for those tests the next day. He wrote me a prescription for pain medication and told me to go home. I left the hospital at around 2:30 A.M. My brother helped me into my apartment and into bed, and I fell asleep—exhausted from a long day.

Three hours later, I woke in searing pain—an 11 out of 10. I moved my bedsheet to uncover my leg and saw that my knee had swollen to the size of a large grapefruit. I broke out in a cold sweat and used all my energy to crawl on the floor toward my phone (this was in the days before cellphones). I called my friend who lived nearby, begging him to come quickly to pick up my prescription and have it filled. It was another two hours before I was finally able to take my medication—each second felt like an hour as I waited for it to take effect.

The next day, I went back to the hospital. Tests on my knee determined I had torn two ligaments and my meniscus and snapped my anterior cruciate ligament (ACL), a key ligament that helps stabilize the knee joint. I was told the knee surgeon at Toronto Western was one of the best—he was the go-to guy for professional hockey players. Now we were getting somewhere. A week later, I woke up post-surgery and the pain hit me immediately. The morphine helped me settle down. After two hours in recovery, I was allowed to return home under my brother's supervision, my leg encased in a temporary brace.

For the next two weeks, my routine consisted of taking my pain medication and having friends drop by to deliver food and help me with basic household tasks. I kept pressure off my knee at all times, if only to keep the pain from overpowering my medication. I had not received a call from the doctor or the hospital during that time, so I called them. The duty nurse I reached seemed surprised, and I could hear concern in her voice. "You should have been seen two days after surgery, and you needed to start moving your knee right away." She scheduled an appointment for the next day.

When I was finally back in front of my surgeon, he informed me the surgery had gone well and that I needed to start rehab right away. Then he told me that after a year of rehab, I would have to modify which sports I could play. I asked him why, as I'd been told his specialty was getting hockey players back on the ice. That's when he told me he had not re-attached my ACL. I was confused. "Why not?" I asked. He told me that because I wasn't a high-performance athlete, he hadn't thought it was necessary. I was so angry I had no words. I had not even been consulted or given the option for my ACL to be re-attached. That was the last time I ever spoke to him.

Because of the delay in starting rehab, my leg muscles had already atrophied; I'd lost significant muscle mass and my knee was stiff. It would take me months just to get to the point where most people are when they begin physiotherapy. And of course, playing soccer, basketball, or tennis would be challenging without a brace of some kind to stabilize my knee. My accident and the poor treatment I'd received would have a major impact on my quality of life—and I was not yet thirty.

Luckily, I had naturally strong, athletic legs and my body did much of its own healing. With the help of a basic neoprene knee brace, and sheer determination, I was able to go on to play the sports I loved—if not at the same competitive level I had enjoyed previously.

Fast-forward twenty-six years to another surgery on the same knee—a small meniscus tear from playing pickup basketball. My new knee doctor (a person of colour) was surprised I was so active given my lack of an ACL; he wondered why my previous surgeon had not re-attached it all those years ago. It should have been routine for someone in his twenties, he noted.

Was I treated differently by the health-care system because I was Black or perceived to be socio-economically undesirable? And if so, should those identity markers have deemed me unworthy of full use of my knee? I believe this particular experience is a perfect example of the intersectionality of factors that contribute to systemic inequality in the health-care system.

Conscious and unconscious biases and prejudices baked into understanding, knowledge, and training in health care across Canada negatively affect how BIPOC patients receive care and result in a wide range of negative outcomes. For most non-BIPOC citizens accessing the health-care system, the realities of systemic racism are invisible—another advantage, and one less barrier, to achieving more positive health outcomes.

What Needs to Change

In his 2019 report, Justice Viens noted that "a systemic problem needs a systemic solution."[33] He said we cannot begin to address the roots of the problem without implementing systemic reforms for "lasting change," rather than taking the kinds of "temporary measures...all too often implemented in reaction to unfortunate events, only to be gradually abandoned." Spot on: less window dressing and more real action are needed to reform the health-care system from the inside out. We must move forward with social policy reforms to resolve the disproportionate levels of food insecurity, food deserts, unsafe and unaffordable housing, and of course, poverty, among BIPOC communities.

We see some efforts being made with investments in housing and demonstrated commitments by some government ministries to uncover the issues and, at a minimum, begin the discussion around reform. Many stakeholders in the health-care sector, from government to academia and public policy, are calling for anti-racism training in the health-care system,[34] as it becomes ever clearer that health-care administrators, social workers, doctors, nurses, and support personnel need the specific training, tools, and resources to learn how to respectfully and effectively engage with patients from marginalized communities. If we recall the Truth and Reconciliation report's Calls to Action, number 25 is to "Make training developed in cooperation with Indigenous authorities that promotes cultural sensitivity, cultural competence, and cultural safeguards available to all public service managers, professionals and employees who are likely to interact with Indigenous peoples." We are a long way from achieving that goal. As I mentioned at the outset, there is so much more involved in this complex problem that it deserves a book of its own. But like all aspects of systemic racism, getting to the root of the problem is key. As individuals, we need to continue to inform ourselves so we can participate in the evolving discourse and hold our governments accountable for the care of all citizens.

As then-Minister of Crown-Indigenous Relations Carolyn Bennet noted in response to the Viens report, "If you can't utter the words systemic racism, then you're probably part of the problem."[35]

---

[33] "Dépôt du rapport final," *Public Inquiry Commission on relations between Indigenous Peoples and certain public services in Québec: listening, reconciliation and progress: Final Report*, Gouvernement du Québec, 2019. cerp.gouv.qc.ca/index.php?id=2

[34] "Ignored to Death: Systemic Racism in the Canadian Healthcare System," Submission to EMRIP the Study on Health by Brenda L Gunn, Robson Hall Faculty of Law, University of Manitoba (n.d.) ohchr.org/Documents/Issues/IPeoples/EMRIP/Health/UniversityManitoba.pdf

[35] Calls for 'Justice for Joyce' after Indigenous woman's death in Quebec hospital" by Julia Page, *CBC News*, September 20, 2020. cbc.ca/news/canada/montreal/joyce-dominique-one-year-after-publication-viens-report-1.5743501

EDUCATION: A FAILING GRADE

SYSTEMIC RACISM IS ALSO PERVASIVE IN OUR EDUCATION SYSTEMS. THE ISSUES are numerous and, taken together, continue to negatively impact racialized students across North America. One of the most egregious issues is "streaming," an institutionally driven process which determines whether high-school-aged students will be directed toward an "academic" track, intended as preparation for college or university, or toward hands-on "applied" studies, to prepare them for careers in the trade or service sectors. Though the process is still used in some Canadian schools—in the provinces of Ontario and Alberta specifically—it has been proven discriminatory toward students in general, and exponentially more for Black students,[36] who are disproportionately streamed to applied programs.

What and how students are taught is also problematic. As we discussed in Chapter Two, much of the curriculum still being taught today has been shown to be biased, disadvantaging non-white students by failing to reflect their lived experiences or histories and emphasizing a white colonial heritage and perspective.[37] To add to these challenges, there is a severe lack of racialized and Indigenous educators in the education systems, due in part to "a lack of diversity hiring based on merit within our education workforce."[38]

Let's unpack some of these realities.

Streaming

In July 2020, the Ontario government announced plans to end streaming in Grade 9. Research had found that the practice "disproportionately impacts Black and low-income students and severely limits their chances of graduating and going on to post-secondary education."[39] A York University study showed that Black students were more likely to be streamed to applied programs rather than academic programs and to experience negative outcomes

---

36 "Ontario to end academic streaming for Grade 9 students starting next school year," *CBC News*, November 11, 2021. cbc.ca/news/canada/toronto/ontario-schools-streaming-academic-applied-1.6245612

37 "Racism: A Hidden Curriculum" by Ratna Ghosh, *Canadian Education Association*, Vol. 48 (4), 2010. edcan.ca/wp-content/uploads/EdCan-2008-v48-n4-Ghosh.pdf

38 "Ontario to end academic streaming for Grade 9 students starting next school year," *CBC News*, November 11, 2021. cbc.ca/news/canada/toronto/ontario-schools-streaming-academic-applied-1.6245612

39 "Ontario to end streaming in Grade 9 and change other 'racist, discriminatory' practices" by Kristin Rushowy, *Toronto Star*, July 6, 2020. thestar.com/politics/provincial/2020/07/06/ontario-to-end-streaming-in-grade-9-and-change-other-racist-discriminatory-practices.html

from that practice. Data showed that 53 percent of Black students went to academic programs, compared to 81 percent of white students and 80 percent of other racialized students. Meanwhile, 39 percent of Black students were in the applied stream, compared to 18 percent of other racialized groups and 16 percent of white students.[40]

There is also a direct correlation between stream and graduation rate for students. Of those who entered Grade 9 in 2006, 88 percent enrolled in the academic stream graduated in 2011; the number who graduated sunk to 59 percent for those in applied courses.[41] The data is clear—streaming negatively affects all students but disproportionally disadvantages Black students. It can no longer be ignored.

The Minister of Education for Ontario, Stephen Lecce, responded in a July 2020 CBC interview by stating, "It is clear there is systemic discrimination built within the education system" and added that "students and teachers deserve an education system that is inclusive, accountable and transparent, and one that by design, is set up to fully and equally empower all children to achieve their potential."[42]

I couldn't agree more, but interestingly, while Lecce re-announced in November 2021 the de-streaming of the entire Grade 9 curriculum, his ministry made public that streaming would remain in place for Grade 10 students, claiming that "additional learning expectations" would help support students transitioning from the de-streamed Grade 9 math curriculum into an applied or academic path. Simply put, the Ontario Ministry of Education was going to delay by one year a policy it admits is discriminatory. At minimum it's a poor communication strategy, but on a larger scale it's devastating news for Ontario's students, who will continue to be negatively impacted by this misguided policy.

∞

My own story with the public educational system is a cautionary tale against streaming, and at the same time a reminder of the negative impact "indifference" can have on young students on a path to adulthood. I attended Victoria High School ("Vic High") in the early 1980s in Victoria, BC. As I remember it, few teachers seemed interested in inspiring their students. This was partly a by-product of systemic inequality rooted in socio-economic discrimination, which I'll elaborate more on shortly. My history teacher, the late Mr. Nesmith,

[40] "Black students in Toronto streamed into courses below their ability, report finds" by Muriel Draaisma, *CBC News*, April 24, 2017. cbc.ca/news/canada/toronto/study-black-students-toronto-york-university-1.4082463

[41] "[Research]" Coalition for Alternatives to Streaming in Education (n.d.). endstreaming.org/research

[42] "Ontario to end streaming in Grade 9 and change other 'racist, discriminatory' practices" by Kristin Rushowy, *Toronto Star*, July 6, 2020. thestar.com/politics/provincial/2020/07/06/ontario-to-end-streaming-in-grade-9-and-change-other-racist-discriminatory-practices.html

was a standout exception—a fascinating character and an excellent educator who knew how to connect with young minds by making learning relevant to our lives. He made me want to show up for class.

I don't recall formalized streaming in Grade 9 or 10, but my high school was known as a great school for trades; there were amazing programs and facilities, with hands-on learning for students who had an interest in becoming a car mechanic, an electrician, a carpenter, or an electrician. Maybe there was more to it than I realized.

Back then, there were many students like me who were just counting down the days to graduation. We were bored and distracted by adolescent priorities and some, like me, were dealing with challenging home lives. In addition, most of us felt that our teachers barely cared whether we attended school or not. I never had a counsellor or a teacher take enough interest to ask me about my future goals (academic or otherwise) or advise me on how to prepare if I wanted to go to college or university. Not a single person.

My early introduction to business and money had struck a chord, but I was so naive and uninformed that, despite making it out of high school, I was shocked when I looked into applying to UBC's Bachelor of Commerce program. Apparently, I needed to be a straight-A student. Even though I'd worked hard for years to save enough money to pay my way, money alone would not be enough to open that door. It was a rude awakening, so instead of going to university I spent two years at Camosun College in Victoria just catching up and learning how to learn. It wasn't until I was twenty-three and enrolled at the British Columbia Institute of Technology (BCIT) in 1989, where I studied marketing and advertising, that I was finally inspired to achieve scholastically—partly because I was able to connect my new knowledge to the years of work experience I now had under my belt. I was excited to see how the pieces of the puzzle were coming together, creating opportunities for me. I found my groove and my passion, which set me up for future success.

Imagine if I had been streamed in high school due to my dismal scholastic performance and attention span. My future opportunities would have been pre-determined or limited by the biased decisions of others; I would not have been given the opportunity to apply my intellect, skills, interests, and willingness to work hard. On the other hand, what more could I have become if I had been encouraged and supported to maximize my academic opportunities? If someone had recognized my academic strengths? I made it despite the obstacles and indifference I had to confront in the educational system, not because any systems or individuals helped me. And that's where we still find ourselves today, nearly forty years later.

Curriculum

Another systemically racist reality in the education system is found in the biased curriculum. In June 2021, Malaika Joudry-Martel, a Mi'kmaw student enrolled in a Grade 10 English correspondence course from Nova Scotia's Department of Education, discovered racist stereotypes about Indigenous people in one of her assignments on First Nations history.[43] Students were asked "to list the advantages and disadvantages of being placed in a residential school." This same assignment asked students to consider questions like, "Why are poverty and alcoholism common problems among First Nations popula-tions?" and "Why is unemployment high among First Nations?" Biased, leading questions that clearly perpetuate negative stereotypes of Indigenous peoples.

Then-Nova Scotia Education Minister Derek Mombourquette apologized, noting that "This was an oversight and it made it out and it shouldn't have made it out."[44] The materials had been created in 2003 and hadn't been revised since. Malaika's class alone had seventy-five students. That's a lot of years of potential harm. But as I've shared previously, racist curriculum goes back a long way.

The version of history still found in most Canadian textbooks goes all the way back to the post-Confederation materials written by influential historians like Henry H. Miles, which were used to teach kids in elementary and middle schools in the early twentieth century. Mills's writings included such broadly racist statements as: "the "Indians...of Canada and New England were all savages and heathens."[45] Other statements congratulated the Jesuits for their noble efforts "to civilise and Christianise the native Indian tribes, by bringing them under the influence of the Church." Mills's many published books, and those of his peers, taught Canadian children a "sanitised account of the litany of injustices committed by Europeans against Indigenous peoples" and "helped indoctrinate generations of Canadians to accept the genocide that had been taking place since Europeans landed in what is now Canada."

This isn't news to the government of Ontario.

In 1994, the province's own Royal Commission on Learning identified systemic racism in public education in its *For the Love of Learning* report.

> Racism is systemic within the educational system. Though often
> unintentional, it frequently results from a lack of awareness of the

---

43   "Grade 10 distance course asks about 'benefits' of residential schools, calls First Nations alcoholism 'common'" by Frances Willick, *CBC News*, June 18, 2021. cbc.ca/news/canada/nova-scotia/n-s-cor-respondence-course-residential-schools-stereotypes-1.6069747

44   *Ibid.*

45   "Textbook Cases of Canadian Racism: Canadian History Books as Captivating Works of Fiction" by Richard Sanders, *Press for Conversion!* 69, Fall 2017. coat.ncf.ca/P4C/69/69_15-18s.pdf

discriminatory effect of many policies, procedures and practices on racial and linguistic minorities, and it can range from learning materials selected, materials that have an inherent negative bias, to teaching strategies and attitudes employed in the classroom.[46]

In 2020, a powerful video produced by the Ontario Black History Society and advertising agency DDB Canada, showed an actual Grade 8 history textbook currently being used in Ontario schools, with all the non-Black history censored. Only 13 of the book's 255 pages remained.[47]

Change is happening, but slowly. New learning resources and teaching materials are being made available to educators so they can incorporate more diversity into their teaching and be more inclusive and sensitive to the perspectives of students from BIPOC communities. But until these materials are prioritized and mandated, educators—and students—will be left in the dark.

Hiring

Systemic racism in the education system also extends to the hiring and training of educators, from the diversity of applicants accepted to teachers' colleges, to the hiring of graduates of diverse racialized backgrounds, to the unconscious bias that some non-BIPOC teachers continue to bring into their classrooms. A chorus of voices is calling for faculties to "embed ongoing anti-racist training and education into their teacher education and leadership development programs"[48]—programs they argue would alert educators to their own bias and prejudices and help change attitudes and beliefs so they can better support racialized students.

As journalist Robyn Maynard explains in a recent *Walrus* article, "teacher expectations play a significant role in the academic engagement of Black students. Black youth in major cities across the country have consistently named their teachers' low expectations as a major factor when it comes to their overall engagement."[49] A 2006 census survey revealed that only 54 percent of Black students felt supported by their teachers. Many said they

---

[46] *For the Love of Learning: Report for the Royal Commission on Learning*, Volume 1, Government of Ontario, 1994. collections.ola.org/mon/25005/176974.pdf

[47] *Ibid.*

[48] "Short-term anti-racist training is not enough to counter systemic racism in Canadian education" by Jerome Cranston, *The Conversation*, February 17, 2021. theconversation.com/short-term-anti-racist-training-is-not-enough-to-counter-systemic-racism-in-canadian-education-152725

[49] "Canadian Education Is Steeped in Anti-Black Racism" by Robyn Maynard, *The Walrus*, November 29, 2017. thewalrus.ca/canadian-education-is-steeped-in-anti-black-racism

felt as if "their presence [was] unwanted." One student went as far as to say, "They don't care if you are there or not."[50]

According to University of Toronto doctor of education student Zuhra Abaw's 2018 thesis, "the teaching staff in Ontario schools do not reflect the increasing diversity of the students who occupy Ontario classrooms today."[51] This "teacher diversity gap" has been discussed in Canada for years. Even in Toronto, for example, where more than half the population identify as visible minorities, only about one-fifth of teachers are non-white.[52]

The Turner Consulting Group published a report in 2014 revealing a wide demographic divide between teachers and students of colour in Ontario, where racial minorities represent 26 percent of the population, yet make up only 10 percent of secondary school teachers and 9 percent of elementary and kindergarten teachers. Similarly, in the GTA, racial minorities represent 47 percent of the population yet only 20 percent of secondary school teachers and 18 percent of elementary and kindergarten teachers.[53]

Simply stated, not enough students with racially diverse backgrounds are admitted into teachers' colleges and, of those who make it through the program, not enough are subsequently hired for teaching positions to proportionately reflect the diversity of the community where they teach—a situation often referred to as "equitable racial representation."[54] If nothing changes, the diversity gap will only grow larger; as Statistics Canada data suggests, Canada is becoming much more diverse, and in the future a larger percentage of the population will be made up of visible minorities.[55]

[50] *Ibid.*

[51] Troubling the Teacher Diversity Gap: The Perpetuation of Whiteness through Practices of Bias Free Hiring in Ontario School Boards by Zuhra Elizabeth Abawi, Graduate Department of Social Justice Education Ontario Institute for Studies in Education, University of Toronto, 2018.

[52] "Schools need BIPOC educators now more than ever" by Helen Vangool, *CBC Saskatoon* [opinion], September 30, 2020. cbc.ca/news/canada/saskatoon/op-ed-sask-diversity-teachers-bipoc-1.5703711

[53] "Teacher Diversity Gap" by Tana Turner, Turning Consulting Group. October 30, 2014. turnerconsultinggroup.ca/blog/teacher-diversity-gap

[54] "Teacher Diversity in Canada: Leaky Pipelines, Bottlenecks, and Glass Ceilings" by James Ryan et. al, *Canadian Journal of Education*, Vol 32, No. 3, 2009. journals.sfu.ca/cje/index.php/cje-rce/article/view/3053

[55] "Canada becoming more culturally diverse: Census," *Canadian Press*, Toronto Sun, October 25, 2017. torontosun.com/news/national/canada-becoming-more-culturally-diverse-census

School Boards:
My Fight for Equality for Vic High

Another issue that doesn't seem to get a lot of attention is the way some school boards in this country contribute to perpetuating systemic inequality, particularly when it comes to socio-economic status. Today, I find myself embroiled in a battle for the equity and equality rights of students at my alma mater, Victoria High. It's a long and winding story, but I feel it illustrates what historically disadvantaged communities are up against, so I want to share it with you.

In April 2018, I received a call from my Vic High friend Taki Niketas ("Tak"), who graduated a year before me, in 1983, as the school's valedictorian. He told me he needed my help to rally the community and the alumni to stop the school board from razing our former high school. The School District (SD61), with support from the provincial ministry of education, communicated three options for the seismic upgrade of the school, characterizing it as the "range of possibilities."

Citing the high cost of preservation, many of us could read between the lines to see that SD61'S preferred path forward was to demolish the historic building and build a new school on a smaller footprint. This option would make the valuable land surrounding the school available for non-educational needs. This was a long-standing point of contention given that Vic High, sitting on 3.5 acres, was already in deficit as per of the provincially mandated student-to-land ratio—an issue that would only be exacerbated by projected significant increases in enrollment.

Vic High is the oldest public school west of Winnipeg and north of San Francisco. Established in 1876, the current edifice was built in 1914 in the Classical Revival style. The school boasts many accomplished alumni, including world-renowned artist Emily Carr (1888), and my friends Moe Elewonibi, an NFL and CFL football star and Superbowl champion (1983), Sam Dunn, an Emmy- and Peabody Award–winning documentary film director and producer (1992), Hans de Goede, a legendary Canadian Rugby Team captain (1971), and Richard Hunt, one of Canada's premier Indigenous artists (1971).

Beginning in the 1970s, Vic High, once an athletics powerhouse with a good reputation as an academic and trades school, began to decline due to a decrease in resources and support, accelerated by budgetary factors and by provincial policies that systemically disadvantaged some schools while prioritizing others. "Systemic classism," an unfortunate holdover from the region's colonial past, remains a reality in Victoria. Over the decades, socio-economic inequality has been a reality for young people from working-class and immigrant households. Many of these youth are disadvantaged simply because of where they live and the economic status of their parents. Vic High just happens to serve this segment of the population.

In the early 1980s, when my friends and I arrived, school spirit at Vic High was at an all-time low after nearly a decade of neglect. The once championship-calibre sports programs of decades past were barely hanging on, and our student body often bore the brunt of jokes by students from other schools. "Slick High" was a popular reference to our high school and the student body—a term rooted in widely held stereotypes that Vic High students were "greasy," druggies, stupid, and poor—our aged and run-down school only amplifying that narrative. We developed a thick skin and took strength in the fact that we were different; we wore our black and gold school colours as a badge of honour.

I left Victoria at age twenty, more than thirty-five years ago now, and have since spent very little time looking back and wondering whether the city has evolved, or whether the disenfranchisement my schoolmates and I experienced was still a reality for students there. So, this new engagement with Vic High brought back the negativity I'd felt all those years ago. I was shocked and furious, and I committed to doing my part to bring about change.

Through the dogged efforts of Esther Callo, a local community activist whose kids attended Vic High, we assembled a treasure trove of documents; they detailed how the school district had in recent years moved full-steam ahead to embrace a policy of selling or leasing away land they deemed "surplus to educational needs." This was done to help shore up their ever-shrinking capital-improvement budgets and, as we would later learn, to paper over some serious fiscal mismanagement. The school district pushed back on our "land grab" assertion, but their subsequent actions—combined with their lack of transparency—would eventually confirm what we'd suspected.

At the behest of Tak and others, in May 2019 I published an op-ed on *Medium*, which was eventually reprinted by the Vic High alumni website, espousing the importance of saving and renovating the historical building, and making the argument for the benefits to current and future students and the community. In the months that followed, my letter struck a nerve and, combined with an online petition and efforts by many other stakeholders, we were able to mobilize the community and raise awareness.

In June 2019, more than a year after the "seismic improvement" consultation, and with increasing headwinds of protest, the BC government stepped in and announced it would properly fund the upgrade to the existing Vic High building, making nearly $80 million available to the school district to do so.[56] "It is long overdue," BC Minister of Education Rob Fleming said.

---

[56] "Victoria High School gets $77.1 million from province for seismic upgrade, expansion" by Jeff Bell, *Times Colonist*, June 27, 2019. timescolonist.com/local-news/victoria-high-school-gets-771-million-from-province-for-seismic-upgrade-expansion-4673918

"This community deserves it." The announcement also made clear that the project would include the "renewal of the sports infrastructure at the school."[57]

We were all excited, especially at hearing that the renewal of Memorial Stadium was being considered. Vic High's track, sports field, and grandstand—collectively known as Memorial Stadium—had been built in 1949 to honour students who had made the ultimate sacrifice in the Second World War. In fact, the Vic High Alumni Association had been championing and fundraising since 2012 to raise money to revitalize the stadium, because after nearly fifty years of neglect, the facilities were decrepit. The vision for the revitalization would include a lighted all-weather artificial turf field (large enough to accommodate multiple sports, including rugby), a field house, a new eight-lane metric track, and a re-imagining of the Memorial Stadium grandstands.

Vic High students could once again train to competitive standards and the school could host sanctioned events like the Lower Island Track and Field Championships. And the new state-of-the-art turf pitch would hopefully contribute to reviving the school's nearly seventy-five-year championship-winning rugby history, which ended in the late 1960s.

At that time, the school district had advised that the plan required an additional twenty metres of land to the west, which was subsequently secured. The district had also given unanimous support for the $7-million upgrade in 2012; in 2014, the City of Victoria had voted unanimously to provide a grant of $250,000 to the project, which, considered alongside other donations and commitments, green-lit phase one of the project. Things were all set—or so we thought.

In September 2020, I received another call from Tak; he was mad as hell. Esther had told him she'd uncovered some disturbing new information. The school board had made a closed-door deal with the City and its community housing organization to lease away land for a housing project. The amount of land to be carved out would essentially make the decades-long plans to revitalize Memorial Stadium impossible. Working hand in hand, SD61 and the City of Victoria orchestrated a plan to dispose of land deemed "surplus to educational needs" at Vic High, to modify bylaws to allow for what they called an "easement," and in the process ensured that key documents about the modified plans were not made public until it was too late for anyone to oppose them.

In an effort to stop SD61's plans, Tak, Esther, and I co-founded the Friends of Vic High (FOVH) in 2020. For nearly two years since, we've worked hard to raise awareness of the issue in the press and via social media. We've rallied former alumni, community members, world-class athletes, and others to our cause. We've secured dozens of documents through Freedom of Information (FOI) requests. These documents validate our assertion of systemic inequality and confirm that the district did not adhere to its own policies regarding the

---

[57] *Ibid.*

disposal of "surplus" land; they also show that the district has ignored its own data, which clearly shows that more educational space will be needed to accommodate an expected growth in student population. And once that land is gone, it's gone forever.

When the school district held public consultations regarding Vic High's proposed new amenities and heritage-preservation priorities, officials did not divulge the land-lease agreement to the public. The public was not "consulted" until June 2019, when an alternative revitalization plan was revealed which included a small playing field (not big enough for rugby), a two-lane walking track (completely unsuitable for track and field), and four beach volleyball courts—a ridiculous add-on in a city renowned for its rainfall, and where competitive high-school volleyball is an indoor sport.

Apparently, the beach volleyball idea was championed by the principal of Vic High, Aaron Parker, who, not surprisingly, wrote a letter endorsing the school district's misguided plans in March 2021, ahead of anticipated critical school district votes on the matter. In the letter, he says, "In my observations and conversations with staff and students, I have not seen or heard of a significant interest in a full-sized track that would be capable of hosting sanctioned competitions."[58] Beach volleyball didn't even register in the Amenities Survey conducted in 2020, while a metric track and revitalized Memorial Stadium were noted as the top three priorities by nearly 1,700 respondents of the survey.

At the Victoria City Council meeting in October 2021, when the bylaws were rubber-stamped by a nearly unanimous vote, a local resident who lived just blocks from Vic High spoke in support of making some of the school's land available for the housing development (and for bylaws to be changed to allow housing). To be clear, my peers and I believe housing is important, but it makes no sense to appropriate land to address one social problem only to exacerbate another.

Interestingly, the local resident also made the FOVH case, noting that her daughter, who should be attending Vic High, "simply would not have it." As a supportive parent, she had worked hard to get an exemption for her daughter so she could attend Oak Bay. That school, located less than 5 kilometres from Vic High, has been traditionally blessed with resources going back nearly a century, and today it boasts university-level athletic facilities and a multi-million-dollar performance centre. We can't blame this young woman for fighting to go to Oak Bay rather than Vic High. She knew what the school board and the City were hoping the public would continue to ignore—that if you go to Vic High, you will be systemically disadvantaged.

58   [Letter from Aaron Parker to Victoria City Councillors], Victoria High School, March 3, 2021. drive.google.com/file/d/15yJvHcl-8e3JQRHlfUC2WBs_EJ5JBh2B/view

According to the 2016 census, the District of Oak Bay has a total population of just over 18,000, with a majority of residents earning well over the median income of \$94,000; it has a demographic mix that includes 1,820 visible minorities[59], or approximately 10 percent. Most people in Oak Bay (41 percent) have a university degree.[60] In contrast, Victoria has a population of approximately 85,000 and a median income of approximately \$53,000. Nearly 14 percent of the Victoria population are visible minorities and 32 percent have a university degree.[61] Curiously, Oak Bay has a student population that is about 400 students greater than Vic High's[62], though it serves a population nearly five times smaller.[63]

Even the Vic High Alumni Association board was co-opted in the effort to systemically disadvantage Vic High students. In June 2019, the Alumni board quietly endorsed the new plans for the memorial revitalization.[64] The board then waited nearly four months before informing their membership of their decision: they would abandon their plans for Memorial Stadium dating back to 2012. All the while, they had continued to fundraise, promoting the original vision. Nearly \$600,000 had been raised over the years from private supporters and alumni, and from the Bays United Football Club, and the City of Victoria had committed to a \$250,000 matching contribution—the latter seemingly working against its own prior commitment. Shameful.

The Vic High Alumni Board of Directors, who have failed the current and future students of Vic High, is currently comprised of all white alumni who graduated on or before 1970 (with one outlier who graduated in 1976). They experienced the golden age of Vic High and have been out of touch as to the growing challenges and systemic inequalities faced by students at the school since the 1970s. Diversity and inclusion appears to be foreign to their own lived experiences.

I've estimated that more than ten thousand students[65] of diverse racialized, socio-economic, and immigrant backgrounds have graduated from Vic High over the past fifty years, so I wonder: how it is possible that the Alumni board is a "private club" made up of white Baby Boomers? They apparently missed one of the core principals of a successful alumni association, which requires the renewal of leadership and the passing of the torch from one generation to the next. They are holding on tight for all the wrong reasons.

---

59   Statistics Canada does not yet fully collect data based on race.
60   [Oak Bay, BC Statistics], Townfolio, 2017. townfolio.co/bc/oak-bay/demographics
61   [Victoria, BC Statistics], Townfolio, 2017. townfolio.co/bc/victoria/education
62   "School Enrolment Numbers 2019–20" sd61.bc.ca/schools/school-enrollment-numbers=
63   I shot a satirical video when I visited family and friends in Victoria with my kids in the summer of 2021. The visual example of systemic inequality between Vic High and Oak Bay is shocking. Take a look for yourself: https://youtu.be/DnEhdLNcSgs
64   Information verified via documents uncovered through FOI.
65   200 graduates per year times 50 years.

Having all schools in the Greater Victoria region provided with equal resources and facilities for optimum learning (and with important athletic facilities that promote healthy lifestyles) in the public system should be priority number one. Parents of public-school students continue to voice their concerns over shrinking school budgets while, in British Columbia for example, the government continues to subsidize private schools in the province to the tune of nearly $500 million annually. How are such blatant disparities even possible?

FOVH are continuing the fight against the systemic inequality the students of Vic High have endured for more than half a century. The City of Victoria, the school district, the housing corporation, and even the Vic High Alumni Association board continue to use the system to protect their untenable status quo and to sell our children's futures to balance their budgets, completely ignoring the realities of systemic racism and the inequality they are in fact helping to perpetuate. The students are the ones who continue to pay the price.

Despite the City's vote to allow the housing development to move forward in fall 2021, FOVH continues to gain momentum through added support from a growing number of influential Parent Advisory Councils in the city, and we have made a public call for the BC Minister of Education to open a formal independent investigation. The fight for the current and future students of Vic High continues. Power to the people!

∞

I've only skimmed the surface of the negative issues at play in the education system. But by now, the picture should be pretty clear—and without our activism, it's bleak. These kinds of challenges are faced in education systems across North America. There is much to do, and for racialized students especially, change can't come fast enough.

Ensuring more and more BIPOC students can graduate from high school and go on to further learning will help increase the pool of racialized people with the skills and knowledge needed to compete for better employment opportunities—opportunities that can in turn transform their lives, the lives of their families, and their communities. Unfortunately, as we'll discuss next, once BIPOC students enter corporate North America, they continue to encounter barriers to success.

BARRIERS TO OPPORTUNITY

Income Inequality

Income inequality continues to significantly disadvantage racialized minorities in North America, where a significant number of people (nearly 8 percent, or 2.6 million people in Canada, and more than 4 percent, or 13 million people in the US) fall into the category of "working poor"[66]—people who mostly work for minimum wage. Currently, there are 2.2. times more Black working poor in Canada than white working poor.[67] This doesn't even factor in all those living in poverty who are unemployed.

In Canada, the minimum wage ranges by province, from a low of $10.45 an hour in Québec for a worker earning tips to a high of $16 an hour in Nunavut, where the cost of living is substantially higher. The median minimum wage is $13.74, with Ontario, Canada's most populous province, clocking in just above that at $14.35.[68] Depending on which city you live in, you could possibly afford a one-bedroom apartment in Québec City (costing an average of $917 a month), which would take about 88 hours' worth of your wages (of a total 160 full-time hours)[69]—and that's without factoring in tax deductions. In Toronto, where a one-bedroom apartment averages $2,000 a month, you'd have to work nearly 140 hours just to meet your rent obligations.[70]

And of course, you need to eat, pay for some form of transportation, a phone, and utilities. You get the picture. Working for minimum wage in North America means that taking care of your most basic needs will be a struggle. Even with a recent push by some government leaders on both sides of the border to raise the minimum wage for workers, the gap between worker compensation and corporate management remains huge.

This reality is even worse south of the border. In Atlanta, Georgia, where the minimum wage is $7.25-an-hour[71], the average price of a one-bedroom

---

[66] "Infographic: Inequalities in working poor Canadians," Pan-Canadian Health Inequalities Reporting Initiative, April 24, 2019. canada.ca/en/public-health/services/publications/science-research-data/inequalities-working-poor-canadians-infographic.html

[67] *Ibid.*

[68] "Minimum Wage by Province," Retail Council of Canada, 2021. retailcouncil.org/resources/quick-facts/minimum-wage-by-province

[69] "November 2021 Rent Report" by Ben Myers, *Rentals.ca*, November 2021. rentals.ca/national-rent-report

[70] *Ibid.*

[71] "Income tax calculator Georgia," *Talent.com* (n.d.). talent.com/tax-calculator?salary=1160&from=month&region=Georgia

apartment is $1,723.[72] A single person earning minimum wage would need to work more than 238 hours a month (or about 60 hours a week) just to afford rent. Obviously, the math doesn't add up for those earning minimum wage, and it would still be challenging with a two-income household. Data shows that BIPOC who are also of lower socio-economic status are disproportionally impacted by low wages and rising costs of living.

A January 2021 paper by the Canadian Centre for Policy Alternatives notes that the average annual income for CEOs ($10.8 million) is over two hundred times that of the average Canadian worker ($53,482).[73] In the US, the disparity between workers and corporate leaders is even more drastic. CEO compensation has grown 940 percent since 1978, while average worker compensation has risen only 12 percent during that same period.[74] Yet the US federal government's efforts to raise the minimum wage from $7.25 to $15.00 an hour (gradually, over several years) failed in 2021[75]—due in part to the massive lobbying efforts of the National Restaurant Association and the Chamber of Commerce, among other corporate organizations.[76] Even though twenty-five states did raise their minimum wage in 2021, twenty have only mandated the federal minimum, while the majority still pay between $8 and $12 an hour.

The minimum wage should not be a benchmark for success—it is, literally, the minimum wage employers are legally mandated to pay their workers. What we need to do is to raise hourly wages to a *living wage*, "the wage needed to provide the minimum income necessary to pay for basic needs based on the cost of living in a specific community,"[77] and contribute to reducing the income inequality between BIPOC and white workers. This will require solutions that take into consideration the unique factors—including cost of living—of each province or state. If those with the power to make this happen were truly bold, they would also be looking to pass legislation to reduce the enormous gap between leadership and average-worker compensation.

[72] "Minimum Wage by State and 2022 Increases," *Paycor*, November 19, 2021. paycor.com/resource-center/articles/minimum-wage-by-state

[73] *The Golden Cushion: CEO compensation in Canada* by David Macdonald, Canadian Centre for Policy Alternatives, January 2021. policyalternatives.ca/sites/default/files/uploads/publications/National%20Office/2021/01/Golden%20cushion.pdf

[74] "CEO compensation has grown 940% since 1978" by Lawrence Mishel and Julia Wolfe, *Economic Policy Institute*, August 14, 2019. epi.org/publication/ceo-compensation-2018

[75] "It's been 12 years since the last federal minimum wage increase. Where efforts to raise the pay rate stand" by Lorie Konish, *CNBC*, July 16, 2021. cnbc.com/2021/07

[76] "Business groups prepare for lobbying push against $15 minimum wage" by Alex Gangitano, *The Hill*, January 26, 2021. https://thehill.com/business-a-lobbying/535957-business-groups-prepare-for-lobbying-effort-against-raising-the-minimum

[77] "Minimum, living and fair wages: What's the difference?" *CUPE*, June 28, 2016. cupe.ca/minimum-living-and-fair-wages-whats-difference

The pushback against efforts to increase the minimum wage is mainly centred around the possible negative effects on small businesses like restaurants. I get it. That's why we need a custom approach. We shouldn't look at a small family-owned restaurant the same way we look at an international franchise. Workers at a one-location restaurant should also be paid a fair wage, and tips should be factored in as part of a living-wage compensation formula.

For those working for huge corporations like McDonald's, whose fiduciary obligation is to maximize profits for shareholders, legislation and/or regulation are the only ways to ensure a fair share of profits is distributed to workers in the form of higher wages and cost-of-living increases. These, too, must be customized to regional economic realities. Someone making $15 an hour working and living in downtown Toronto cannot provide for themselves in the same way as someone making the same hourly wage and living in London, just two hours down the road.

Pushing Through the "White Ceiling": BIPOC Diversity and Inclusion

As a society, it seems we are most familiar with the challenges women continue to face in the workplace—pay equity, for example. Women are still paid less than men for equal work, an average of $0.87 for every $1. In twenty years, from 1998 to 2018, the gender-equity pay gap narrowed by only 5.5 percent.[78] As I've previously noted, Black men are paid significantly less than white men and women—and it's an even worse story for Black women.

In July 2020, the *Globe and Mail* published an article called "Why Are There Still So Few Black Lawyers on Bay Street?" This story came at a time when many people were awakening to the Black Lives Matter movement and many businesses, including law firms, were making public their support for diversity and inclusion. Strikingly, the article revealed 2016 data that showed only 63 out of the 1,050 Black lawyers in Ontario (6 percent) were partners, representing only 0.2 percent of all lawyers in the province. Conversely, 18 percent of white lawyers (4,800 out of nearly 27,000) were partners.[79] This highlights two concurrent issues in the legal field in Ontario: a general lack of diversity, and inequality in leadership positions.

---

[78] "The gender wage gap in Canada: 1998 to 2018" by Rachelle Pelletier, Martha Patterson, Centre for Labour Market Information, Statistics Canada and Melissa Moyser, Centre for Gender, Diversity and Inclusion, Statistics Canada, October 7, 2019. www150.statcan.gc.ca/n1/pub/75-004-m/75-004-m2019004-eng.htm

[79] "Why are there still so few Black lawyers on Bay Street?" by Christine Dobby, *The Globe and Mail*, July 17, 2020. theglobeandmail.com/business/article-why-are-there-still-so-few-black-lawyers-on-bay-street

The article goes on to highlight the racism experienced by Black lawyers—from overt discrimination to microaggressions, including:

> drawing scathing rebukes for minor errors that white colleagues don't seem to face; being mistaken for an assistant rather than a litigator; enduring comments about their hair and clothing, or blatant accusations of tokenism; being ignored in a circle of white colleagues, and left out of after-work drinks and client meetings.[80]

This is the kind of corporate racist bullshit that sends the message to BIPOC employees that they don't really belong. The legal profession is not alone, of course. This is an issue across many public and private sectors, some of which I've already touched on. But some progress has been made. We have seen some corporations being compelled to make a more concerted effort to enshrine diversity, equity, and inclusion (DE&I) into their corporate DNA, and to address systemic discriminatory policies and pay equity issues. The public is watching, and we're holding corporations to account.

My friend Jesper Bendtsen, former Head of Global Talent Acquisition at Thomson Reuters (TR), a Canada-based multinational media conglomerate with more than twenty-five thousand employees worldwide, shared insights on the company's blog about its approach to diversity and inclusion. "Developing a diverse workforce isn't just a nice thing to do anymore," he says. "It's an essential business practice that helps ensure longevity in a time of rapid change."[81] As such, the company is committed to doing so with transparency and accountability. TR's former Head of Diversity and Inclusion for the Americas, Linda Hassan, emphasized during her tenure the importance of having leaders "consistently deliver messages supporting diversity and inclusion and provide evidence they're taking steps to promote those two values."[82] When we spoke in 2021, Jesper added that TR was also looking at different approaches to link executive compensation to diversity and inclusion goals. In short, not meeting the diversity and inclusion goals set by the organization would have a negative impact on an executive's overall pay.

To date, Starbucks is one of the few companies (McDonald's is another) to institute a long-term executive incentive program around DE&I. In October 2020, the international coffee chain announced it would adjust its annual bonus plan to create "a more direct tie between executive compensation and

---

[80]   *Ibid.*

[81]   "Inclusive diversity—what does it mean? Why does it matter?" Inside Thomson Reuters (n.d.). thomsonreuters.com/en/careers/careers-blog/inclusive-diversity.html

[82]   *Ibid.*

the goal of creating a more inclusive and diverse company...holding senior leaders individually accountable."[83]

Refinitiv, one of the world's largest providers of financial market data and infrastructure that tracks DE&I, reported that "organizations that prioritise a diverse and inclusive environment and worker satisfaction outperformed both financially and in the equity markets."[84] Those trends are continuing but are being shaped in new ways. Refinitiv's metrics demonstrate that diverse boards also correlate to outperformance for equity investors "by a considerable margin."[85]

Refinitiv publishes an annual D&I Index, ranking the top one hundred organizations in the world (out of more than eleven thousand reporting companies), with an objective to "transparently and objectively measure the relative performance of companies against factors that define diverse and inclusive workplaces."[86] Key metrics roll up into four categories: the Diversity Pillar (which details gender board diversity), the Inclusion Pillar (inclusive of data on people with disabilities), People Development (which includes management training), and News and Controversies (which includes data on working conditions). In Refinitiv's 2021 Index, The Gap ranked number one, or most diverse, and the Royal Bank of Canada number two. Two other Canadian financial institutions, the Bank of Nova Scotia and Toronto Dominion Bank, ranked in the top twenty.[87]

Outside of large corporations, Black entrepreneurs in Canada are also facing barriers to success partly as a result of systemic racism. A study conducted and published by Abacus Data in May 2021 revealed that the main barriers to growth and sustainability in Black-led and Black-owned businesses were "systemic racism, access to capital and the lack of a business network."[88] Almost half of Black entrepreneurs who responded believed their race had been a factor in a supplier or vendor refusing to do business with them, while 45 percent believed they had been denied funding because they were Black.

Less than a week later, the Canadian government seemingly validated

---

[83]   "More Companies Use DE&I as Executive Compensation Metric" by Allen Smith, *SHRM. org*, July 12, 2021. shrm.org/resourcesandtools/legal-and-compliance/employment-law/pages/dei-as-executive-compensation-metric.aspx

[84]   "Investment Insights: Navigating Diversity and Inclusion," *Refinitiv*, September 14, 2021. refinitiv.com/perspectives/future-of-investing-trading/navigating-diversity-and-inclusion

[85]   *Ibid.*

[86]   Top Ten Most Diverse and Inclusive Companies", *Refinitiv*, September 14, 2021. refinitiv.com/en/media-center/press-releases/2021/september/refinitiv-announces-the-2021-d-and-i-index-top-100-most-diverse-and-inclusive-organizations-globally

[87]   The Refinitiv D&I Index is just now being modified and expanded to measure racial inequality in corporate organizations. We'll see how adding "race" to the equation impacts these rankings in 2022.

[88]   "Pan-Canadian Survey Finds Black Entrepreneurs Face Significant Barriers to Success," *Abacus-Data*, May 26, 2021. abacusdata.ca/black-entrepreneurs-canada-inclusive-entrepreneurship

the findings of the study. Mary Ng, the federal Minister of Small Business, Export Promotion and International Trade, announced a $291.3 million fund to be administered by the Federation of African Canadian Economics (FACE), a coalition that consists of several prominent Black business and community organizations, including the Black Business Professional Association (BBPA). The fund provides loans of up to $250,000 for Black business owners and entrepreneurs, who "continue to face systemic barriers in starting and growing their businesses."[89] This is a much-needed equity measure and a welcome boost for Black entrepreneurs across Canada.

Sadly, a July 2021 analysis by the *Globe and Mail* found "a vast majority of companies that made a high-profile public commitment last July [2020] to combat anti-Black systemic racism by boosting diversity within their ranks and elevating Black people to leadership roles, have shown little or no tangible progress in meeting those goals a year later."[90]

The companies had signed on to the BlackNorth Initiative, created by Black Bay Street entrepreneur and philanthropist Wes Hall in the summer of 2020, at the peak of the Black Lives Matter protests around the globe. It was a challenge aimed at CEOs with the aim of tackling racism over the subsequent five years, "primarily by hiring more Black people and elevating existing Black employees to senior leadership roles." However, data from the 105 companies (out of 209 companies that signed onto the initiative) revealed that after one year, a substantial number had "neither increased the number of Black employees in their workforce or elevated Black people to executive roles or to the board level."[91]

Based on Mr. Hall's track record of success and tenacious perseverance, he doesn't strike me as someone who will let initial headwinds get in the way of achieving his objectives, so I remain hopeful this and other tangible actions will soon begin removing barriers to opportunity for the BIPOC community.

The Generational Wealth Gap

More than $68 trillion of generational wealth[92] is expected to be passed down in the US in the next twenty-five years, with less than 3 percent (based on

---

89 "[Press Release] Minister Ng announces the launch of the Black Entrepreneurship Loan Fund," *Newswire.ca*, May 31, 2021. newswire.ca/news-releases/minister-ng-announces-the-launch-of-the-black-entrepreneurship-loan-fund-878271213.html

90 "Companies show little progress on diversity a year after committing to BlackNorth Initiative" by Vanmala Subramaniam, *The Globe and Mail*, July 20, 2021. theglobeandmail.com/business/article-companies-show-little-progress-on-diversity-a-year-after-committing-to

91 *Ibid.*

92 "US$68-trillion wealth-transfer tsunami in the next 25 years, says Cerulli" by Leo Almazora, *WealthProfessional.ca*, November 26, 2018. wealthprofessional.ca/news/industry-news/us68-trillion-wealth-transfer-tsunami-in-the-next-25-years-says-cerulli/251066

household wealth data) expected to benefit the Black community.[93] Shockingly, estimates show that at current rates, it would take 228 years to close the wealth disparity between Black and white Americans.[94] It's estimated that the situation is mirrored in Canada, but on a much smaller scale based on population alone. Interestingly, Statistics Canada is just beginning to collect economic data based on race, so we can't yet get a full read on the situation.

Why should we care about generational wealth inequalities? Because the generational wealth gap prevents racialized communities from competing on an equal footing in capitalistic societies like Canada and the US. Let's take a simple example like housing.

In recent years, the real-estate market in most cities in the US and Canada has exploded. Values of homes have risen exponentially, in part because of speculative buying by affluent investors, but also because of population growth and a diminishing housing inventory. In one West End Toronto neighbourhood, for example, semi- and fully detached homes sell for anywhere between $1.5 and 2.5 million, and prices continue to rise. To purchase a home even at the low end of this scale, you'd need a minimum of $150,000 for a down payment. Housing prices across the GTA continue to break all-time records, with detached-home prices increasing about 30 percent annually.[95]

Many Generation Xers and Millennials have only been able to get into the real-estate market because their parents have given or loaned them the down payment, from savings or from equity on their own homes. In a March 2021 article in the *Globe and Mail*, financial institutions in Canada estimated that between 50 and 60 percent of "young people applying for mortgages today have received assistance from parents."[96] Mortgage brokers suggested the number is likely closer to 90 percent.

In short, the economic opportunities available to many first-time home buyers in Canada is a direct result of generational wealth. But many in the BIPOC community are unlikely to participate in generational-wealth transfer anytime soon. When you consider that for nearly four hundred years most Black people in North America owned no property because they *were* property, it makes a disturbing kind of sense.

Post-slavery, and continuing well into the twentieth century, many BIPOC were legally prohibited from buying or were discouraged from owning a home in certain

93   "Closing the racial wealth gap requires heavy, progressive taxation of wealth" by Vanessa Williamson, *Brookings*, December 9, 2020. https://www.brookings.edu/research/closing-the-racial-wealth-gap-requires-heavy-progressive-taxation-of-wealth

94   "The Average Black Family Would Need 228 Years to Build the Wealth of a White Family Today" by Joshua Holland, *The Nation*, August 8, 2016. thenation.com/article/archive/the-average-black-family-would-need-228-years-to-build-the-wealth-of-a-white-family-toda

95   "Toronto Housing Market Report," *WOWA*, December 3, 2021. wowa.ca/toronto-housing-market

96   "The great generational wealth transfer is on the way" by Gary Mason, *The Globe and Mail*, March 12, 2021. theglobeandmail.com/opinion/article-the-great-generational-wealth-transfer-is-under-way

neighbourhoods—many of them in the same neighbourhoods where homes have increased substantially in value. Many other racialized people were simply turned away by banks who would not approve a mortgage. Meanwhile, Indigenous peoples were forced onto reservations situated on undesirable land and found themselves living in poorly built houses—many in communities without safe drinking water—with little chance those properties would appreciate in value.

This generational—and racial—wealth gap continues to have major ripple effects, making it challenging for BIPOC to invest in themselves and their families because of a lack of access to funds for post-secondary education, to finance new business ventures, or for housing.

So how do we fix this four-hundred-year-old problem?

In 2017, a UN expert panel recommended that the Government of Canada "issue an apology and consider providing reparations to African Canadians for enslavement and historical injustices."[97] This wasn't the first time the idea of reparations had been called for. As we discussed in Chapter Two, Canada does have a history of acknowledging past wrongs and making reparations to those affected by discrimination; the apology and reparations paid to Japanese Canadians and to Indigenous people who survived residential schools are notable examples. However, in June 2020, more than two years after the United Nations called on Canada to apologize "for its history of enslaving black people" and asked the country to "consider paying reparations for the abusive practice," Prime Minister Justin Trudeau would not commit to offering either.[98]

South of the border, US Senate Majority Leader Mitch McConnell made it clear in June 2019 that he opposes reparations (a sentiment broadly shared by Republican politicians in that country), noting,

> I don't think reparations for something that happened 150 years ago for whom none of us currently living are responsible is a good idea....We've tried to deal with our original sin of slavery by fighting a civil war, by passing landmark civil rights legislation. We elected an African American president.[99]

As my buddy Ted would say, "Thanks—what a pal."

In February 2021, Congressional Democrats renewed their push for a federal study of racial reparations—a centuries-old idea. First introduced in

97 "Trudeau won't say whether Canada will apologize for history of slavery or pay reparations" by Marieke Walsh, *The Globe and Mail*, June 2, 2020. theglobeandmail.com/politics/article-trudeau-wont-say-whether-canada-will-apologize-for-history-of-slavery

98 *Ibid.*

99 "McConnell opposes paying reparations: 'None of us currently living are responsible' for slavery" by Ted Barrett, *CNN*, June 19, 2019. cnn.com/2019/06/18/politics/mitch-mcconnell-opposes-reparations-slavery/index.html

1989 and now re-introduced in a House Judiciary subcommittee hearing, Bill H.R.40 would establish a commission "to study slavery and discrimination in the United States and potential reparations proposals for restitution."[100] The bill was sponsored by 170 representatives in congress but, as of November 2021, the Biden administration has not made it a political priority.

The bill's name has quite a history; it refers to an 1865 order by Union Major General William T. Sherman that "land confiscated from Confederate landowners be divided up into 40-acre portions and distributed to newly emancipated Black families."[101] Unfortunately, after President Lincoln's assassination, the order granting "40 acres and a mule" was struck down by President Andrew Johnson, and most of the land returned to white landowners. It was a monumental missed opportunity and a betrayal with huge consequences for Black people—a broken promise still waiting to be honoured 150 years later.

Back in Canada, Rhoda E. Howard-Hassmann, professor emeritus in the department of political science at Wilfrid Laurier University, published an op-ed in June 2020 on "why reparations and apologies to African Canadians are necessary."[102] In it, she suggests the establishment of a fund, which could be used to "redress discrimination from before and after 1960," the year racial discrimination was prohibited in Canada under the Canadian Bill of Rights. She specifies that these reparations "would not have to take the form of a financial payment to every individual African Canadian," but that reparations for victims of specific harms, past and present, should be considered a viable option.

In my October 2020 op-ed published in the *Globe and Mail,* I echoed Howard-Hassmann's suggestion, noting that,

> instead of doling out individual cheques to Black Canadians, Canada should instead establish an on-going stream of investment in Black-owned businesses and start-ups, offer financial assistance for post-secondary education and subsidize the purchase of residential and commercial real estate.[103]

---

[100] "Democrats Push For Reparations Bill, Testing White House Support" by Gina Heeb, *Forbes*, February 17, 2021. forbes.com/sites/ginaheeb/2021/02/17/democrats-push-for-reparations-bill-testing-white-house-support/?sh=557928a3c9db

[101] "What slavery reparations from the federal government could look like" by P. R. Lockhart, *NBC News*, May 12, 2021. nbcnews.com/news/nbcblk/slavery-reparations-federal-govera-tions-looks-2021-rcna900

[102] "Why reparations and apologies to African Canadians are necessary" by Rhoda E. Howard-Hass-mann, *The Conversation* (n.d.). theconversation.com/why-reparations-and-apologies-to-african-ca-nadians-are-necessary-140527

[103] "If Canadians hope to achieve a more just society, let us eliminate 'white advantage'" by Stephen Dorsey, *The Globe and Mail*, October 9, 2020. theglobeandmail.com/opinion/article-if-we-hope-to-achieve-a-more-just-society-canadians-must-stop

After its publication, I continued to flesh out this idea in collaboration with my financial advisor, Andrew Sheppard, and his team at Flatiron Wealth Management. The plan, currently being structured, is rooted in the development of a social opportunity fund for Black Canadians (managed professionally, much like the Ontario Teachers' Pension Fund or Caisse de dépôt et placement du Québec). It would be initially funded by government and private-industry grants, supplemented by enrolees (with contributions tiered, to make participation accessible to varied income earners), and eventually funded by growth from its own investments.

Underpinning this envisioned opportunity fund would be three specific strategies to address immediate, medium-term, and generational-wealth issues. To address immediate issues, the fund would make lending available to the Black community for the purchasing of businesses and property. To address medium-term issues, the fund would create and sustain scholarships for wealth-management and education programs. Apprenticeships would be coordinated to provide entry-level positions in the financial-services industry and a clear path to advancement. Finally, the use of a variety of insurance policies (fuelled by the fund) would ensure that parents and their children participate in the program. A blend of term, permanent, and participating life insurance policies would be utilized, depending on the individual's needs.

For example, a participating life insurance policy would provide immediate coverage to the life insured, while using investments to generate dividends that are then used to purchase more coverage every year within the policy. This creates a positive feedback loop where the benefit amount increases annually and the dividend generated also increases, the growth becoming exponential and tax-free. These policies are very useful for providing coverage for children, and have the potential to contribute to a major generational wealth transfer. I've personally been successfully investing in this kind of insurance-based strategy for my family for more than a decade.

Many people have suggested potential solutions, and some have already moved ideas forward with action. In March 2021, Wes Hall's BlackNorth Initiative announced a new effort, this time a plan to launch the BlackNorth Homeownership Bridge Program, "aimed at tackling the large gap between white and racialized Canadians in relation to home ownership." Through "shared equity and special mortgage arrangements," the program aims to give working-class Black families the opportunity for home ownership.[104] As Hall explains, "When you own a home, and you're able to leverage your home—to start a business, to send your kids to university—it's much easier to rise....Everything that comes with success in this country comes, for the most part, with real estate."[105]

[104] "A plan to boost home ownership by Black families" by Alex Bozikovic, *The Globe and Mail*, March 5, 2021. theglobeandmail.com/real-estate/toronto/article-a-plan-to-boost-home-ownership-by-black-families

[105] *Ibid.*

For Indigenous peoples in Canada, decades-long efforts to negotiate settlements with the federal government have seen some First Nations secure self-government agreements (SGAs). What many Canadians may not know is that Indigenous peoples have "an inherent right of self-government," as per Section 35 of Canada's 1982 Constitution Act.[106] These SGAs give Indigenous governments the power to make decisions about their own communities, including how to best deliver programs and services. This, importantly, includes the power to make decisions on linguistic and cultural protection, education, land management, and job creation.

Because every Indigenous community is different, agreements need to be customized and negotiated on a nation-by-nation basis. To date, there are twenty-five SGAs across Canada involving forty-three Indigenous communities.[107] Eleven of these are located in the Yukon alone.

In 2008, as part of the Governor General's Canadian Leadership Conference, I had the privilege to be invited to visit Old Crow on Vuntut Gwitchin First Nation (VGFN), a fly-in community of three hundred located north of the Arctic circle. It is a breathtaking place to visit. Chief Joe Linklater and several elders took great pride in touring us around their many newly built facilities, including a modern school with all the standard amenities, a medical clinic, and even an indoor ice rink. The Vuntut Gwitchin First Nation self-government agreement, signed in 1993 by Chief Robert Bruce Jr., outlined many provisions, including the right of the VGFN to hold decision-making powers over settlement land (both above and below the earth's surface[108]), addressing everything from fish and wildlife to education and health care—jurisdictional powers similar to those accorded to provinces and territories across Canada.

I recall Chief Linklater telling us how the VGFN had also negotiated implementation supports which would see the Yukon Territorial government provide resource support for a pre-determined period of years until the VGFN could build enough capacity to independently manage and deliver services to its citizens across its educational and health-care systems.

In addition to legally reclaiming rights to their land, the VGFN also received financial compensation of just over $36 million that made it possible for them to acquire a 49 percent interest in Yukon airline Air North.[109]

---

106 "Self-government," Government of Canada, August 25, 2020. rcaanc-cirnac.gc.ca/eng/1100100032275/1529354547314

107 "Self-Governing First Nations in Yukon" by Jocelyn Joe-Strack and Kirk Cameron, *The Canadian Encyclopedia*, March 18, 2021. thecanadianencyclopedia.ca/en/article/self-governing-first-nations-in-yukon

108 "First Nation Community Profiles: Vuntut Gwitchin First Nation–Community of Old Crow," *Yukon.ca*, Vuntut Gwitchin First Nation (n.d.). yukon.ca/sites/yukon.ca/files/ybs/ybs-forms/fin-vuntut-gwitchin-first-nation-census-2006.pdf

109 *Ibid.*

This investment has provided both sustainable jobs and a transportation lifeline to Old Crow.

In her article published in June 2021, Gabrielle Slowey, an associate professor in the department of politics at York University, and the inaugural Fulbright Chair in Arctic Studies at Dartmouth College, noted that the SGAs in the Yukon are "ground-breaking and far-reaching"[110] in that "they protect and enhance Indigenous culture, economy, and lifestyle, and have made First Nations equitable partners in the governance of Yukon society." She suggests that although most Canadians are unaware of Indigenous self-government in the Yukon, "if Canadians are serious about reconciliation, they need to learn more about this important work."

∞

So, there you have it. Canada does know how to make settlement agreements as well as provide reparations to historically marginalized communities. It's really a matter of will and want. A big question, of course, is whether non-racialized North Americans will support having billions of taxpayer dollars allocated to these reparations. We need action on that scale to make an impact.

If you are a member of the BIPOC community, waiting another 248 years for the generational wealth gap to miraculously close will simply not cut it.

Let's get on with it. Opportunity is knocking.

110 "Indigenous self-government in Yukon holds lessons for all of Canada" by Gabrielle A. Slowey, *Policy Options*, June 28, 2021policyoptions.irpp.org/magazines/june-2021/indigenous-self-government-in-yukon-holds-lessons-for-all-of-canada/

Chapter Eight

Systemic Inequality: Québec Exceptionalism

PART I: SYSTEMIC RACISM AND RELIGIOUS DISCRIMINATION

A FEW YEARS AGO, MOTIVATED BY A STRONG DESIRE TO UNEARTH MY FAMILY roots, I was bitten by the genealogy bug. I focused on my maternal line as it offered the clearest path to discovery, even with the limited first-hand information my mother could provide. Through the meticulously detailed—and, luckily for me, digitized—marriage and baptismal records of the Catholic Church, I was able to trace the Moore family, which had originally settled in Montréal, back to 1852, when my ancestors lived in Lévis, Québec.

In the spring of 2021, I received an alert that another member on the genealogy app shared some relatives with me. Not only did we share the same Moore line, but he had traced the family all the way back to 1550, to Dover—the town noted for its iconic white cliffs—in County Kent in the United Kingdom, . Thomas Moore, a sailor born there in 1654, immigrated to Québec sometime prior to 1690, and became the first family member to settle on Île-d'Orléans, the island located in the middle of the St. Lawrence River off the shore of Québec City. Records show he was married on April 6, 1690, to Jeanne Lemelin at Notre-Dame de Québec Cathedral-Basilica—the oldest church in Canada, which still stands today.

For nearly two centuries, many members of the Moore family were sailors who worked for the Hudson Bay Company, ferried goods between settlements, and were engaged—as needed—to help protect the colony in times of war. Like many Scottish, Irish, and English families who immigrated to Québec, the Moores started out as Protestant anglophones and, through generations, morphed into Catholic francophones, contributing to the unique cultural mix of the region. It's likely, however, that my brother Chris and I are the only Black descendants of our long and wide branch of the Moore family tree.

I expect none of my ancestors could ever have imagined that possibility.

In short, my roots in Québec run deep. Much of my immediate and extended family—including members of the Moore, Lefevre, Charette, Paquin, Morin, Marchand, and Guertin families—still lives in and around Montréal (in Longueuil, St. Bruno, and Valleyfield). And over the decades, I've forged lasting friendships there with members of the Jutras, Quesnel, Lussier, Theberge, and Pelletier families, to name but a few.

Québec is my native home filled with people I love. Much of my identity as a bilingual, biracial man was forged there. And it was for those very reasons that I felt the need to expose the province's history of systemic racism. I needed to dig deep to make sense of it for myself and for others.

Questioning the motives and actions of the people and places we hold dear can be challenging, but I think it's an important exercise that each of us has a responsibility to undertake—if only to know where we all stand on important issues of our time. In fact, I believe it's an act of love and care.

With foundational elements of liberal democracy under attack around the world (voter suppression in the US and the limiting of individual freedoms in Québec come to mind), I believe it's our democratic duty to try and find connection with fellow citizens on both simple and complicated issues before they lead to deeper divisions that threaten our entire political system. Just because some things have always been, doesn't mean they should continue to be. Especially if, as I believe, our society continues to advantage some over others.

Some may wonder why I've dedicated an entire chapter to the issue of systemic inequality in the province of Québec. My answer is simple: discrimination against minorities in Québec, as Canada's only predominantly French-speaking province, is even more multi-layered than you'll find in the rest of the country. For those outside Canada, it might be helpful to view the province of Québec through the lens of the state of Texas, which has flirted with secession from the union, and where some local leaders believe that, as State Representative Kyle Biedermann says, "the People of Texas should be allowed the right to decide their own future."[1]

In Canada, this pursuit of independence is the life's work of the Bloc Québécois. The federal political party devoted to Québec Nationalism and sovereignty (separating from Canada) is currently led by Yves-François Blanchet, and holds nearly 10 percent of the seats (34 out of 338 as of the 2021 election) in Canada's Parliament. There are several other political parties in the province with a nationalistic focus, including the Coalition Avenir Québec (CAQ), which has governed the province with a strong majority since 2018.

---

[1] Texas can't legally secede from the U.S., despite popular myth" by Aneri Pattani, *The Texas Tribune*, January 29, 2021. texastribune.org/2021/01/29/texas-secession

Other nationalist movements in Spain (in the Catalan and Basque regions), Belgium (the Flemish movement), and Scotland are often cited in the context of Québec's aspirations for independence. Two referendums, in 1980 and 1995, were held in Québec, asking citizens to vote on their desire to secede or not. The most recent attempt failed by a margin of less than 1 percent. (We'll discuss the referendums in more detail in Part II.)

In addition to the many systemic barriers to equality in Canada, Québec has its own unique barriers. These are rooted in part by the core belief, held by many in positions of power, that the essence of French Canadian culture should be protected within prescribed constructs of the francophone heritage of the province's majority—an untenable position for those in the minority. Essentially, this desire to protect French Canadian culture comes at the detriment of everything, and everyone, that is *not* French Canadian—or, in the minds of some, not the "right kind" of French Canadian.

The populist provincial regime in power today, the CAQ, continues to publicly deny that systemic racism even exists in Québec. It is also the only province, territory, or state on the continent to pass legislation that explicitly restricts the individual rights of citizens to publicly express their religious faith in key sectors of employment. And to make matters even more complicated, since the mid-1970s, the Province of Québec has passed a series of laws that have effectively made its minority English speakers second-class citizens, their equal rights subjugated by the French-speaking majority.

It's a lot to unpack, but I believe it's important to do it if we want to effect tangible change as it relates to systemic inequality—including addressing systemic racism. I have a vested interest in Québec being a full partner in Canada because my own Canadian heritage is woven into the history of the province. I was born here and raised within a French Canadian family that embraced bilingualism and grew up to love the cultural differences and unique character that make Québec a special place in Canada.

∞

In Québec, the issue of systemic racism is further complicated by the intersectionality of race, religion, and language that creates a unique blend of discrimination and disadvantage. Systemic inequalities are perpetuated through policies promoted by government and enshrined in law. As we've discussed elsewhere, one of the first steps in working toward change at the individual level is to admit that you may hold unconscious bias. Governments need to be held to the same standard. Like many Canadians, I am infuriated at the government leadership in Québec that continues to deny the existence of systemic racism. Is it possible that Québec is the only region in Canada without it? Of course not.

François Legault, the premier of Québec at the time of writing, and his ministers are too intelligent not to grasp the indisputable facts. Their intentional blurring of the issue, noting "lack of consensus," is disingenuous and only works to serve their political and policy objectives. Their "denial" tactic is pulled straight out of the playbook of climate change deniers, who often claim "scientists are still debating whether climate change is real" even when it is clear that the debate has long been put to bed by overwhelming scientific evidence. Today, even some of the more right-wing anti–carbon tax advocates have finally, if begrudgingly, acknowledged that climate change is real and that it is caused by humans. When it comes to systemic racism in Québec, though, Premier Legault and his ministers are simply being intellectually dishonest, guided by their ideological and political motivations—because if there's no such thing as systemic racism in Québec, then there's nothing wrong with the system. Nothing to fix.

Benoit Charette, the Minister of the Environment and the Fight Against Climate Change, was appointed Minister Responsible for the Fight Against Racism in 2021 (managing two huge portfolios at the same time) with a priority to see implementation of key recommendations in a commissioned report released in December 2020 titled *Racism in Quebec, Zero Tolerance.* The task force, known as the "Groupe d'action contre le racism," was mandated to submit concrete recommendations to the government to fight racism by identifying which sectors—particularly public security, justice, school systems, housing, and employment[2]—have high-priority needs in this area.

The architects of the report, among them accomplished people of colour, sidestepped the issue of systemic racism, arguing that "there is no consensus in Québec society on what the term 'systemic racism' means or on the actions that arise from it."[3] They claim that "the debate is still open" and that "as its very name clearly indicates, [the task force] was mandated by the government to recommend concrete actions, not to settle the debate on the matter of 'systemic racism.'"[4]

In an article published in Québec's prominent French-language publication *Le Devoir* on December 15, 2020, titled "Manque de Vision" (Lack of Vision), columnist Emilie Nicolas wrote that the report "seems to sweep away in advance any debate that [the government] wished to avoid. The Premier and the 'group' tell us they do not want to speak of systemic racism, but they also don't tell us what they want to talk about."[5] Ms. Nicolas correctly points

---

2   *Racism in Quebec: Zero Tolerance.* Report of the Group d'action contre le racism. December 2020. cdn-contenu.quebec.ca/cdn-contenu/politiques_orientations/Groupe_action_racisme/ RA_GroupeActionContreRacisme_AN_MAJ.pdf?1608750405.

3   *Ibid.*

4   *Ibid.*

5   "Manque de vision" by Emile Nicholas. *Le Devoir*, December 15, 2020. ledevoir.com/opinion/ chroniques/591727/manque-de-vision

out the obvious. The report makes recommendations for various measures but without providing concrete solutions for implementation. It also doesn't make clear which systems were examined—most notably missing is any kind of investigation into Québec's police system.

Failing to address systemic racism, the central issue of the civil rights reckoning of our time, is a major missed opportunity for the government and the people of Québec. More than that, it's a slap in the face to all those from racialized communities who hoped that we had arrived at a historical inflection point—one that demanded a serious examination and acknowledgement of the facts. As Marisa Berry Méndez, a coordinator with Amnesty International, notes, "to not acknowledge systemic racism not only will stand in [Charette's] way in terms of taking action...but also in terms of being seen as credible or legitimate by the communities that are impacted."[6] Furthermore, this lack of acknowledgement of a racist system means any action taken will not get to the root of the issue, or to the dismantling of the elements within the existing systems that perpetuate racism.

No society lives in a bubble. There is plenty of available data to be referenced in Québec and from across Canada, the US, and beyond to instruct the province on how to make institutions more transparent. It's clear the government of Québec was motivated by other priorities; their lacklustre efforts never intended to get to the heart of the matter. Of the twenty-five recommendations the report highlights, Ms. Nicolas notes, and I paraphrase, that a dozen could be summarized as information and educational tactics, among them the development of a national anti-racism awareness campaign to keep the public informed about racism and discrimination. Again, no specific action plan is provided.[7]

Of the remaining recommendations, many lack clear objectives. As Ms. Nicolas further paraphrases from the report, the province wants to increase, within five years, the number of visible minorities in leadership positions in the civil service. The report doesn't provide a quantifiable goal or even a process by which to achieve that objective. To illustrate her point, Ms. Nicolas draws a parallel to the issue of global warming, noting how absurd it would be if the government's approach to addressing racism in Québec was applied to climate change. To paraphrase Ms. Nicolas, imagine if countries around the world did not set specific targets for the reduction of carbon (as stipulated in the Paris Agreement—the legally binding international treaty on climate change), and even went as far as to refuse to investigate the *causes* of climate change,

6   "Premier appoints Benoit Charette, environment minister, to lead fight against racism" by Antoni Nerestant, *CBC News*, February 4, 2021. cbc.ca/news/canada/montreal/anti-racism-commissioner-quebec-1.5925915

7   "Manque de vision" by Emile Nicholas. *Le Devoir*, December 15, 2020. ledevoir.com/opinion/chroniques/591727/manque-de-vision

arguing the "lack of consensus" on whether or not humans play a role. The tactic to combat climate change would instead be to *hope* that information campaigns targeted at citizens are sufficient to affect change. That's essentially where we are left with the report on racism from the government of Québec. It would be laughable if it were not so serious.

Other parts of the report are quite revealing of the mindset of the Group d'action which authored the report. They note that "...other organizations and individuals cautioned that ideologies and movements associated with the term 'systemic racism' could ultimately undermine anti-racism and social cohesion efforts."[8] It's unclear who they are referring to as "other organizations," as they never disclose this in the report. Here, the report appears to be making an incredibly general statement about how activist groups and movements pushing for the acknowledgement and dismantling of systemic racism are, in fact, the very organizations we should be wary of. Is this gaslighting on a provincial scale?

And they double down, adding that, "fundamentally, no clear and undisputed definition of the concept was presented." What experts did they call to testify on this issue? Again, they don't tell us. And for the *coup de grâce*, they finish by noting that "the task force also found that in most cases, the positions expressed are quite polarized, leaving no room for compromise."[9] A compromise that would dilute the truth because some refuse to acknowledge that systemic racism exists in Québec? The group's perspective seems to be that doing nothing about the core issue is better.

To be fair, the report does call for some positive change, for example partnering police with social workers in community policing, an approach I myself endorse, but again, there are no details as to how this will actually be put into practice. The recommendation detailing how the province can better integrate immigrants into the workforce (including devising a better approach to recognizing foreign credentials) is actually a good idea, one which aligns with the federal government's Foreign Credential Recognition Program, which in part looks to simplify and harmonize the process and make it easier for a doctor from Afghanistan or an engineer from Peru to be allowed to practice in Canada. But these suggestions are few and far between and offer nothing that isn't already being done on a national scale outside of Québec.

Armed with a very flawed report, Minister Charette is now charged with implementing the recommendations, guided by Premier Legault's intransigence on the non-existence of systemic racism in Québec. "What bothers me with the expression [systemic racism], there are many elements to this, it gives

---

8   *Racism in Quebec: Zero Tolerance.* Report of the Group d'action contre le racism. December 2020. cdn-contenu.quebec.ca/cdn-contenu/politiques_orientations/Groupe_action_racisme/ RA_GroupeActionContreRacisme_AN_MAJ.pdf?1608750405.

9   *Ibid.*

a false sense of security, [allowing some] to lay blame on others," he said. "If we base ourselves solely on a concept that is very vague, and not well defined, it takes away a bit of the responsibility that we have."[10]

A concept that is very vague? In fact, there is a broad consensus, in Canada and around the world, on the meaning of systemic racism. In a June 2020 a poll conducted by Abacus Data revealed that more than 60 percent of Canadians—including 50 percent of citizens living in Québec and the Atlantic Provinces—believe systemic racism exists in Canada.[11] Every provincial and territorial government in Canada (except for Québec) has acknowledged the irrefutable data that suggests systemic racism is present across many institutions.

In June 2020, Prime Minister Justin Trudeau acknowledged that "systemic racism is an issue right across the country, in all our institutions, including in all our police forces; including in the RCMP,"[12] and that the way forward "is recognizing that the systems we have built over the past generations have not always treated people of racialized backgrounds, of Indigenous backgrounds fairly through the very construction of the systems that exist."[13] Statistics Canada has collected and analyzed troves of data that validate the reality of systemic racism and inequality in Canada.[14] This data shows lower personal income, higher rates of unemployment and poverty, and much higher rates when it comes to being targets of hate crimes for Black Canadians. So the proof is there in black and white, if you want to see it. Apparently, Mr. Legault and his ministers do not.

To complicate matters further, in June 2019 Québec's National Assembly passed Bill No. 21, An Act Respecting the Laicity of the State, otherwise known as the Secular Act. The legislation bans Québec public servants—such as teachers, police officers, judges, lawyers, and government workers—from wearing religious symbols such as crosses, hijabs, turbans, and yarmulkes when carrying out their civic duties. The law also prevents people from receiving public services with their faces covered. The law was created in the name of "religious neutrality of the state," but I agree with the Canadian Civil Liberties Association that Bill 21 is a "law against religious freedom that

[10] "Premier appoints Benoit Charette, environment minister, to lead fight against racism" by Antoni Nerestant, *CBC News*, February 24, 2021. cbc.ca/news/canada/montreal/anti-racism-commission-er-Québec-1.5925915

[11] "Almost two-thirds of Canadians believe systemic racism exists in the country: poll," *City News*, June 11, 2020. edmonton.citynews.ca/2020/06/11/racism-discrimination-canada-poll/

[12] "Systemic racism exists in all institutions, including RCMP: Trudeau" by Sarah Turnbull, CTV News, June 11, 2020. ctvnews.ca/politics/systemic-racism-exists-in-all-institutions-including-rc-mp-trudeau-1.4979878

[13] *Ibid.*

[14] "Five charts that show what systemic racism looks like in Canada" by Graham Slaughter, CTV News, June 4, 2020.

is problematic in fomenting systemic inequality against racialized and religious minorities."[15] As a 2019 article explains, "Premier François Legault has insisted that the Bill is consistent with the views of most Quebecers that the state ought to be religiously neutral."[16] Again, Premier Legault chooses to lean into the assumed populist position instead of showing support for minority rights. As the Toronto-based journalist Ahmed Sahi insightfully points out in his 2019 *Maclean's* op-ed: "You know something is all about politics when it does absolutely nothing for people's livelihood, education, prosperity or quality of life."[17]

Let's unpack some of these terms. *Secularism* is the idea of something being not religious or not connected to a church or other religious organization. For example, the federal governments in many democratic nations, including Canada and the United States, are independent of any religion. The counter to this would be a country like Iran, a nation guided and governed by a fundamentalist Islamic theocracy. In the former, religion does not factor into government decision-making; in the latter, it underpins everything the government does.

As explained in the chapter "Trying to Understand French Secularism" in the 2006 book *Political Theologies*, "To be fully part of a democratic community, citizens holding different religious beliefs (or none) must share values that reflect the unity of the state, that enable them to have a common political life. Without shared values there can be no integration [and therefore] no political stability, no justice, no freedom, and no tolerance."[18] In Canada, we are united around shared values as codified in the Charter of Rights and Freedoms (part of Canada's constitution) and in the US, the values found in the Bill of Rights and amendments in that country's constitution set the tone.

Québec has a history of turning to its colonial roots in France on issues regarding language rights, identity politics, and governance. Instead of embracing all of Canada's Charter-enshrined protections of rights and freedoms (including those related to religion), Québec looked to emulate France's new secular law, which was put into effect in 2004, and which prohibits the wearing of attire associated with any religion in schools. As many rightly pointed out, the new secular law in France was clearly intended to discriminate against

---

[15] "Bill 21: The Law Against Religious Freedom." The Canadian Civil Liberties Association. ccla.org/bill-21/

[16] "Québec's Bill 21 misapplies religious neutrality principle" by Kristopher Kinginger, *Policy Options*, May 7, 2019. policyoptions.irpp.org/fr/magazines/may-2019/Québecs-bill-21-misapplies-religious-neutrality-principle/

[17] "Québec's unthinkable Bill 21" by Ahmed Sahi, *Maclean's*, April 9, 2019. macleans.ca/opinion/Québecs-unthinkable-bill-21

[18] *Political Theologies: Public Religions in a Post-secular World*, edited by Hent de Vries and Lawrence Eugene Sullivan, New York: Fordham University Press, 2006.

Muslim women who wear head (hijab) or face and body (burqa) coverings as part of their faith—religious symbols that many French citizens dislike, and which some would even go as far as to say do not fit their view of *being French*. France's new law overreaches, mischaracterizing the principle of secularism as it was written in the country's own constitution in 1905. As a 2020 *Euronews* article explains, "The legal definition demands religious neutrality of the state, not individuals, so long as they are not disrupting public order."[19]

Originally, France's 1905 *laïcité* (secularism) law was put in place to limit the power of the Catholic Church in governmental affairs. Ironically, Québec struggled with this separation of church and state for hundreds of years. Up to the late 1960s, the all-powerful Catholic Church was ubiquitous in almost every aspect of the lives of French Canadians. However, as Stéphanie Hennette Vauchez and Vincent Valentin, legal scholars based in France, pointed out in 2014, "The new laïcité is coming to limit not only the actions of the state, but also the freedom of individuals."[20]

Let's be clear. France is not a beacon of diversity and inclusion. As a country, it remains very segregated, and has grappled for decades with how to build a truly multicultural society that fully embraces immigrants—many of whom are originally from former French colonies in northern Africa, including Algeria and Tunisia. Emmanuel Macron, the President of France since 2017, acknowledges that "France...failed its immigrant communities, creating 'our own separatism' with ghettos of 'misery and hardship' where people were lumped together according to their origins and social background." He adds, "We have thus created districts where the promise of the Republic has no longer been kept."[21]

I witnessed this French dichotomy first-hand during a short holiday to Paris in 2019. I love almost everything about Paris; it's one of my favourite places in the world. Wandering its pristine and historic streets without a destination is my favourite way to enjoy the city. There are approximately 11 million people living in the greater Paris area, which is often cited as one of the most diverse cities in Europe. An estimated 23 percent of the population migrated there sometime after they were born, while 20 percent are first-generation immigrants, and at least 40 percent have one parent who is a first-generation

19 "What is secularism and why is it causing such divisions in France?" by Emma Beswick, *Euronews*, September 12, 2020. euronews.com/2020/11/05/what-is-secularism-and-why-is-it-causing-such-divisions-in-france

20 "The contradictions of French secularism" by Joan Wallach Scott, *The New Statesman*, November 18, 2020. newstatesman.com/world/europe/2020/11/contradictions-french-secularism

21 "What is secularism and why is it causing such divisions in France?" by Emma Beswick, *Euronews*, September 12, 2020. euronews.com/2020/11/05/what-is-secularism-and-why-is-it-causing-such-divisions-in-france

immigrant.[22] An estimated 6 million foreign-born citizens live in France, which constitutes nearly 10 percent of the total population. The downtown core of Paris, though, feels very white—there, you'll find mostly affluent Parisians who can afford to live in one of the most expensive cities in the world. You do see some people of colour mixed in, as well as a diverse array of tourists from around the world. But they're rare enough that you notice them.

One late afternoon, I decided to change things up and use the Métro to get back to my hotel. Descending the steps of the nearest station was like stepping into The Land of Oz, except in reverse. All of a sudden, Paris transformed from a vibrant, colourful city into a dull grey, dingy basement packed with people. The majority of Parisians I saw in the "underground" were shades of Black; most were blue-collar workers heading home to the suburbs after a hard day's labour. The station and trains were crowded and dirty, and the air was suffocating on this hot summer day. It was a sharp contrast to the manicured streets and buildings above, and a far cry from the comparatively pristine subway systems I'd travelled in Toronto and Montréal. It was a shocking dose of reality. A tale of two cities.

Paris is not alone in this "informal" racial and economic segregation. In the United States, cities like Atlanta and Boston come to mind—cities divided by race, where certain neighbourhoods are predominantly Black while others are mostly white. If Black and white citizens interact at all, they do so during mostly brief, service-related transactions—in restaurants, at the mall, or at the gas station, for example. Communing between races does happen, but it is the exception.

This is also a reality in many Canadian cities, towns, and villages. Take Toronto for example, a very multicultural city which, even to me, seems like a place where people "mix" well. Research published in 2018 by professor David Hulchanski and his team at the University of Toronto revealed, however, that "new demographic charts show a strikingly segregated city, with visible minorities concentrated in low-income neighbourhoods and white residents dominating affluent areas in numbers far higher than their share of the population."[23]

Using the 2016 Canadian census data, Hulchanksi's team found that, in a city where whites make up 49 percent of the total population, they make up only 31 percent of the population in neighbourhoods where the average individual income is $32,000, while 68 percent of residents in these same neighbourhoods are visible minorities. "High-income neighbourhoods are

[22] "World Population: Paris," *Worldpopulation.com*, worldpopulationreview.com/world-cities/par-is-population

[23] "Toronto is segregated by race and income. And the numbers are ugly" by Sandro Contenta, *Toronto Star*, October 1, 2018. thestar.com/news/gta/2018/09/30/toronto-is-segregated-by-race-and-income-and-the-numbers-are-ugly.html

almost a reverse image," the article says. In neighbourhoods with an average pre-tax income of $102,000, 73 percent of residents are white, disproportionate to their share of the city's population. The rest are visible minorities, of whom only 3 percent are Black.

The 2011 Martin Prosperity Institute (MPI) report, *Segregated City*, measured the intersectionality of over seventy thousand census tracts, ranking economic segregation across major US cities. Interestingly, the nation's three largest metropolitan areas—New York, Los Angeles, and Chicago—ranked among the top ten most segregated cities, leading the report to claim that "large metros have higher levels of economic segregation than smaller ones."[24] The report also suggests that the growing trend of income inequality—and its associated income segregation—should be addressed head on.

This kind of racial, cultural, and economic segregation is largely informal and unacknowledged. Still, it has a negative effect on the lives of those who are pushed to the margins and segregated in low-income areas with few services and opportunities. But what happens when policies are put in place to further segregate minorities? That's exactly what's happening in Québec today.

∞

For most of Québec's history over the past two centuries, no government had ever expressed a need or been compelled to prohibit individual religious expression in institutions such as in schools or police forces. For much of the province's history, the Catholic faith was a dominant force in Québec society. The Christian crucifix was prominently featured in the Québec legislative assembly from 1936 until 2019, when it was removed. Why the province's sudden rush to impose restrictions on the religious freedoms of its citizens? Former Calgary Mayor Naheed Nenshi, the city's first Muslim mayor, noted in a 2021 *Politico* op-ed that "Bill 21 restricts what job you have based on your faith. That's not secularism, that bigotry, and we need to call it out no matter the political risk."[25] I couldn't agree more. Federal government leaders of all stripes—except for members of the Bloc Québécois—expressed their displeasure with the enactment of Bill 21, but none actually specified what they would do protect the Charter rights of those Canadians affected. Prime Minster Justin Trudeau was the only political leader who did leave the door open to intervening, noting that the federal government would look at its options once all court challenges brought by other parties had concluded.

---

[24]   *Segregated City* by by Richard Florida and Charlotta Mellander, Martin Prosperity Institute, February 23, 2015. 2.rotman.utoronto.ca/mpi/wp-content/uploads/2015/02/Segregated-City_Insight_15-02-11.pdf

[25]   "Mayor Naheed Nenshi to Canadians: 'We need to talk'" by Naheed Nenshi. *Politico*, April 28, 2021. politico.com/newsletters/corridors/2021/04/28/mayor-naheed-nenshi-to-canadians-we-need-to-talk-794935

I was particularly perplexed by Jagmeet Singh's position on the issue. Mr. Singh, leader of the New Democratic Party of Canada since 2017, is a practising Sikh of Punjabi descent who wears a turban and a small, sheathed ceremonial knife called a kirpan as symbols of his faith. During Canada's 2019 federal election, only months after the passing of Bill 21 by Quebec's legislative assembly, Mr. Singh said he would not interfere in the matter if he were prime minister. But on behalf of all Canadians, I have to ask: if you are the leader of a federal party in Canada, seeking to become the prime minister, is there a more important obligation than protecting the rights accorded Canadian citizens as prescribed by the Charter of Rights and Freedoms? If not them, then who?

In the spring of 2021, the Québec Superior Court upheld Bill 21, exempting only the English school board on the basis of minority language rights protected under the Charter. In his ruling, Justice Marc-André Blanchard noted that "Quebec's secularism law violates the basic rights of religious minorities in the province, but those violations are permissible because of the Constitution's notwithstanding clause."[26] The notwithstanding clause, or Section 33, allows Canada's Parliament or provincial or territorial legislatures to temporarily override certain portions of the Charter. This means that while it can be argued that Bill 21's very existence violates Canadians' Charter rights, this clause allows it to be upheld and re-enacted every five years and any number of times.[27]

Like France's laïcité legislation, Bill 21 was clearly devised to intentionally marginalize and disadvantage immigrant and racialized communities whose personal beliefs and faiths are honoured in part through their religious dress, most commonly in the Muslim faith. In my view, Bill 21 is a law in search of a problem that doesn't exist. It is an ideological choice that imposes systemic inequality on certain religious and racialized communities under the guise of a supposed need for "neutrality" in expression of individual faith. It's evident that the bill will have little impact on citizens whose symbols of faith—such as the Catholic crucifix—can be easily concealed underneath clothing. When the garments themselves are the religious symbol, what is one to do?

---

[26] "Quebec Superior Court upholds most of religious symbols ban, but English-language schools exempt" by Jonathan Montpetit, Benjamin Shingler, *CBC News*, April 20, 2021. cbc.ca/news/canada/montreal/bill-21-religious-symbols-ban-quebec-court-ruling-1.5993431

[27] "Canadian Charter of Rights and Freedoms," *Wikipedia*, wikipedia.org/wiki/Section_33_of_the_Canadian_Charter_of_Rights_and_Freedoms

Immigration & Multiculturalism

Canada is home to a vast number of immigrants. Data from the 2011 National Household Survey (NHS) shows that one in five Canadians is foreign-born—the highest percentage of any G8 country.[28] It's helpful to compare Québec to Ontario, which leads Canada in immigration. Québec is in second place, though on a per-capita basis, it ranks sixth in Canada for newcomer intake.[29] Ontario has a population of 14 million, with nearly 7 million living in the Greater Toronto Area alone. In contrast, Québec, a province with 30 percent more land, has a population of nearly 8.5 million, with the Greater Montréal area, the province's most populous city, accounting for 4.2 million people.

Ontario has welcomed nearly 1 million immigrants over the past five years (including reduced numbers in 2020 due to COVID-19). Some of these were racialized immigrants who faced the same kinds of systemic challenges experienced by racialized Canadians—most notably in securing employment, although even that reality is improving. Data collected by the Government of Canada that tracked Syrian refugees resettling in Canada between November 2015 and December 2016, for example, shows that the majority of refugees were able to integrate effectively within Canadian society.[30]

According to the data, overall immigrant and refugee earnings match the Canadian average about twelve years after arrival, while some economic immigrants (those selected based on specific professional credentials or investment criteria) catch up within their first year. In 2016 one-third of all immigrants in Canada were volunteers and two-thirds were members of social organizations. The data also shows that two out of three immigrants became home owners after ten years; these respondents have the highest citizenship uptake, with 89 percent choosing to become Canadian citizens.[31] In fact, Toronto, whose citizens represent over 230 nationalities and over 180 languages, is recognized as one of the world's most multicultural cities. In contrast, Québec, at 50 percent the size, welcomed less than 25 percent as many immigrants as Ontario during the same time period.

---

[28] "Immigration and Ethnocultural Diversity in Canada." Statistics Canada, July 25, 2018. www12. statcan.gc.ca/nhs-enm/2011/as-sa/99-010-x/99-010-x2011001-eng.cfm

[29] Québec needs 80,000 immigrants per year, not 50,000" by Kareem El-Assal, *CIC News*, November 4, 2019. cicnews.com/2019/11/Québec-needs-80000-immigrants-per-year-not-50000-1113097. html#gs.chaquv

[30] "Syrian Outcomes Report," Government of Canada, Immigration, Refugees and Citizenship Canada, June 2019, canada.ca/en/immigration-refugees-citizenship/corporate/reports-statistics/ evaluations/syrian-outcomes-report-2019.html.

[31] "#ImmigrationMatters: Canada's immigration track record." Government of Canada. canada.ca/ en/immigration-refugees-citizenship/campaigns/immigration-matters/track-record.html

One major issue that impacts immigrants across Canada is the lag time in the federal government's recognition of foreign professional credentials—of medical and engineering licences for example—which means that in the interim, many people have to take work outside their fields of expertise, often in the service industry. But setting the issue of professional credentials aside, it seems that Canada has done a relatively good job integrating immigrants from all over the world.

Since 1971, when Canada's federal multiculturalism policy was adopted, the country has remained focused on developing and promoting a multicultural society, one that respects its citizens' diversity of language, religion, and culture. And one could easily argue that the importance of multiculturalism is only growing. In an April 2018 *Globe and Mail* op-ed, Erna Paris noted that "in 1985, when asked what made them proudest of their country, Canadians placed multiculturalism way down the list—at No. 10. By 2006, it was in second place—above hockey. Multiculturalism had evolved into a shared identity—a loose identity—Canadian style."[32] Ms. Paris also noted the following:

> One of the most important reasons for Canada's success is the fact that we have eschewed demands for total assimilation to a defined identity in favour of integration. Integration is the foundation of the support we offer newcomers. Its most salient feature is that no one attempts to alter the core identity of an individual or group. Canada's contemporary, multicultural success stems in large part from Pierre Trudeau's vision that no singular culture could, or would, define Canada and that there would be no overriding cultural identity to assimilate. As populism and intolerance increase elsewhere, it is this deliberate looseness when it comes to identity, this unique approach to pluralism, that will help to protect us—if we remain vigilant.[33]

In contrast, a country like France has experienced a concerning increase in populism and intolerance of the "other"—people whose ethnic, cultural, and religious identities don't align with that of the colonial French identity.

French government policies have purposefully interfered with the pluralistic evolution of the nation—an evolution that would see French society embrace diverse groups of people, ideas, religions, and more. They've done so by introducing state-mandated assimilation laws anchored in a tightly defined and prescribed French "identity." This approach is widely understood to have failed because it has, in effect, led to a growing segregation of racialized,

---

[32] "Canada's multiculturalism is our identity" by Erna Paris. *The Globe and Mail*, April 27, 2018. theglobeandmail.com/opinion/article-canadas-multiculturalism-is-our-identity

[33] *Ibid.*

immigrant French citizens along ethnic, cultural, and religious lines. Sukhada Tatke relates her experience engaging in France's civic training for new immigrants—after taking a French-language test—in a recent *Al Jazeera* article called "Not French Enough":

> Simply put, the essence of Frenchness rests on the troika of liberty, equality and fraternity....And yet, while pluming itself as one that champions these republican values above all, France remains twisted in a skein of injustice, inequality, and exclusion towards immigrants and people of colour.[34]

Although Québec began the multicultural experiment (though not without pushback) with the rest of Canada more than fifty years ago, the province followed France's lead over the decades, defining the province around French identity and culture, and mandating that immigrants from other cultures assimilate. Québec argues that this approach is necessary to protect the erosion of the French language and culture in Canada. I believe that objective could be met differently, and that this approach is only going to hurt Québec in the long run.

Between 1971 and 1991, attempting to appease separatist sentiment, the federal government allowed the Government of Québec to renegotiate its provincial powers four times, to claim more autonomy in immigration matters. In 1991 the Canada–Québec Accord became the most important agreement ever made between Canada and Québec in matters of permanent and temporary immigration. The agreement gave the province significant power, including the ability to select and accept economic immigrants and to do so within specific provincial integration and francization (expansion of French-language use) constraints. In other words, Québec now had the power to manage the numbers of its future permanent residents. For decades, other Canadian provinces and territories have been asking the federal government for a similar right to control immigration—most recently in 2020, mainly because "they believe they are each best placed to decide exactly what is required in terms of immigration for their individual economies."[35] This want is driven by "a pressing need for skilled global talent in the workforce across Canada."

Like many Canadian provinces, Québec is combating a major decline in population growth. This is the result of a number of factors, including fewer births (-3 percent), more deaths (+10 percent), and fewer immigrants and

---

[34] "'Not French enough': What it means to be an immigrant in France" by Sukhada Tatke, *Al Jazeera*, March 2, 2021. aljazeera.com/features/2021/3/2/not-french-enough-what-it-means-to-be-an-immigrant-in-france

[35] "Canada's Premiers: Give Us the Same Immigration Powers as Québec," *Immigration.ca*, February 6, 2020. https://www.immigration.ca/canadas-premiers-give-us-immigration-powers-Québec

permanent residents moving to the province, for a total growth in population of only 19,300, compared to 2019's 110,000.[36] According to a 2019 report by CIC News, Québec needs 80,000 immigrants a year.[37] It would make sense, then, that Québec attract more immigrants, particularly French-speaking immigrants, to shore up its labour force and ensure the French language continues to flourish in Québec. Statistics Canada projections published in 2011 suggest fewer Québecers will speak French at home in the future, from 82 percent in 2011 to around 75 percent by 2036.[38]

Recently published reports estimate that there will be 700 million French speakers globally by 2050, 80 percent of whom will be in Africa. Today, there are about 140 million French-speaking Africans; with the median age on the continent being 19.7, this means there are nearly 70 million potential immigrants aged twenty or younger, a rich pool of people that could be welcomed into Canada's stellar post-secondary education system and encouraged to contribute to the innovation economy. For Québec, attracting more immigrants from Africa, including those with existing French-language skills, seems like a no-brainer. Why this is not already happening at a rate commensurate with its demographic needs, however, is curious.

Imagine if Québec welcomed at least 350,000 French-speaking immigrants over the next five years to meet its needs. This would dramatically increase the amount of French spoken inside and outside the home, making it unnecessary for the government to continue to impose restrictions on the individual rights of English-speaking Canadians in the province for protectionist reasons. According to a 2019 *Financial Post* article, "allowing immigration to rise 1 percent would allow GDP growth to hover between 1.7% and two percent."[39]

And imagine the positive impact this would have on the economy across the country. Immigration increases contributions to the Canada Pension Plan (especially important as our country is aging) and to our health-care system. It would also help to mitigate the projected labour gap that Canada will experience over the next two decades, when "13.4 million people are projected to exit the workforce and only 11.8 million people will finish school and join the workforce."[40]

36 "Significant slowdown in Québec's population growth in 2020," Statistics Canada. statistique. Québec.ca/en/communique/significant-slowdown-in-Québecs-population-growth-in-2020

37 "Québec needs 80,000 immigrants per year, not 50,000" by Kareem El-Assal, *CIC News*, November 4, 2019. cicnews.com/2019/11/Québec-needs-80000-immigrants-per-year-not-50000-1113097. html#gs.chaquv

38 "Language Projections for Canada, 2011 to 2036; Chapter 3. Population projections by language group." Statistics Canada, February 2, 2017. www150.statcan.gc.ca/n1/pub/89-657-x/2017001/chap3-eng.htm

39 "All the reasons why Canada needs immigration—and more of it" by Gabriel Friedman, *Financial Post*, October 3, 2019. financialpost.com/news/economy/all-the-reasons-why-canada-needs-immigration-and-more-of-it

40 *Ibid.*

While all of this information is readily available to Québec's leaders, it means nothing if there is no political will. This point was illustrated perhaps most clearly by the COVID-19 pandemic that began in 2020. The global health crisis exposed the hypocrisy of Québec's secular law, specifically with regard to religious facial coverings. Bill 21 cites the need to enforce the law "for the purpose of identity or security verification," but with COVID mask mandates put in place by the Québec government to fight the spread of the virus, hospital workers relied on identification cards and medical documents alone to know who they were interacting with—and of course, they conducted their work while wearing masks themselves. No one decried COVID masking as a safety or security issue. Worst of all, this double standard seemed completely lost on the provincial government. It just goes to show: only if the civil rights of the majority are at risk is the Québec government is willing to compromise.

Québec remains the only jurisdiction in Canada that has secularism laws limiting individual expressions of faith.[41] Employment discrimination based on religion is against the law in Canada and the United States. So, where do we go from here?

PART II: FRENCH ADVANTAGE

THE ISSUE OF SYSTEMIC RACISM IN QUÉBEC IS MADE EVER MORE COMPLICATED by the disadvantages experienced by the province's English-language speakers for more than four decades. The province has limited which citizens can attend English schools and created oppressive signage laws enforced by the "language police." Since January 2020, Québec's immigration policies include Bill 9, a legally mandated "values test" about Québec culture, as expressed by the provincial Charter of Human Rights and Freedoms, that new immigrants to the province must pass in order to remain in the province.

Québec's language-rights laws are, first and foremost, protectionist toward French culture; because of this, Québec's government espouses a singular vision of inclusiveness built upon the supposed superiority of the province's colonial French heritage. This approach completely disregards the Indigenous peoples for whom Québec is traditional territory and unceded land—the Abenaki, Algonquin, Atikamekw, Cree, Haudenosaunee, Huron-Wendat, Innu, Mi'kmaw, Mohawk, Naskapi, and Wolastoqiyik First Nations[42]—the Métis, immigrants and refugees, as well as descendants of colonial English settlers,

---

[41] "Religious discrimination." US Equal Employment Opportunity Commission. eeoc.gov/religious-discrimination

[42] "Reserves in Québec" by Peter di Gangi. *The Canadian Encyclopedia*, March 27, 2021. thecanadianencyclopedia.ca/en/article/reserves-in-Québec

who, similarly to the French, consider their heritage tied closely to the history and territory of the province.

To understand the current realities in Québec, you have to go back to the mid-twentieth century, when French Canadians both within and outside the province sought equity measures to achieve equal cultural and societal rights within the Canadian federation—an era that became known as the "Quiet Revolution" (Révolution tranquille).

During the late nineteenth and early twentieth centuries, powerful forces converged to effectively keep French Canadians in Québec (primarily in rural areas) socio-economically oppressed. By the 1930s the autocratic, populist regime of Premier Duplessis and his Union Nationale party, which lasted nearly twenty years, saw the government of Québec work hand in hand with the Catholic Church, itself a dominant institution in the province at that time, to keep a tight grip on the francophone population, particularly in the areas of education and social services. The party actively suppressed modern liberalism (civil liberty and equality with support for social justice) favouring social conservatism (a limiting of individual rights and promotion of state-mandated edicts such as the decertification's of unions and the arbitrary closing of businesses). A complicity between the Duplessis government, the francophone bourgeoisie, the Catholic Church, and the English power-elite further suppressed opportunities for upward mobility for most Québecers at the time.

The era during which Duplessis was in power (1936–1939; 1944–1959), known as *la Grande Noirceur* ("the Great Darkness"), also saw Duplessis use his populist mandate to repress political and civilian opponents, such as Jehovah's Witnesses and communist sympathizers—the latter putting him in direct conflict with the province's trade unions. Furthermore, his policies saw him sell out the economic interests of his constituents to the benefit of US–based corporations. The entrenched power elite of the day—the majority being white, anglophone Québecers—saw no reason to relinquish the advantages they had accorded themselves since the British conquest of Québec in the mid-eighteenth century. They fought hard to preserve what they had.

After Duplessis's death in 1959 and the victory of the provincial Liberals in 1960 under Jean Lesage, a great fracturing began; many Québecers felt a desire to split from the authority of the church, ruralism, and the patronage that characterized the Duplessis era. Opposition forces favoured political, cultural, social, and economic democratization and gave rise to social justice by championing broader civic engagement.[45] What followed was an exposure of the untenable advantages of the white anglo elite, a social reckoning that opened up discourse for reform and change.

---

[45] "La Grande Noirceur (the Great Darkness)" by Serge Dupuis. *The Canadian Encyclopedia*, December 15, 2020. thecanadianencyclopedia.ca/en/article/grande-noirceur

Sound familiar? Think about the issues being examined today, in the Black Lives Matter era. I'm not the first to make the correlation between systemic anti-Black racism in North America and the systemic inequality of twentieth-century working-class French Québecers. In his 1968 essay, "The White Niggers of America" ("Nègres blancs d'Amérique"), Pierre Vallières, a journalist, author, and leading member of the intellectual wing of the separatist terrorist organization Front de libération du Québec (FLQ), argued that working-class French Canadians were being disadvantaged and discriminated against by the Anglo-Saxon power-elite and the francophone bourgeoisie—both of which were in cahoots with Duplessis's populist regime. Through the efforts of union activists and influential intellectuals, and with the growing support of an awakened citizenry, the Quiet Revolution pushed the government of the day to acknowledge the systemic inequality experienced by working-class French Québecers and to take action. But the most dominant, and aggressive, actions were taken by the FLQ.

The FLQ (established in 1963), whose members were known as *felquistes*, operated under the belief that Québec must liberate itself, through armed struggle, from anglophone and capitalist domination. Between 1963 and 1970, the militant arm of the FLQ perpetrated a string of terrorist attacks in the province, planting bombs in places like mailboxes in wealthy anglophone Montréal neighbourhoods, the downtown Eaton's department store, and the residence of Montréal's mayor, Jean Drapeau. One of its most violent actions was the bombing of the Montréal Stock Exchange in 1969, injuring twenty-seven people. The violence culminated in what became known as the October Crisis.

On the morning of October 5, 1970, the FLQ kidnapped a prominent British diplomat, Commissioner James Cross, from his Montréal home, and made a series of demands on the Québec government for his release: notably, the release of twenty-three FLQ "political prisoners" as well as the publication of its manifesto and safe passage to Cuba or Algeria. Police raids were conducted and over thirty arrests made in the following days, and the Québec government refused to comply with FLQ demands, offering only safe passage out of Canada. Shortly after the deadline for negotiation had passed, on October 10, the FLQ kidnapped Deputy Premier Pierre Laporte; he was found dead days later in the trunk of an FLQ member's car. By October 16, Prime Minister Pierre Trudeau had invoked the War Measures Act, suspending citizens' civil liberties for their own protection, and made membership in the FLQ illegal. In total, between 1963 and 1972, the FLQ was responsible for more than two hundred bombings and six deaths.[44]

---

[44] "Front de libération du Québec (FLQ)" by Marc Laurendeau and Andrew McIntosh. *Canadian Encyclopedia*, August 11, 2013. thecanadianencyclopedia.ca/en/article/front-de-liberation-du-Québec

The Quiet Revolution had led to this reckoning; the measures brought about were initially intended to achieve much-needed equality for francophone Québecers. Compounding concerns were the decline in birth rate throughout the 1960s, as well as the tendency for new immigrants to adopt English rather than French, and to send their children to English schools. Because of this, according to the Centre for Constitutional Studies, "some demographers predicted that Montréal would again become a mainly English-speaking city, as it briefly had been in the mid-nineteenth century."[45] These realities, followed as they were by the era of the FLQ and the October Crisis, sparked something substantial in Québec's identity. That said, subsequent laws passed in the 1970s and beyond by various Québec governments would go far beyond delivering equity measures, and instead work to favour francophone Québecers in the province—the results of which have negatively impacted Québec and the rest of Canada for decades.

French Above All

In the 1976 Québec provincial election, the separatist Parti Québécois was elected with a mandate to lead the province out of the Canadian federation. The provincial government immediately enacted new laws addressing the francophone-equity measures that had been proposed for many years. In 1977, Bill 101, the Charter of the French Language, made French the official language of the Québec government, as well as education, commerce, and the workplace. The bill's core intent was to put French on equal footing with English across all private and public provincial institutions. Through this lens, many of the provisions in Bill 101 can be viewed as objectively necessary equity measures. But some sections of the bill went much further, imposing discriminatory policies that clearly disadvantaged Québec's English speakers—including the prohibition of English signage on business storefronts, the imposition of "stringent French language tests for admission to the professions,"[46] requiring businesses to operate mainly in French, and requiring that all collective agreements be written in French. The pendulum was now swinging too far the other way.

With the introduction of the Canadian Charter of Rights and Freedoms in 1982 and its protection of minority language rights, several sections of Bill 101 were successfully challenged and subsequently ruled unconstitutional by the Supreme Court of Canada. Further amendments were made to Bill 101

[45] "Bill 101." Centre for Constitutional Studies, University of Alberta. constitutionalstudies.ca/2019/07/bill-101

[46] *Ibid.*

and new bills were introduced; for example, by 1993 English could be featured on business storefronts—as long as it was secondary in size and presentation to the French. These policies created a language-based systemic inequality that has further complicated the issue of systemic racism in the province. The government's actions—and, in many cases, inaction—have made it clear that the rights of French Québecers supersede the rights of all others in the province, including racialized citizens—a double standard that cannot be lost on Québec's government.

In May 2021, the Québec government tabled Bill 96, a sweeping language bill that would impose new restrictions on English linguistic rights in the province, and which would see French recognized as the only official language in the province, meaning that all government services would be provided *only* in French. The bill, which has not yet been made law at the time of writing, would create a French Language Ministry and a French Language Commissioner. The latter would provide an avenue for francophones to lay formal complaints in instances where Québecers are not offered services in French. The office of the commissioner would have the power to sanction (with some exclusions) any non-compliant businesses.

There are other problematic elements in the bill which directly undermine the Canadian constitution, including the unilateral declaration that Québec is a "nation." (The latter issue deserves a chapter in itself, though we won't focus on it here.) The bill also includes a provision limiting francophone access to English CEGEPs (colleges). This is due to the government's view that too many francophone students are choosing to study in English after high school. The government would have the authority to set arbitrary quotas, setting an imposed cap on overall enrollment—regardless of demand. In addition, English CEGEPs would be mandated to prioritize admission for anglophone students. In essence, the bill is intended to mitigate and suppress English-language education for Québec francophones.

The restriction of civil rights under the guise of protecting the French language seems to have renewed vigor in this populist era. For example, the curtailing of an individual's right to study in the language of preference—unless it's French—is antithetical to the broad principles of inclusion and diversity, and in my opinion, detrimental to the democratic principles of Canada as codified in the Charter. I would argue that the incremental erosion of the rights of English Canadians living in Québec, and the decades-long appeasement by federal leaders, threatens Canada's very democracy. The limiting of access to English education via discriminatory and exclusionary provincial laws is but one example of the continued exacerbation of this issue. It may seem counterintuitive, but generations of young French Canadians in Québec—including French-speaking immigrants—are put at a disadvantage when they do not have the choice to educate themselves in English if they so desire.

As a Québécois, there is no doubt in my mind that many of the decisions made in Québec are done under the guise of language protection. I also realize that the francophones of Québec have at heart the protection of their language, and I am wholeheartedly with them. Canada will always be better if it remains multilingual, a country that celebrates English, French, and, I hope one day, Indigenous languages. However, I disagree with the idea that French is under attack. There is no law in Canada preventing anyone from studying in French, like what we see in Québéc for the study of English. Could the federal and provincial governments do more to subsidize French schools and encourage French across the country? Certainly. But no one is actively trying to destroy the French language in this country. And while it may seem that inaction is the norm, in reality, interest in French is real and strong in Canada. What I want to avoid more than anything is seeing the issues of inequality, discrimination and racism disappear behind the smokescreen of language protection. Maybe French is in trouble in some parts of Canada, but this is a challenge whose solution will never be more discrimination and more racism. Québec must stop hiding behind the language issue to justify measures that violate the fundamental liberal democratic rights of individuals in the province of Québéc that should be accorded to all Canadians.

To be clear, I believe native English speakers in Québec should also look to study in French at some point in their educational career; a mastery of both languages offers enormous advantages in an officially bilingual country. I submit myself as Exhibit A of the benefits of bilingualism. Being able to speak both French and English has had an immensely positive impact on my personal life and career. In a world where English has become the language of international commerce, limiting the right to access English-language education for protectionist reasons is detrimental to the future of everyone living in Québec, no matter their native tongue. Ultimately, it is detrimental to Québec society as a whole.

During the February 28, 2021, edition of the popular Québec talk show *Tout le monde en parle*—which reaches an average of 1.3 million viewers weekly—host Guy A. Lepage was interviewing Benoit Charette, the Minister of the Environment and the Fight Against Climate Change, who had recently been named Minister Responsible for the Fight Against Racism. Mr. Lepage referenced a long list of validated data on the socio-economic disparities between racialized and non-racialized citizens—which Minister Charette acknowledged to be fact—including gaps in minimum wage, employment, and housing. He asked Minister Charette if those examples were not "the very definition of systemic racism.[47]

---

[47]   French-to-English translations of Minister Charette's interview provided by the author.

Minister Charette pushed back, noting that because some wanted to label Bill 101 and Bill 21 as forms of systemic racism, the government could not endorse the term. "It's the adjective 'systemic' that is problematic given the many definitions we have. And many of our leaders who believe in systemic racism go so far as to say that Bill 101 is evidence of systemic racism, go so far as to say that the Secularism Act is systemic racism. So with a definition of that nature, we can't endorse it." Minister Charette also noted that the government is prioritizing the fight against racism, which "unfortunately is still present within certain individuals"—clearly missing the pressing and negative reality of the pervasive, top-down racism within private and public institutions. Mr. Lepage responded with a tongue-in-cheek summarization of the government's approach, noting that was in fact "a systemic fight against racism."

More recently, in a now-infamous press conference on October 5, 2021, Premier Legault doubled down on his stance on systemic racism after Québec coroner Géhane Kamel, who led the inquest into the death of Atikamekw woman Joyce Echaquan, responded "I think so" when asked whether Echaquan would still be alive today if she were a white woman.[48] The Indigenous mother of seven had documented her experience in a Joliette, Québec, hospital on Facebook. Staff had made a snap judgment that she was suffering from opioid withdrawal and "failed to properly evaluate the medications she was taking and ignored the symptoms she described, including heart palpitations."[49] She was then strapped to her bed after becoming agitated and deemed "theatrical." The final report indicated that Echaquan was the victim of prejudice and that her death was "unacceptable." Kamel demanded in her own press conference that "Quebec recognize the existence of systemic racism in its institutions."

During the press conference, Legault used a prop—the common *Petit Robert* French dictionary, to parse the definition of the word "systemique"—noting that the definition's institutional "top-down" criteria was not present in the province's health-care system or other provincial institutions. But this was only another distraction by the premier to avoid confronting a deeper reality.

Sepratism & the Seeds of Inequality

As it's likely clear by now, the pushback and obfuscation by the Québec government on the very definition of systemic racism remains, to this day, an excuse for not acknowledging its existence, thereby making it impossible for them to

---

48 "Québec coroner feels Joyce Echaquan would be alive if she were a white woman" by Daniel J. Rowe, *CTV News: Montreal*, October 5, 2021, montreal.ctvnews.ca/Québec-coroner-feels-joyce-echaquan-would-be-alive-if-she-were-a-white-woman-1.5611303.

49 *Ibid.*

address the issue in any meaningful way. In fact, Québec seems to be caught in a vicious cycle, where discriminatory laws enacted to protect the province's language and presumed culture contribute to maintaining a fundamentally discriminatory state, preventing the government from acknowledging this discrimination for fear of having to address the laws.

Minister Charette's comments reminded me of 1995, when Canada was gripped by a constitutional crisis: the province of Québec was holding a referendum that would see Québecers decide whether or not to separate from Canada. Out of the more than 4.7 million votes cast, the NO side (voting not to separate) received 50.58 percent—a very small margin of victory, but enough to keep Québec in the Canadian federation. Most Canadians, including me, let out a sigh of relief.

The sovereigntist Québec premier of the day, Jacques Parizeau, who was championing the YES side, made an infamous concession speech that night. You could feel the rancor in his voice when he said what many knew he was thinking, blaming "the money and the ethnic vote"—a direct reference to Jews and immigrants—for the loss. I recall vividly wanting to jump through my TV screen to slap him across the face. Just three days earlier, I had taken the day off work and flown from Toronto to Montréal to take part in the Unity Rally, answering the call to join thousands of others to demonstrate support for the NO side. I felt it was my responsibility to fight to keep Québec in Canada; I truly believed—and still believe—that we would be a lesser country without Québec. I'd like to think the collective efforts of the more than one hundred thousand of us who rallied that day made a difference.

Parizeau's concession speech, though, put a spotlight on Québec's long history of alienating any citizen who doesn't conform to its colonial French identity. The controversial term *pure laine*, which literally means "pure wool," refers to those Québecers who can claim exclusively colonial French ancestry, which many Québec nationalists viewed as superior. The term was once openly used but today, much like the term "Old stock Canadian," it's not spoken in polite company. However, it remains a hardline mindset for some francophone Québecers with nationalist and sovereigntist leanings. This separation of Québec's citizens into pure and, by default, impure, continues to fuel much of the systemic racism and inequality in the province.

"All animals are equal, but some are more equal than others," wrote George Orwell in the ground-breaking political satire *Animal Farm*. Its central conceit was to highlight the perils of preaching equality for all but making exceptions that only advantage some. This hypocritical mindset, as the book demonstrates, only leads to failure. Supporting and promoting the French language and culture in Canada—both inside and outside Québec—is critically important, not only because we are officially a bilingual country, but because it is integral to Canada's identity.

And it is true that bilingualism outside of Québec is not where it should be by a large margin. This is partly the result of demographic growth—the English-speaking population outside Québec is growing more rapidly, reducing the numbers of French-speaking and bilingual citizens—and partly because the population growth is largely due to immigration, where the mother tongue of new immigrants is neither French nor English. In 2016, the bilingualism rate for people with a native language that was not French or English was 11.7 percent, a proportion that has not changed since 2011. That said, outside Québec, the English–French bilingual population rose 6.6 percent between 2011 and 2016, with those with French as their first language representing 53.2 percent[50]; this population had a bilingualism rate of 46.2 percent, up almost two percentage points from 2011. Those with English as their first language had a bilingualism rate of 9.2 percent in 2016, an increase of 0.3 percentage points compared to 2011.

Some success in the growth of French outside Québec is happening organically in our education system, where French immersion is so popular (there were nearly 450,000 students enrolled the 2016–2017 schoolyear, and increase of 59 percent since 2006[51]) there aren't enough qualified teachers to satisfy demand.[52] In Ontario for example, demand for French immersion has increased by nearly 40 percent over the past five years, putting a strain on school boards to meet the demand. I know this first-hand through my daughter, whose school's French immersion classes are often made up of split grades because of the shortage of French teachers.

The Office of the Commissioner of Official Languages notes that eight out of ten Canadians believe more needs to be done to help Canadians become bilingual.[53] This is good news. As discussed in Part I, French remains a Top 10 global language today, with a future global footprint estimated at 700 million speakers by the year 2050.[54] No matter where we live in this country, we need fewer restrictions and increased access to education in French.

I come to this debate from the perspective of someone who was raised French Canadian and educated in English schools, while happily immersed in the rich culture of Québec. To this day, I cherish those memories of a youth

[50] "English–French bilingualism reaches new heights," Statistics Canada, August 31, 2017. www12. statcan.gc.ca/census-recensement/2016/as-sa/98-200-x/2016009/98-200-x2016009-eng.cfm

[51] "Enrolments in French immersion programs, public elementary and secondary schools, Canada." Statistics Canada, October. www150.statcan.gc.ca/n1/daily-quotidien/201015/cg-a001-eng.htm.

[52] "Demand for French immersion grows as spots shrink. Here's what's happening" by Katie Dangerfield, *Global News*, February 13, 2019. globalnews.ca/news/4922887/french-immersion-school-canada-demand-teachers/.

[53] *Ibid.*

[54] "The case for French immersion" by Irvin Studin. *Toronto Star*, February 20, 2018. thestar.com/opinion/contributors/2018/02/20/the-case-for-french-immersion.html.

nourished in part by an amazing, French-based creative arts culture showcased in film, television, theatre, music, and comedy, and the many cultural celebrations unique to the province. I think of community-based traditions like la cabane à sucre, where we indulged in maple syrup and enjoyed traditional folk music (my brother Chris can still give'r on the spoons). I also remember the neighbourhood fêtes that brought people together to celebrate and create community—one of my favourites being our annual *épluchette de blé d'Inde* (corn boil party), where families gathered in a neighbour's backyard and we all pitched in to shuck bags and bags of corn. We'd boil it in huge pots and eat as many as we could—with tons of butter and salt. It was a fun communal event that hearkened back to simpler times.

As an adult, I've spent many memorable occasions in Québec with my family over the decades. I've also visited Montréal and the region with many anglophone friends and enjoyed the province's culinary delights and world-class events that offer unique experiences with that extra dose of joie de vivre— including Cirque du Soleil, the Montréal Jazz Festival, Just for Laughs, the OSHEAGA Music and Arts Festival, and Carnaval de Québec. In fact, in 2016 I published a discussion paper on strategic innovation titled, "Winning in the New Economy: Seven Steps Toward a Canadian Digital Innovation Strategy,"[55] where, in part, I called for Canadians to learn from Québec's very successful French-language creative and cultural industries and use this model to enhance and amplify Canada's multilingual culture both nationally and abroad.

Unfortunately I've also witnessed, from near and far, the insular tendencies of some French-speaking Québecers—those who continue to hold on to long-standing historical grievances (some valid, as previously noted) and deep-seeded beliefs of victimhood. These feelings are standing in the way of the progress and evolution of Québec culture, which, to truly thrive, requires a more open and equitable integration of diverse peoples.

In early 2021, a professor at the University of Ottawa published his personal views on Bill 21 on his Twitter account, calling out Québec culture as racist. He rhetoric didn't stop there; he levelled similar critiques against institutions like the Royal Canadian Mounted Police. In reaction, government officials inside and outside Québec, including some political pundits in the media, called for a stop to "Québec-bashing." The truth is that there is no widespread Québec-bashing going on in Canada. It's a red herring, but one that politicians of all stripes leaned into to ingratiate themselves to Québec voters—especially nationalist-leaning voters—in the 2021 federal election.[56]

---

55 "Winning in the New Economy: Seven Steps Toward a Canadian Digital Innovation Strategy" by Stephen Dorsey, *Dorseystudios.ca*, July 6, 2017. dorseystudios.ca/dorseyondigital/2017/7/6/discussion-paper-wining-in-the-new-economy-seven-steps-toward-a-canadian-digital-innovation-strategy

56 "Why the English election debate tripped the Québec campaign" by Emilie Nicholas, *Maclean's*, September 15, 2021, macleans.ca/opinion/why-the-english-election-debate-tripped-the-Québec-campaign.

As *Montreal Gazette* journalist Basem Boshra notes in a December 2015 article, "accusations of Québec bashing are often a way for those with a vested interest in maintaining the status quo in this province to shout down important discussion of any uncomfortable realities of life here."[57] To call criticizing systemic inequality and discriminatory policies in Québec "bashing" is a gross oversimplification.

That said, many Canadians express a core frustration about Québec, and a fatigue that issues around separation and identity have dragged on for nearly half a century. They wonder how some Québecers can justify that they should be *more* equal than other Canadians. Isn't our democracy built upon the foundation that we are all equal under the law? I have yet to hear a logical argument from any nationalist in Québec that addresses this conundrum. Where does the basis for this linguistic superiority argument stem from? Is it that French Canadians in Québec have a greater claim to the land they occupy because they have been settled on this particular land longer than other peoples? If that's the basis for their "advantage," then logically the Indigenous peoples, whose traditional land Québec occupies, should supersede the French. The Algonquian people's claim to their land (and that of other First Nations in the territory) goes back thousands of years.

Is the argument of these Québecers based on their right of "discovery" or "conquest"—the "taming" of the land? From the time French Europeans established permanent settlements in Québec City in 1604 to the territory ceding to British rule in 1763 (following French defeat in 1760 at the Battle of Sainte-Foy on the Plains of Abraham), the French had been in Québec for nearly 200 years. From the British conquest of 1763 to today, English-speaking Canadians in Québec can trace their heritage in the province back more than 250 years. Is the argument that 250 years of English heritage in Québec doesn't count? Why is there a need to minimize the heritage of others in order to celebrate and promote the French heritage, culture, and language in Québec?

As history has shown us, there is a long-standing tradition of cultural groups assuming the supremacy of their heritage over another group as an excuse to claim rights to a territory. How did this mythology become "un fait accompli" in the minds of some Québecers? Is this not similar to our current discourse around white advantage? As Canadians, do we not carry our equal rights with us no matter where we choose to live or travel within our country's boundaries? Of course we do. What of the equal rights for other founding cultures of Canada in Québec? Why are the province's provincial governments tilting the balance toward one group and away from others? How can this not be seen as discrimination and inequality?

---

[57] "Are you a 'Québec basher?' Find out using this handy checklist" By Basem Boshra, *Montreal Gazette*, December 21, 2015. montrealgazette.com/opinion/columnists/are-you-guilty-of-Québec-bashing-consult-our-handy-checklist

The nationalist arguments of many Québec politicians are not based on logic but rather on emotion—namely, fear, fuelled by a convenient mythology that the English majority in Canada continues to oppress French Canadians across the country. Playing the victim continues to feed the nationalist narrative, and widens the gulf between the people of Québec and the rest of Canada, directly serving to achieve their agenda of a sovereign Québec. Without this us-versus-them mentality, it cannot survive. This is compounded by the fact that some francophone Québecers continue to live with the fear that increasing change in society will make it impossible to maintain their cultural identity, their language, and the unearned advantages the system has accorded their majority in the province. This fear is preventing some from embracing the natural evolution of culture that has contributed to elevating diverse communities to new heights and created more opportunity for all citizens, despite the pervasive barriers of systemic inequality that remain.

A May 2018 report called *Multiculturism: Its Contribution to Canada's International Trade and Investment Activities,* published by Canada's House of Commons Standing Committee on International Trade, says,

> Immigrants to Canada, and their offspring, have made—and will continue to make—positive economic and other contributions to Canada, including through their ownership or operation of some of the country's firms. Among other benefits, these firms sell to, buy from, and invest in countries around the world. They create jobs and pay taxes that help to finance a range of public policy priorities. They develop innovative products that improve business competitiveness and respond to consumers' needs, while also contributing to the socio-economic development of local communities throughout Canada.[58]

But in Québec, the wound of attempted sovereignty is festering. Decades of divisiveness have resulted in a government that leverages populist rhetoric to gain support for increasingly discriminatory policies. Some francophone Québecers continue to see an advantage in positioning themselves as an oppressed minority in Canada. The truth is, the societal reckoning that began in the 1950s and culminated in the 1970s led to francophone Canadians in Québec successfully securing the equality they rightfully demanded. And subsequently, many of the federal government–led laws extended those rights to francophone Canadians across the country. It's not my place to deny anyone

---

[58] "Multiculturalism: Its Contribution to Canada's International Trade and Investment Activities." Report of the Standing Committee on International Trade. House of Commons Canada, May 2018. ourcommons.ca/Content/Committee/421/CIIT/Reports/RP9819495/ciitrp10/ciitrp10-e. pdf

their dreams or aspirations—even of some citizens in Québec believe they would have it better if they lived in a separate country. But I will say this: Be careful what you wish for.

We need to ask ourselves: if what we are seeing today is an indication of the evolution of Québec society, what would the country of Québec really look like—especially if there were zero opposition to divisive and discriminatory laws disadvantaging minority groups? Perhaps it would become a country guided by the unbridled nationalistic impulses of its government officials (carrying the mandate of the majority) with a clear focus to advantage those citizens that have been deemed to be superior. With diminished opposition, such a government could enact laws crafted with the sole purpose of advantaging its French-speaking citizens above all else, and within a narrow, prescribed notion of heritage, cultural identity, and values.

Who would want to immigrate to such a country? Certainly not people from racialized and religious minority communities; they would clearly not be welcomed as equals. If they were Muslim or Sikh for example, what other career opportunities would eventually be closed to them simply because they choose to express their faith?

In an era when businesses are competing for the best global workforce, how would Québec attract that diverse multicultural talent that the rest of Canada and other countries are competing for? Why would international corporations want to invest in and grow operations in a country with such an insular and exclusive mindset, protected by law? Many Fortune 500 companies either have made or are moving toward making diversity and inclusion standards a core component of organizational growth and success. According to a 2020 survey designed "to help Fortune 1000 companies quickly assess their standing in the D&I [diversity and inclusion] landscape," inclusive and diversified companies enjoy 2.3 times higher cash flow per employee; 43 percent of companies with diverse boards noticed higher profits; and racially and ethnically diverse companies are 35 percent more likely to perform better.[59] These companies could not even contemplate investing in Québec if they intend to honour their commitment to diversity and inclusion.

∞

In 2006, when I was planning my return to Canada after years of working in Seattle, I seriously considered moving back to Montréal to put down new roots, with hopes of meeting "the one," starting a family, and building my entrepreneurial business. Toronto and Vancouver were also in the mix. I love Vancouver and would have been closer to family and great friends there,

---

59 "Diversity & Inclusion Survey for Fortune 1000 Companies." *The Bassiouni Group*. bassiouni-group.com/diversity-and-inclusion

but there was not as much opportunity for my consulting business in that market. By all accounts, Montréal seemed to be ascending after many decades of stagnation. Tech and media innovators and businesses were establishing footholds, the relative affordability of real estate was attractive, and I liked the idea of being able to reconnect more fully with relatives and friends in the province.

As I've expressed, I have a deep love for La Belle Province and its French culture. When I dug a little deeper, I found that even though there appeared to be little appetite for independence from Canada (or for another referendum on the issue), the "nationalist" issue was clearly far from settled, and in fact a populist movement seemed to be growing, moving the nationalist and secular agenda forward. My instincts were proven correct, of course. The move to Toronto made more sense from that perspective alone.

What about all those people already living in Québec who now fall outside the norms of the envisioned country I've described? Most would come to realize they would have little choice but to move out of the "country" of Québec because, they would be deemed less-than and with new laws like Bill 96 and Bill 21, their individual rights would continue to be eroded. They would be faced with what Fareed Zakaria, the well-known American journalist, author, and CNN political commentator, calls an "illiberal democracy," a term referring to "western democracies (with duly elected officials) that are increasingly limiting the freedoms of the people they represent."[60] Notably, leaders of illiberal democracies tend to ignore the will of the minority, something Premier Legault seems intent on, citing the notwithstanding clause in order to exempt minorities from the protection they're legally entitled to under the Charter.

The good news? This bleak scenario does not need to come to pass. That's why it's a perfect time for Québecers to have a "remise en question," to choose a new path that propels them to engage differently with the rest of the country and to contribute to moulding Canada into a country that promotes equality for all of its citizens, including francophone Canadians, from coast to coast to coast. As I've detailed in previous chapters, Canada has much work to do to address the imperfections of its democracy. But we need *all* Canadians to be part of that enterprise.

Acknowledging that systemic racism in Québec exists, as it does in the rest of Canada, will inevitably lead to a broader reckoning on the issue of systemic inequality as it relates to the "protection" of the French language and the discriminatory secular laws that disproportionally affect some religious minorities in the province. Tellingly, a 2020 Leger survey noted that 66 percent

---

60 "The Rise of Illiberal Democracy" by Fareed Zakaria, *Foreign Affairs*, November/December 1997. foreignaffairs.com/articles/1997-11-01/rise-illiberal-democracy

of Québecers polled are "fine" with the use of the term "systemic racism,"[61] despite its rejection by political leaders.

It is also critical that any citizen looking to protect their own minority rights in Canada—whether on the basis of gender, ability, race, religion, or language—also advocate for the minority rights of others. Recognizing whatever advantage you have and using it to amplify the voices of those who are disadvantaged is something we can and should all do.

∞

Québec is, of course, not alone when it comes to the issue of systemic inequality. But unlike Québec, Canada's other provinces have recognized that systemic racism exists, and some have started to proactively address the issue. In November 2020, the British Columbia government released a damning 236-page report that that concluded its health-care system has a "deeply rooted" system of racism, discrimination, and bias in how it treats Indigenous patients, prompting BC Health Minister Adrian Dix to offer an "unequivocal apology" to the First Nations, Inuit, and Métis peoples in the province.[62] The report made twenty-four recommendations, and while the minister acknowledged there was a long road ahead, he felt encouraged, stating, "We have to begin somewhere. And today is the beginning."[63]

The Notwithstanding Clause

So how does Canada make things right for all Canadians living in Québec who feel like their future in that province is now limited? With the Québec government once again threatening to use the Charter's notwithstanding clause (Section 33) to pass even more regressive language-rights laws in 2021, many, including myself, have called for the abolishment of the notwithstanding clause. I'm not an academic, but I consulted with my much more informed friends who live and breathe the Charter, and they shared with me the actual mechanics of how this could be achieved fairly and responsibly—not just to deal with the issues facing Québec today, but to curtail the flagrant abuse of Section 33 by other provinces in the future.

---

[61] "Québecers are fine with use of term 'systemic racism,' despite rejection by political leaders: study" by Rachel Lau, *CTV News: Montreal*, September 30, 2021. montreal.ctvnews.ca/Québecers-are-fine-with-use-of-term-systemic-racism-despite-rejection-by-political-leaders-study-1.5606348

[62] "Widespread systemic racism in B.C.'s health-care system: report" by Rob Shaw, *Vancouver Sun*, November 30, 2020. vancouversun.com/news/politics/widespread-systemic-racism-in-b-c-s-health-care-system-report

[63] *Ibid.*

The notwithstanding clause, which, as a reminder, allows Parliament or provincial legislatures to temporarily override (or essentially ignore) sections of the Canadian Charter of Rights and Freedoms they do not like, was written into the Charter back in 1982. Its genesis is rooted in the first ministers' conferences of 1980 through the 1982 patriation of the Constitution. As *CBC News* describes:

> Various factions in the discussions argued over whether the new Constitution should include an entrenched charter of rights. Pierre Trudeau, who was then prime minister, argued against the idea of a notwithstanding clause but faced opposition from provinces that wanted a way to override some charter guarantees and some who were worried about potential judicial overreach.[64]

At long last, on the evening of November 4, 1981, Justice Minister Jean Chrétien and Saskatchewan Attorney-General Roy Romanow developed what was known as the "Kitchen Accord," "a compromise that included an entrenched charter of rights along with notwithstanding provisions."[65] Although Québec would refuse to sign it, nine provinces joined the federal government in signing the constitutional accord on November 5—notwithstanding clause included.

By eliminating Section 33 from the Charter, the protection against overreach would instead have to be baked into government legislation in a manner that was consistent with the Charter. This way, the onus would be on provincial governments, for example, to craft and pass legislation that protects equality but also allows for equity measures to be considered as necessary as per Section 15 of the Charter.

Part One of Section 15 of the Charter details that "every individual is equal before and under the law and has the right to the equal protection and equal benefit of the law without discrimination and, in particular, without discrimination based on race, national or ethnic origin, colour, religion, sex, age or mental or physical disability."[66] The word "particular" is important, as it reflects that the included list is just sampling of the protected rights of Canadians. For example, it wasn't until 2005 that the federal government passed the Civil Marriage Act, making same-sex marriage legal across Canada (British Columbia and Ontario had allowed it as of 2003). The legislation was consistent with Section 15, Subsections 1 and 2 of the Charter—the latter noting that an equity measure can be put in place that "does not preclude any law, program or activity that has as its object the amelioration of conditions of disadvantaged individuals

---

[64] "Canada's notwithstanding clause—what's that again?" *CBC News*, September 18, 2018, cbc.ca/news/canada/canada-constitution-notwithstanding-factsheet-ford-1.4817751.

[65] *Ibid.*

[66] "Guide to the Canadian Charter of Rights and Freedoms," Government of Canada, June 8, 2020. canada.ca/en/canadian-heritage/services/how-rights-protected/guide-canadian-charter-rights-freedoms.html

or groups including those that are disadvantaged because of race, national or ethnic origin, colour, religion, sex, age or mental or physical disability."[67]

This is the mechanism that French Canadians could leverage to support well-crafted legislation to enact equity-based policies addressing their minority-language status in Canada—those same policies specifically intended to promote and sustain the French language in Québec and across Canada; the policies that align with the principles of the Charter, and which, most importantly, do not discriminate against other citizens.

Bill 21 doesn't come close to measuring up to the Charter and should be stricken in its entirety. It's clear that key sections of Bill 96 should be challenged under Section 15 of the Charter, and the only way to do so at this stage would be to amend the Charter. Premier Legault's government's insistence on invoking the notwithstanding clause to shield itself and its flawed legislation (Bill 96 and Bill 21) goes against the fundamental liberal democratic principles of this country. On a personal level, I find it galling to see it being used in such a cavalier manner by a provincial government that refuses to sign on to the Canadian Constitution.

It is worth noting that Québec is not alone in its ability to flex its populist power and invoke the notwithstanding clause. Ontario Premier Doug Ford—brother of Rob Ford, the infamous "crack mayor of Toronto"—threatened to invoke the notwithstanding clause of the Charter as a pre-emptive measure to stave off any potential challenges to his petty, revenge-fuelled legislation to cut the size of Toronto City Council by half. His threat came in the middle of a declared municipal election. (He was reportedly upset at many councillors whom he felt had treated him badly when he was a city councillor.)

Ford did recklessly evoke Section 33 in June 2021 to pass Bill 307, legislation that would "double the restricted pre-election spending period for third-party advertisements to 12 months before an election call."[68] The Ford government argued this restriction, under the same legislation Ontario Superior Court Justice Edward Morgan had previously ruled unconstitutional, was necessary to "protect elections from outside influence."[69] Ford defended his actions, stating simply, "We're fighting for democracy. I'll work all day, all night to protect the people."[70] In reality, it was purely a political move to hamstring the ability of opposition parties to raise monies to fight future elections.

---

[67] *Ibid.*

[68] "Ontario passes election spending bill with notwithstanding clause" by Holly McKenzie-Sutter, *CP24*, June 14, 2021, cp24.com/news/ontario-passes-election-spending-bill-with-notwithstanding-clause-1.5469529?cache=%3FcontactForm%3Dtrue%3FclipId%3D89926%3FcontactForm%3Dtrue.

[69] *Ibid.*

[70] "Ford government pushes through controversial election spending bill with notwithstanding clause" by The Canadian Press, *CBC News*, June 14, 2021, cbc.ca/news/canada/toronto/notwithstanding-clause-vote-ontario-1.6064952.

Here's why Canadians should be concerned. The notwithstanding clause essentially holds us hostage to the intransigence of populist provincial governments, and as we've experienced recently with Québec and Ontario, it threatens the very foundation of our liberal democracy and the rights it accords all Canadians within our constitution. If you're still not convinced, remember this: If you are amenable to limiting the rights of others today, what is stopping anyone from doing the same to you tomorrow?

Where Do We Go From Here?

As far as what is possible regarding Québec's current policies, it's heartening to see that some have spoken out, with individuals and organizations, such as the National Council of Canadian Muslims (NCCM) and the Canadian Civil Liberties Association (CCLA), submitting court challenges. In September 2019, Calgary's then mayor, Naheed Nenshi, introduced the Resolution Against Bill 21, which states, in part, "the wearing of signs or clothing as a religious symbol is a fundamental right in the exercise of 'freedom of thought, conscience and religion,' as written in *Article 18* of the [United Nations's] *Universal Declaration of Human Rights*."[71] Soon after, he told CBC that "the federal government has the constitutional right to disallow provincial legislation. It is very rarely used, but they could do it. They could do what the United States federal government did when certain states were being recalcitrant on civil rights legislation, which is withhold federal funding."[72]

Personally, I'm not sure if that is where we should begin, but I certainly wouldn't take that option off the table. As an immediate measure, all federal party leaders should come together, agree to stop appeasing the nationalist Québec government, pledge to Canadians that they will stop at nothing to protect their rights, no matter where they live, and defend the Constitution and the freedoms it accords all citizens. Enough is enough. The Government of Canada should prioritize an immediate commitment to forcefully challenging Bill 21 and the sections of Bill 96 that discriminate against minorities in Québec. The federal, provincial, and territorial governments of Canada should organize an urgent summit to negotiate an amendment to the Charter that would provide redress to individual rights, as I've suggested, or to determine another formula that achieves the long-term fix we

---

[71] "Notice of Motion: Resolution Against Bill 21," Mayor Nenshi Chahal et. al, September 30, 2019. pub-calgary.escribemeetings.com/filestream.ashx?DocumentId=108651

[72] "It's terrifying: Naheed Nenshi calls for national groundswell against Québec secularism bill" by David Bell, *CBC News Calgary*, October 2, 2019, cbc.ca/news/canada/calgary/nenshi-opposi-tion-Québec-bill-21-1.5305955.

need. These and other measures have to be considered if the Government of Québec doesn't curtail its flagrant assault on the Charter and the rights of all Canadians living in the province of Québec. Challenging these bills would further protect all Canadians against similar actions being taken in their own provinces.

But true unification must come from within Québec. Imagine the potential if a majority of Canadians living in Québec stood up and came together to demand equality rights, setting aside their fear of those who don't look like them, pray like them, dress like them, or speak like them. Together, they could rally to elect new government representatives that would have a mandate to repeal both Bill 21 and the most flagrantly discriminatory sections of Bill 96, and ask that their representatives acknowledge and take action to address systemic racism in the province. It would also take politicians brave enough to run on a platform of social justice (with equity and equality as central and fundamental tenets), pushing back against protectionist populist forces and appealing instead to the sense of justice embraced broadly by the people of Québec. I may be an idealist, but I think this path would deliver the most positive outcomes, not just for Québecers but for all Canadians.

∞

I am heartened by the fact that there are leaders in Québec who have been swimming against the populist tide, providing some hope to racialized communities that help and change are on the way. Montréal mayor Valerie Plante and her administration have been vocal in affirming the existence of systemic racism and discrimination in the city. And she has taken action to uncover some of the most egregious forms of systemic racism, most notably by commissioning a report, released in May 2021, which focused on unionized blue-collar workers in various commercial enterprises (including the trucking industry) in the Montréal-North neighbourhood.

The report detailed specific incidents of racism and discrimination, including access to overtime and preferential assignment of equipment for those in the trucking industry, noting the complicity of some union and company leaders, the majority of them white. Plante called it "a deplorable situation." She committed to taking "tangible action by setting up a committee that can recommend practical reforms." A positive step in the right direction.

In my research for this book, I also stumbled upon the history of *Le Devoir*, a francophone daily newspaper published in Québec and viewed by many today as nationalist-leaning. I learned more about its founder, Henri Bourassa, who, beginning in 1910, acted as the publication's first managing editor. Surprisingly, Mr. Bourassa was in fact opposed to the notion of a separate francophone state, believing instead in "an Anglo-French concept of Canada in which French-speaking Canadians would see their culture recognized as equal and protected and encouraged from coast to coast."

For the most part that vision has been achieved, but French is still not part of everyday life for a majority of Canadians outside Québec. Canada has come a long way to make this a reality, but I acknowledge more work is needed on the "encouragement" front. By engaging fully, Québecers of all stripes will have more opportunities to play a proactive role in continuing to shape the Canada of the future and improving our union for all Canadians. Québec's tomorrow, and Canada's as a whole, will be defined by the important moral and ethical decisions made at this critical moment in history.

My hope is that many francophones in Québec who have passionate nationalist inclinations might be ready to turn the page on the past and join the rest of Canada on a new path forward, a path that respects rather than fears difference and celebrates true equality for all. To be part of rather than to remain apart. To shed the tired narrative of victimization and embrace the possibility of what it could mean to be a francophone Québecer within Canada's vibrant, dynamic multicultural community. To step out of these constraints of their own making and realize the opportunities in a community of diverse languages, races, genders, abilities, and religions. It's time for Québecers to stop hedging. Canada needs the energy, talent, and passion of all the people of Québec to make our country all it can be. Let's rally around all that unites us. Let's do the work to uncover and rid ourselves of systemic inequality. If the COVID-19 pandemic taught us anything, it's that most of us have the ability to modify how we approach our lives and to make the necessary adjustments for the betterment of others. We all have the ability and will to make change happen.

There is so much potential for Canada with the full participation of an open and more inclusive Québec. The support and promotion of French language and culture in Canada must be at the core of reframing this relationship. It's not going to happen overnight, but we need to put effort to purpose. I for one will be an enthusiastic champion, advocating for bilingualism across the country, and especially in majority English-speaking provinces. We are already seeing how French is being embraced by English Canadians in an organic manner outside of prescribed and mandated government policies or programs. This is exemplified, as previously noted, in the exponential rise in the demand for French immersion learning in Ontario. No one mandated that English-speaking parents send their kids to learn primarily in French. They made that choice on their own accord with an understanding of the value and benefit for their children's future.

My foster father shared a loving lesson when I was a teenager. One Saturday over coffee while reading the newspaper, I asked him how he managed to share his love with all his children equally. How did that work? What I was really asking, of course, was how he could make room to love one more: me. Ralph explained to me that love is indivisible. If you have three children, you don't love the first two with 33 percent of your heart and the third with 34 percent, you give each child 100 percent of your love. I never forgot that. And today, as a father of two lovely souls, his wisdom resonates with me even more deeply. We are all part of a big—and, yes, dysfunctional—Canadian family. But for the most part, it works. You can love and be proud of being Canadian and equally love being a francophone from Québec.

Imagine what would happen if all Canadians in Québec committed to Canada and the common values enshrined in the Charter. Imagine a majority of Canadians pulling in the same direction. Imagine a more diverse and open Québec, where people worked together to remove systemic barriers to opportunity and equality. Canada is always going to be a work in progress, but the only thing standing in the way of this vision reflected in the Charter, is our collective commitment of what this country *can* be.

The French-language issue has been a hot topic of discussion between my white, French-Canadian cousin Luik, a successful businessperson based in Valleyfield, Québec, and me for nearly two decades now. For fifteen of those years, we've gathered at my home in Toronto for Thanksgiving to celebrate family. Like "brothers" do, we have passionately voiced our perspectives on the Québec issue. He's shared how he feels that his native language is disrespected inside and outside Québec, and I have just as passionately made my own case. We haven't solved the issue, but we've kept talking and caring for each other with love and mutual respect. More recently, he and I have had dialogue around systemic racism and the reckoning around the Black Lives Matter movement. I wasn't surprised that we aligned on this issue and I was interested to hear his perspective, as he was mine. The conversation continues.

I expect there will always be a small contingent of Canadians who hold biases and prejudices against francophone Québecers. My hope, though, is that many more people will want to actively reflect, perhaps even in ways unfamiliar to them, and do the heavy lifting necessary if we are to create a better society for all.

It's challenging to face difficult truths and acknowledge our advantages—especially the unearned advantages we may not be aware we hold; some buried in the traditional systems that govern our society. But in a democracy that proports to be inclusive and just, taking action on the issue of systemic racism is imperative. We simply cannot have some citizens be more equal than others. For those Québecers who still believe that French is going downhill, despite Bill 101, maybe it's time to think of another solution. And the answer is not Bill 96 or Bill 21.

Now, I think, is the time to really think about something new. Societies and cultures do not remain static. They evolve. The francophone society of Québec today looks nothing like it did two hundred or even one hundred years ago. Social norms have changed, opportunity has shifted, and even the way French is spoken in Québec has evolved. You can try to artificially stagnate the evolution of culture, but it's like trying to hold back the tide with your bare hands. It simply isn't possible.

Chapter Nine

I'm a Black Man in a White World

IT WAS NO ACCIDENT WHEN I FOUND MYSELF SUDDENLY IN THE ROLE OF hotline operator for the BLM movement. It was my little sister, Elizabeth, who first artfully dubbed me the "connector" back in the late 1980s. The way she described it, I was like the string that connects the thumbtacks on many points of a map. I'm proud that she saw that in me, and I pride myself on being someone who has always connected people to each other, no matter their differences. From my earliest years, I've had a deep desire to understand people—to discover the unique value of each person, the essence that makes them who they are, and to enthusiastically champion them. It's a fundamental part of who I am, and this purposeful action has brought me much joy.

Over the decades, I've enthusiastically curated a network of friends, acquaintances, peers, colleagues, and even new family members. I've discovered profound fulfillment in creating this "found family." I'm grateful that I recognized a need in myself and sought belonging outside of the traditional structures of family. Nurturing these relationships has not only helped me work through the negative circumstances of my youth; these people have enriched my life in immeasurable ways and helped shape the person I am today—because I didn't always realize what I was up against and that as a Black man, I would have to work twice as hard. My Blackness would be a reality I'd need to transcend.

∞

By the time I was sixteen, I had already lived what felt like many lives. I was in a bad way. I was also managing all the usual coming-of-age upheavals—pushing back against authority, witnessing the transformation of my body, figuring out girls and sex, and looking to fit in and connect with like-minded people. Not only was I trying to figure out who I was, I was trying to find my tribe and my place within it. As a result, I found myself going through life with a ball of angst tightly wound inside me. This manifested in part through my purposeful provocation of others; I engaged in verbal confrontations anytime I could. My bad attitude even extended to my relationship with my foster brother, Paul, who had championed me to his family. A chill developed between us that, for a short time, led to arguments about everything and nothing. I wasn't sure why I was being so antagonistic, but I wonder now if I was trying to make everyone else feel as badly as I did.

Intuitively, I always knew that my negative behaviour ran counter to my true nature. As a young boy, I had always been a happy soul who loved to laugh, who sought out moments of fun and joy, and who liked being around other people. I reminded myself of how I'd countered my stepfather's treatment of me, turning a negative into a positive. Now, I felt myself becoming the bully. I knew deep down that despite all my troubles, my true, positive, and sunny self was still there inside me, ready to be reclaimed and shared once again.

One day in my sixteenth year, a few months after moving in with the Viponds, something clicked. I still vividly remember that morning. I sat up in bed and made a promise to myself that today was the day I would stop being angry. I knew that my anger was rooted in my perception of myself as a victim, and I didn't want to let my past challenges define my future; I wanted to define it on my own terms and honour my inner light. I'm not sure what prompted this level of self-awareness or self-healing, but it worked.

As soon as I allowed my true self to shine through again, my natural charisma and warm and approachable nature, combined with intellectual curiosity and a natural gift for communicating, allowed me to navigate the world around me in a more authentic manner. I hadn't realized how exhausting denying my true nature had been. This breakthrough allowed me to find joy in many aspects of my everyday life—playing sports, hanging with my friends at the arcade and at the movies, and going dancing at the many underage clubs that had popped up in that era. My new aura brought others into my orbit, and this would open amazing opportunities for me. But as with all good things, there were negatives.

My earliest professional successes came about in the restaurant industry, where I would go on to have a fourteen-year international career. At age thirteen, my friend Colin—one of the few other Black kids I knew—and I were hired as dishwashers at a very busy, touristy restaurant in Victoria's inner harbour. If you've never worked in a restaurant dish pit, it is a stressful, dirty job. Wave after wave of bus pans full of disgusting dishes and food are constantly coming at you. I saw it as a challenge, and worked hard to keep my stainless-steel space as clean as possible. Once I got past handling other people's leftovers with my bare hands, the trick was to see how fast I could handle the super-hot dishes coming out of the industrial dishwasher. My hands eventually got used to the searing sting of hot water, and if sorting hot cutlery was an Olympic sport, I would have won a gold medal. My strong work ethic didn't do me any favours, though. The owner and his cooks decided I wasn't working quite hard enough. When I had a second to breathe, I would now have to prepare garnishes for the cooks. So between washing endless dishes, I had to keep my eye on the prep table—or risk being yelled at by the head cook.

But the end of the night was even harder. All the pots and crusty sauce containers would be piled high, waiting to be soaked in scalding hot water before I could get to cleaning them. And for some reason, I was also responsible for cleaning the deep fryer. Not only a dangerous, but a dirty and difficult job, especially for a thirteen-year-old kid. By this time in the day, I'd been on my feet for more than eight hours. And then the *coup de grâce*: I was in charge of disposing of all the garbage from the restaurant—bags filled with a mixture of solid and liquid sludge, and piled into a four-foot-high, wheeled container. I was only five foot eight and skinny as a rake, and I had to wheel this thing down to the garage. The container was so high that I had no choice but to tip it over once I got there, strewing overstuffed garbage bags all over the floor, some exploding in the process—a stinking mess I would have to clean up. I then had to pick up each garbage bag one at time and do a kind of hammer throw to get them into the main garbage disposal. This herculean effort took me nearly an hour each night. Exhausted after my nine-hour shift, I'd then change out of my whites—which were more of a brown mess by that point—wash my hands and face, change, and start my twenty-minute walk home. I'd fall into bed after midnight, and when I finally got to sleep, I dreamt I was washing dishes.

After a week of this routine, Colin and I realized the owner was working us to the bone. The following Monday after school, we went by the restaurant office to pick up our meagre share of the tips. The owner was there, and we approached him. I told him we were both quitting—effective immediately. "You're not going to give me two weeks' notice?" he asked, incredulous.

"Are you kidding me?" I responded. I told him he should be ashamed of taking advantage of two thirteen-year-old kids and working them like slaves. I looked at Colin and gestured that it was time to leave. Hasta la vista, baby.

Two days later, Colin and I were hired as busboys at a place called Waxy's, owned by our friend Marci McNeil's dad. It was a steakhouse on lower Yates Street just up from Wharf, a touristy stretch along the waterfront dotted with stores and restaurants. We learned our roles quickly, and within weeks we were a well-oiled machine. Water, bread, and butter for the table, cleaning, and amplifying the servers' customer service. In fact, it wasn't unusual for customers to tip Colin and me directly on the side. We realized early on that the service game was a performance and that we each had a part to play. And the better we performed, the more money we would make.

One day after school, a year into our tenure at Waxy's, Colin and went down to pick up our weekend tips from the office. When we got there, a server who happened to be the manager's girlfriend met us in the lobby. She immediately started lecturing us about our work ethic. We were both fourteen years old by then and had had jobs since age ten, so we understood what work was about and always pulled our weight. She told us we hadn't earned our tips; she was tired of us "fucking the dog and making puppies." We told her to give us the tips we'd earned. She said if we kept it up, we'd lose our jobs and she'd make sure we wouldn't be able to get another in this town. We laughed at her, which made her even madder—but in the end, we left with our money.

A couple of days later, I was at Colin's house for dinner. His mother, Noreen (a "boss lady" originally from Antigua), had made us traditional curried chicken. As we ate, we discussed the encounter we'd had with our co-worker. Noreen was angry. "After school tomorrow, I'm meeting you both and we are going to go see this woman." This was not going to be good.

The next day, just as promised, Colin's mom was waiting for us in front of the restaurant. She grabbed both of us by the hand and we walked in. "Are you the person who told my kids off?" she asked. The server nodded. Noreen raised her voice. "Don't you ever talk to my babies like that again!" She said much more, but by this time Colin and I were focused on trying not to laugh. I looked up towards the second floor to see Marci busting up too. In short, the server had never "warmed up" to us and was jealous that we were so confident and popular with customers. Her overt racial prejudice had clouded her judgement. She had tried to put us in our place, and we—and Colin's mom—had pushed back. Another lesson learned: always stand up to the bully.

Colin and I knew we were very good busboys. We worked hard, we took pride in our jobs, and we made great money. In fact, by the time I was sixteen (and a ward of the government), I was making about $1,200 a month—working every Thursday, Friday, and Saturday night. I had no living expenses, so it was entirely disposable income. And I disposed of it all! For the first time in my life I could buy whatever I wanted, whenever I wanted—clothes and sneakers, records, movies and arcade games, junk food—without having to ask permission from anyone. It was an empowering feeling that would remain at the core of my drive for success for years to come. I realized at that young age that money bought access and could help me overcome obstacles.

My brother Chris and a handful of others, including Colin, loved eating at all of Victoria's best restaurants. One time, we decided to go to the city's most expensive restaurant, a French place called La Petite Colombe. It featured a very traditional French menu that included escargot and frogs' legs. It was a beautiful, intimate place with about eight tables, Versailles-influenced decor, and red velvet everywhere—a place sophisticated adults would take a date for a special occasion. We were all underage, but we knew food and wine from our years in the business. We requested the wine list and asked questions of the sommelier. It was clear that we knew our stuff and could afford to eat there. We ordered the wines we wanted, and they served us—no questions asked. Lesson learned: a combination of money and acting like you belong could provide access—even to those spaces that seemed off-limits.

We never went back to Waxy's after the tip incident, and that same week Colin and I were hired at a restaurant called Gallagher's, where we had a good run. A year later, I jumped at the opportunity to work at high-end hotel on Victoria's picturesque harbour. Within just a couple of months, I was promoted from busboy to banquet- and room-service waiter, a role that came with a special vest—a symbol of my elevated status at the hotel. Things were going well until the owner (who happened to be one of Victoria's richest businesspeople) decided to target me. I was the only Black person working in the hotel at the time. The only other people of colour were a few women, originally from the Philippines, who worked in housekeeping.

One morning I was checking over a dining room—a large space where hundreds would sit for brunch hours later—that had been set up the night before. I was going about my business when the owner, a man his early sixties with what seemed like a permanent scowl on his face, suddenly appeared. He was verbally assaulting me about something that displeased him. A napkin out of place, a missing fork—something trivial. I immediately walked toward him to see what was wrong, only to be met with a rant as to why I was bad at my job. He never bothered to call me by my name, even though it was plainly visible on my name tag. I stood there and took it. I said, "Yes sir"; "No sir," and fixed issues I'd had no hand in creating. I told myself I wasn't going to let him push me into reacting. I liked working there, I was making good money, and I needed the job. And the optimist in me hoped I could find a way to change his mind.

Over the next few weeks, the owner seemed to pop up wherever I was to point out something I was doing wrong. I remember picking up the phone in the service area and answering as per protocol. He was on the other end and—surprise—was unhappy with how I'd answered. Before I could apologize, he hung up. In the six months I worked there, I never saw this man raise his voice at another staff member. Often his tirades would occur in front of others, who did their best to pretend they didn't see, though some were clearly upset I was being unfairly singled out. Still, I held my tongue. I kept my head down. I worked hard.

It was now summer, and Victoria was jumping with tourists; the hotel was full, and more staff had just been hired. I was returning from delivering room service when the gift shop manager, a woman in her late fifties, told me she needed to speak to me right away. I was busy, but she said it was important. She was the owner's "friend"—I'd seen them chatting intimately on many occasions—so I knew better than to say no a second time. She proceeded to tell me that business was slow and the hotel would be making some cuts. She then told me I was being let go. I knew it was a lie, and I knew she didn't even have the authority to fire me, but I was stunned and beyond frustration, so I unbuttoned my waiters' jacket and tossed it at her. I told her how sad it was that a woman of her age would lie to a young person like me to gain points with the boss. I told her I would never walk into that hotel again so long as that man owned it. I walked out with my head held high. It would be nearly twenty years before I'd set foot in that hotel again, the owner long dead by then.

I made another promise to myself that day: no matter where my life took me, I would never compromise my ethics and morals or treat others poorly in pursuit of financial success. I would never become like the man who belittled and bullied me every day I worked for him. I've stuck to that promise my entire career and I know for a fact that some of the decisions I have made as a result have cost me financially. But I also know that I am a much happier person because of my choices. In the end, no matter how good you are at what you do, it may not be enough to overcome the biases of those wielding power over you.

∞

For the most part, my restaurant career was very fulfilling. I was lucky to work in great places with amazing people and make the money I needed. After high school, I worked several jobs and saved up enough to pay my way through college. I studied commerce at Camosun College for two years and then at BCIT for two more, graduating with a diploma in advertising and integrated marketing. I was the first member of my family to ever graduate from college.

I moved to Vancouver at the age of twenty, where I secured a job at the 1986 World Exposition on the strength of my service experience and my bilingualism. At the time, Vancouver was still seen as a sleepy little town, but Expo 86 was the catalyst for its transformation into an international metropolis. Likewise, my next job was a bit of a catalyst for my life. The Unicorn Pub, an Irish pub through and through, was owned by the Irish Rovers, a folk band that had—via its popular TV variety show and hit songs, including "The Unicorn Song" and "Wasn't That A Party"—parlayed its success in 1960s California into an international career and a loyal following in Canada.

The Unicorn would become the busiest bar in North America for the six-month run of the Expo. It held nearly eight hundred people and had a permanent eight-hour lineup. Sales were nearly $70,000 a day. More importantly for me, it was an incredibly fun summer, working with a staff of three hundred other young people who were all making and spending money at the most amazing "party" the city had ever held.

But it was also the place where I would come face to face with overt racism. One memorable customer exchange I had was with two couples sitting in my section. I sized them up as I got closer. It was clear they were not "downtown people"—so they were fish out of water, if you will—and I asked if they'd like some drinks. They'd waited hours to get in and had one of the best tables in the house, and I was there to make sure they had a good time. The men ordered beers for themselves and pina coladas for the women. I explained to them that we did not offer those kinds of drinks as we were a traditional Irish pub. The alpha at the table gave me an angry look and said, "Listen, you fucking nigger, get us the fucking pina coladas." My instinct was to punch him in the face, but I knew that would be the wrong choice for all kinds of reasons. I had served thousands of people during the Expo—I'd even taken some shit from assholes, most of them very drunk, but this was the first overtly racist comment I'd had to confront. My professional response was measured and delivered with confidence. I calmly told him that not only was I not going to get them the fancy drinks they wanted, but they would need to leave immediately.

More insults flew my way, but they didn't faze me; these were no longer people I had to "care for." I then explained to them that the next person to ask them to leave would not be nearly as polite or understanding. The insults continued as I walked away. What I knew and they didn't was that we had a dozen security staff—most of whom who were off-season football and rugby players. Big guys who loved to hit things. I relayed the situation to the head doorman and just a few minutes later, I saw the racist guy about four feet off the ground, literally flying out the door. Two of our biggest guys had handled the situation. It felt good to know my team had my back and that the pub's no-tolerance policy was exactly that. I made sure to always take care of those big guys—buying them drinks and introducing them to people of note (mostly, female friends of mine they wanted to meet). My formative experience engaging with the big kids at Vernon cadet camp continued to serve me well.

No matter your ethnicity, race, gender, or sexual orientation, every one of us who worked at the Unicorn knew that our safety came first. As a twenty-year old, I wasn't fully aware of how special this kind of policy was—looking back, it was clearly not the norm in the 1980s. Many businesses in that era and prior had informal expectations that their employees would simply suck it up—take the verbal or physical harassment without having management intervene. Black people had been programmed to accept this silent suffering through centuries of slavery and discrimination. As it turns out, I'd landed with an organization led by some good people.

Two years later, the Irish Rover corporation recruited me to work at the Canadian Pavilion bar and restaurant at the World Exposition in Brisbane, Australia.

It was dream job for a twenty-two-year-old: travel, good money, and the chance to meet people from all over the world. Australia was celebrating its bicentennial and experiencing a national reckoning with its relationship with the land's original peoples. That said, it was immediately clear to me that in Brisbane, long-standing colonial attitudes were still negatively impacting the lives of immigrants, people of colour, and Aboriginal people. Not to mention that sexism and misogyny were rampant in 1980s Australia. The Sex Discrimination Act had only just passed, in 1975.

I was always on the lookout for discrimination while navigating my life in Brisbane. There seemed to be a general disdain for the Aborigines (the name used for the Aboriginal people at the time), and widespread prejudice toward what many called the "boat people"—referring to the city's growing Asian population, many of whom were refugees from Vietnam and Cambodia. A Canadian friend who had worked with me at Expo 88 recently reminded me of a conversation we had soon after our arrival. She mentioned how I had worried about being mistaken for an Aboriginal person. I had wondered out loud whether I should cut my long curly hair to downplay my Blackness. The fear of being targeted was weighing on my mind; I was in unknown territory. In the end, I didn't cut my hair. I continued to wear my Lionel Ritchie–inspired curly mullet, disguising my fear with an outward appearance of pride.

The Canadian Pavilion was very popular with visitors, including members of the Brisbane police. The chief was a regular patron of our bar, and he became so friendly with the staff that he invited a group of us to his home one afternoon for a "barbie"—shrimp and all. It was a broad mix of nearly seventy-five guests, including officials from the Canadian Pavilion, managers and staff from the restaurant, government officials, and members of the local police force. As was often the case, I was the only person of colour. I was having a drink by the pool when two newly minted police cadets in uniform approached me. After some small talk, I asked them what it took to become a police officer in Brisbane. They described the training and added that they had to be very good at "Abo-bashing." They laughed, seemingly unaware of the offensive nature of their comment, and I took that as a cue to walk away.

These types of encounters occurred over and over throughout my life. Some white people seemed to feel completely comfortable expressing their racist and bigoted views to me; they seemed either unaware that I was Black or simply didn't care whether I would be offended. Part of the reason for this is that on most occasions, no one would hold the person spouting racism to account. No one would stand up and say, "What you're doing and saying is wrong," so they continued with impunity. Other times, I realized that some people didn't see me as a Black person—perhaps they saw me as a white guy with a good tan because of how I spoke and the lighter shade of my skin.

I was never sure how others saw me. Many times, I, too, said nothing, not wanting to create a scene or a public confrontation.

One incident that really sticks with me occurred in the winter of 1988. Chris and I were living and working in the ski-resort town of Whistler, British Columbia. One afternoon, a friend had given us access to the outdoor hotel hot tub in the village. After fifteen minutes of soaking, a white couple joined us. They appeared to be in their twenties, like us. We said hello, asked them how they were enjoying Whistler and where they were from. They were visiting from Montgomery, Alabama, and asked us if we knew of the place. I said yes, noting that it was the cradle of the civil rights movement and that many Black people lived there. "That's not what we call them," chirped the young woman. Suddenly, her husband gave her a bug-eyed look and they quicky jumped out of the tub. My brother Chris insists to this day that he peed in the hot tub before they had time to step out.

As I was making my way to leave the barbecue that day in Brisbane, the police chief took me aside, asking to speak to me privately. He thanked me for coming, and for the hospitality I always extended to him when he visited my bar, and said he hoped I would have a great time in Australia and "continue to be safe." He then handed me his card and told me to always keep it with me. If anything ever happened, I was to pull it out and make it clear to whomever that he and I were friends and they should call him immediately. I appreciated the gesture but also recognized it for what it was: a warning. I would have to be extra vigilant in navigating a society that was still a very dangerous place for people like me. Thankfully, even though I did experience some racism in Australia, I never felt compelled to pull out that literal "race card."

∞

Four years later, after completing college and graduating from BCIT with my diploma, I was in search of a marketing job amidst a deep recession. The former management team I had worked for at Expos 86 and 88 drafted me to work at the 1992 Universal Exposition in Seville, Spain. It was another dream job. I was hired to build and manage the Jamaican Pavilion bar. It didn't matter that I was not Jamaican and had never even visited the island; my Expo coworkers joked that I was the perfect hire: I spoke French and English and could probably learn Spanish quickly, I had the experience, and of course, I just "happened to be the right colour." I didn't take any offense; my friend Richard, who I had worked with at two to other Expos, was like family and this type of joke was part of our repartee. For once, it seemed that my race would be a benefit to me, and I jumped at the opportunity.

But I knew my history. I knew that Spain had been a fascist dictatorship until the late 1970s. I also knew that in countries like Spain, which have a history of military policing, the use of intimidation tactics lingers, especially for Black people and people of colour. I'd have to be cautious.

The Reggae Bistro turned out to be a special place. For six months, we welcomed people from all over the world who enjoyed amazing music, tasty rum concoctions, and ice-cold Red Stripe beer. More importantly, it was the place where I'd forge lifetime friendships with great people from Holland, Spain, Australia, Columbia, and of course, Jamaica. Seville was another city trying to catch up to the rest of the world economically and socially. The country was also on high alert, dealing with internal terrorist threats from ETA (Euskadi Ta Askatasuna, "Basque Homeland and Liberty"), the militant wing of the Basque nationalist movement seeking independence from Spain and France. The city was amazingly beautiful, but it felt like a military fortress. There were hundreds of police checkpoints and machine gun–wielding military police wherever you looked. Tanks stood guard at the entrances to the Expo site and outside Expo City, the fortified compound where I lived with an international staff of ten thousand—a similar set-up to an Olympic Village. I was stopped constantly by authorities while walking the city streets, travelling by train, and driving my car. I lost count of how many times I had machine guns pointed at my chest and face while being questioned aggressively by police, who demanded to know where I was from and what I was doing in their country. I was asked so many times for proof of my Canadian citizenship, I joked to my friends I should tattoo my passport on my arm. It was obvious to everyone that I was being targeted because I was Black.

I found the younger officers the worst of all, as if they were constantly trying to impress the ranking officer on the scene. If you've never had that experience, I can tell you that it is very scary. And it never got easier. Every single time, thoughts raced through my mind as the adrenalin coursed through my body—*What if the officer's machine gun accidentally fires? What if they squeeze the trigger a little too hard from a sudden rush of adrenaline? What if my answers are "lost in translation"?*

Unfortunately, contact with the officers was unavoidable for me. As part of my manager's role at the bistro, I had to coordinate the overnight delivery of supplies into the Expo site. On many occasions, I had to drive the company van through security at one o'clock in the morning when the site was closed to visitors. I had gotten to know many of the security officers personally because they drank at my bar. This came in handy, as it was their job to check vehicles for bombs, and in my case, to make sure the van's inventory cargo matched the manifest. On most occasions, we'd share pleasantries, they would do a routine check of my vehicle, and they'd send me on my way. But when one particular officer was standing guard in his observation tower, things didn't go so well for me.

My security buddies would approach me, giving me an apologetic heads-up that I would be subjected to "special" treatment from the "jefe." Sure enough, he directed his officers to have me unload the van and carry every single box of bar supplies—sometimes up to thirty of them—up the forty steps to the X-ray machine. My security buddies were under strict instructions not to help me. Each box was scanned, and I was then escorted to a security room where I was patted down and then questioned by the big boss himself, all while he gave me a smug look of superiority.

He seemed mostly to want to remind me that I was a guest in his country and he was in charge. We both knew he had the power. I had a visa and the fine print noted that it could be revoked at the discretion of the authorities. Like so many before me, I just had to sit there and take his abuse at the risk of losing my work visa, going to jail, or being deported. So I gritted my teeth and smiled. What should have taken me fifteen minutes took nearly two hours, and this ordeal seemed to occur once every few weeks—whenever the feeling struck him.

I remember driving away after the first time. I was humiliated and angry. For most Black people, my story is typical of their lived experience, not the exception. I recognized in that moment that I was someone who hadn't grown up in "the 'hood" and under constant police harassment, and I began to better understand the negative impact of this systemic form of racism.

Despite everything, I was a young man in Spain, and I made sure to enjoy myself. I used some of my time off to visit Canadian friends who were running a seaside bar just a few hours from Seville in Portugal's beautiful Algarve region. During one visit, two friends and I were driving to a small town for lunch in search of a piri piri chicken place everyone was raving about. Suddenly, a military police Jeep cut us off. We had to swerve and brake hard to avoid hitting them. My Portuguese Canadian friend Jorge was driving. He quickly stepped out of the car and met the two police officers in front of the car. They looked angry, machine guns at the ready. My friend Brent and I stayed inside, me in the back seat.

We couldn't hear the exchange, but the officers kept pointing in my direction. As it turned out, I had US $1,500 in my pocket as I hadn't had time to find a bank when we got to Portugal. All I could think about in that moment was that they would arrest us, take us to their station or somewhere remote, steal my money, and rough us up for good measure—possibly worse. Suddenly, one of the officers poked his head through the driver's seat window, looked around, sneered at me, and then went back to his partner and Jorge. And then, just like that, the officers walked back to their Jeep and sped away.

When Jorge turned back toward the car, I could see the stress on his face. As soon as he was back behind the wheel, I asked him what the officers had said, what they wanted. He wouldn't answer. I pressed him, and he finally told me. The officers had pulled us over because they wanted to know why he was driving "with a nigger in the car." He'd told them I was a friend from Canada, and they'd asked him for money in exchange for not arresting us for some arbitrary reason. Jorge had been quick on his feet and convinced them we were poor college kids with barely enough money to put gas in the car. Crisis narrowly avoided.

The last night of Expo in Seville was bittersweet. My expo friends from all over the world came by to have a final drink and express the hope that we would see each other again soon. But five minutes after the site closed for the last time, the military police encircled the pavilions; they had been instructed to escort staff off the site. It felt weirdly oppressive. We grabbed all the money, shut the lights off, locked the doors, and my entire staff and I walked towards the exit gates. All the while, the guards were shouting at us, machine guns in hand, telling us to move faster. I couldn't wait to get out of there. It was a sad ending to a complicated, but memorable, few months.

∞

Soon after arriving home, I left behind my fourteen-year career in the hospitality industry when I landed my first professional marketing role with Bose Corporation. A family friend working for the company had put my name forward, and after a three-month letter campaign (this was before email), I secured an interview with management in Toronto. After more interviews and more letters, I sat in a Toronto lobby for my final interview. I waited three hours. I remember the office manager, Susan, was impressed by my patience. I told her I wasn't leaving without the job. Two hours later I was on my way to the airport with the job in hand. I moved to Toronto a few months afterward to begin the next chapter of my life and career.

Working for Bose was an amazing opportunity; it was one of the most respected brands in the world, known for audio innovation and quality sound. I would be responsible for all marketing activities nationally. We had a great team led by a charismatic and mentoring boss, and together we would drive the Canadian business to new heights. But there was one side to the business that surprised me. Although the company was founded by Dr. Amar Bose—a brilliant second-generation, mixed-race Bengali American—the company the former MIT professor founded was as white-bread as you could get. Senior management and the MIT-heavy engineering team were mostly white men, whose uniform of choice was khaki Dockers and penny loafers, finished off with a Bose-branded collared shirt. Women were present in many of the downstream supporting roles but were rare in upper management, and there were very few people of colour anywhere. I stood out as a Black man in the organization, the only one in the Canadian division. Would I need to work twice as hard?

Over my three years with the company, I had some important successes, helped along by a very supportive boss who gave me all the responsibility I wanted and the authority I needed to get the job done. All he asked was that I take accountability, make him look good, and not hesitate to ask for his help. Working with many talented collaborators, my efforts contributed to exponential sales growth year after year. My biggest claim to fame would be spearheading the development and launch of Bose Corporation's first global website in 1995.

Despite my successes, I faced some heavy headwinds from a key member of the North American leadership team. My boss tried to shield me from this person as much as possible, but for some reason I was always in his cross-hairs. Even my boss was at a loss, and he continued to encourage me to seek face time with this person (whom he reported to) to try and resolve it. At one point, after I had been at Bose for about a year, I was summoned to a meeting with this powerful individual. He cut to the chase: he was going to move me to sales—totally discounting my background in and passion for marketing. It was an uncomfortable conversation, as he didn't provide any reasoning. I pushed back hard, which, in hindsight, was brave for someone with little experience. But I could sense that whatever the issue was, it wasn't about my work ethic or my abilities. I left that meeting with my position intact, and we never spoke about it again.

At the time, I'd begun working with many project teams in the US, gaining experience and knowledge I was expected to bring back to the Canadian marketplace. On one occasion, I found myself in Atlanta at COMDEX, a technology trade show targeted at businesses. We were launching a series of new products and technologies including the Bose MediaMate, a premium computer speaker system that was ahead of its time.

Our massive, two-thousand-square-foot booth included a twenty-seat presentation theatre. There were about thirty of us working the booth, and we were each expected to take our turn presenting the product. When it was my turn, I hesitated—I had a case of stage fright. But I knew I had to prove my worth. It wasn't enough to do what was expected—I had to exceed expectations. So I gave myself a big kick in the ass at the beginning of day two of the show, and I volunteered for the next session. And the next. And the next. Before I knew it, I'd presented to various groups—from the US Postal Service to the US Military—for more than four hours straight, honing my script and skills as I went. The last day of the show, I did another four-hour marathon session (to the delight of my colleagues, who were now off the hook), closing our successful showing.

The senior business manager in charge of our show presence, Allan Evelyn, a white New Englander in his early fifties, let me know how impressed he was with my team approach. He wanted to take me out for drink in the city after our team dinner—wherever I wanted to go. It was my first time in Atlanta, so I didn't know the city. I did know that Atlanta had a major Black population, but the city was very segregated (and still is). I asked my hotel concierge for recommendations, and he suggested a club that was popular at the time.

Allan and I peeled off from the group after dinner and caught a cab. The doorman greeted us with a nod. Once I walked inside, I was blown away by what I saw. The dancefloor looked like the set of *Soul Train*—beautiful Black people dressed to the nines in wonderfully colourful outfits; the room was sparkling with light and the music funky and soulful. I'd never seen anything like it in real life. I looked over at Allan who was grinning, happy at where we had landed. He was the only white person in the entire place, but it didn't faze him. It was the first time I'd ever been in a Black club—or any place where everyone looked like me. I felt electrified. In that single moment I felt a connection with my Blackness I'd never experienced before. And I was there with my new brother, Allan. We had a blast drinking, talking, and grooving to the music.

Weeks later, I received a corporate letter from Allan, who had copied every other member of the senior management team just short of Dr. Bose himself. He described my exceptional contribution at the show and said my efforts merited added recognition. It felt amazing to have my work seen and validated, so it was a surprising to me when I never received a single note, email, or even a passing comment from anyone else copied on that letter. It was like it had never happened. This was in stark contrast to the corporate recognition and accolades I'd often witnessed my white colleagues receive. It was what today we'd call a "microaggression." I learned another valuable lesson from this. There are good people everywhere who will look to uplift and support you, while others will continue to ignore your abilities no matter how hard you work. Focus on the good people. People like Allan.

The most unsettling time at Bose when my race came into play was at one of our legendary annual weeklong conferences. It was the spring of 1995, and about two hundred employees were in Boston for the event. I was, as usual, one of just a handful of non-white employees attending. One night, two members of my Canadian sales team and I joined some of our American colleagues at an Italian restaurant. As our first course arrived, the two Canadians—both white, one from BC and the other from Québec—began discussing civil rights in America (apparently, they were experts) and the challenges that continued to plague Black people. I tried to ignore them, but I could tell they were looking for me to engage. One began talking about how, even though civil rights laws had been passed in the mid-1960s, Black people were still complaining. "Why don't they just get on with things? Look at Chinese people. They come here with nothing, start a small corner store, save money, buy a house, send their kids to college. Black people have the same opportunity as everyone else, but they'd rather complain and ask for government help and support."

That was it. I couldn't let this drivel continue unchallenged. I looked up from my plate and spoke to them directly. First, I noted that thirty years is not a very long time and that many of the outcomes envisioned with the passage of civil rights legislation—equal access to college education, white-collar leadership opportunities, broader economic prosperity, and equal access to housing—had yet to become a lived reality for Black people, and that systemic (though I didn't use that word then) racism persists. I noted that even though the Chinese people who came to America in the 1800s and beyond were treated horribly, they had retained their names, their culture, their religion, their heritage, and ultimately their freedom. Black people came to America as slaves—stripped of everything and kept as property for nearly four hundred years. You can't expect Black people to rebuild their entire culture and community in just a few short decades. You need equity measures over time and across social systems to ever achieve true equality. This is exactly what we are still talking about today.

The Québec sales guy added that he thought Black people should just work harder, not be so lazy, and complain less—pull themselves up by their bootstraps. I was now fuming as I twisted my pasta onto my fork. I asked him if he thought I was lazy. They both answered almost in unison: "You're not really Black, Stephen."

I can't tell you how many times over the years I have heard that same message—a double-barrelled insult that served to both offend me and excuse others' racial bias. Their point of view reminded me of a scene in Spike Lee's 1988 film *Do the Right Thing*. Lee's character, Mookie, is arguing with the Italian pizzeria owner's son, played by John Turturro, who claims he doesn't like Black people—with a few exceptions. Turturro's character then makes the distinction that famous athletes like Michael Jordan are not really Black because they are famous and successful—the idea being that their meteoric success has given them a "pass" of acceptance by the white majority. This resonated with me; I saw my continued achievements as a way to transcend any potential barriers baked into the perceived shortcomings of my Blackness.

At this point in the conversation, I'd had enough. I picked up my plate and went to another table to finish my meal.

The next day as I was walking through the hotel lobby, I saw my boss walking earnestly towards me. I could tell that whatever was about to come out of his mouth was serious. "I need to talk to you," he said, leading me to a nearby stairwell. He told me a dozen people had spoken to their managers to say that they'd overheard the conversation at the restaurant and were appalled. I was disappointed to hear that, as no one had come over my table to interject, ask me if I was okay, or attempt to diffuse the conversation. He asked me what had happened. At first I said that nothing had happened, fearing my Canadian teammates could get in trouble—perhaps even lose their jobs. He assured me that he appreciated my team mindset but the cat was out of the bag and he wanted to hear the whole story directly from me. So I told him, and he thanked me. That was the end of the conversation. Period.

I never heard from any other senior manager or from human resources on the matter. I didn't receive a written or verbal apology from my teammates. They were never reprimanded. It would be many years before corporations across the board managed diversity and inclusion in a manner that offered protection and recourse for Black employees. It was clear to me then that, as much as my boss had my back, I was on my own. I had to seriously consider whether this company could be part of my future.

That same afternoon, all two hundred of us boarded half a dozen luxury buses on our way to the John F. Kennedy Presidential Library and Museum, where we would be hosting top dealers from across North America. En route, our bus took a wrong turn and we ended up driving through one of the poorest neighbourhoods in Boston—and of course, it was a Black community. It looked like a bombed-out, war-torn country. Young children were playing amongst garbage on the sidewalks, their toys made of scrap plastic, string, and discarded pieces of wood. I had never seen this level of poverty before. It gave me an idea. I got up from my seat and turned to the Canadian teammate from BC, who was sitting in the back row. "Hey," I said, "there's your equal opportunity."

When we arrived, our surroundings were in complete contrast to what we had just experienced. The Kennedy museum is not only an amazing space celebrating one of America's most significant presidents, but it is also classically opulent—everything is immaculate. I could feel its importance as soon as I entered the door. We were there for a dinner, followed by speeches from the higher-ups, including Dr. Bose.

Per protocol, every Bose sales and marketing person was assigned to chaperone and dine with a specific dealer to ensure they felt appreciated as a partner. My nemesis now had something in store for me. He called me over and personally introduced me to Arnold Frieman. A Jewish businessman from Winnipeg, Arnold was one of the most successful one-location Bose dealers in North America. He was legendary, known throughout the company as a tough negotiator and notoriously difficult to please. It was left to me to walk him and his lovely wife, Myra, through the museum and dine with them afterwards.

As we walked through the exhibits, I used my knowledge of political history to try to impress them. I began a dialogue about President Kennedy, asking Arnold his views on the former president's many legacies. He barely paid attention to me. I was a young kid to him, and I got the strong sense he felt he'd been pawned off on a minor-leaguer. Still, I didn't give up. At one point, we were passing by an exhibit about Kennedy's role in the civil rights era and I mentioned something about the struggle for equality. "What do you know about struggle?" he snapped back. His words hit hard. But instead of lashing out or going quiet, I decided to share part of my backstory with him. It was greatly condensed, but I let him know that I had overcome significant challenges in my youth and had worked hard to achieve the success I was now experiencing.

I could see an immediate change in him. He stopped walking and turned to me. And that's when he shared his own story with me. He'd grown up as an Orthodox Jew in Hungary and was only eleven years old when the Second World War began. He was a concentration camp survivor, and most of his family had perished under the Nazis. Postwar, he lived through harrowing conditions before escaping a Russian labour camp. He went on to volunteer in the Air Force for Israel in the 1948 War of Independence and finally emigrated, penniless, to Canada. It was there, in Winnipeg, that he'd built an amazing business from the ground up. A truly self-made man.

We both were, and now we both knew it.

In that moment of sharing our stories, a bond was created between us. For the rest of our tour, Arnold was like a grandfather to me, a mentor passing on the pearls of wisdom he had accumulated over many decades. I had taken a chance to be honest, authentic, and genuine and it paid off. It was a lesson I'd carry forward.

Finally, we were all seated in the gilded dining room with all the accoutrements of a fine restaurant. The service staff wore smart jackets and white gloves. With my experience working in fine dining, I was always evaluating the level and sophistication of the service I received. This was the major leagues. As we were finishing our first course, I noticed that Arnold and Myra's wine glasses were nearly empty. A server with bottles in hand was standing at a table behind me. I tried to get his attention to no avail, so I stood up and walked towards him. I asked him if he could please refill my guests' glasses. He looked at me dismissively, said it wasn't his table, and walked away. I sat down. But Arnold had also paid attention. He asked me what the server had said, and when I tried to deflect, he pressed me. I detailed the brief conversation. Arnold sat up, spotted the waiter across the room, and walked towards him briskly. He was barely five foot tall but carried himself like a king.

I worried my management of Arnold Frieman was about to cause a major incident, and my nemesis's objective to see me fail would win out. From a distance, I could see Arnold gesturing angrily at the server. By now, other members of the staff had gathered to see what was up. Suddenly, the server took off his jacket, handed it to someone, and walked away. He had been fired on the spot.

When Arnold made it back to the table, he said something that stuck with me forever: "Never let someone treat you or speak to you like you're not worthy of respect. Never!" One minute later, a team of five severs completely turned our table, and our wine glasses were never empty again.

That Boston trip was a key learning moment in my professional career and a harbinger of things to come for a Black man living and working in a white world. There were going to be bumps in the road—many bumps, unfortunately—simply because of the colour of my skin.

∞

I left Bose after three years. I had enjoyed working with many smart and talented people and had gained many professional skills within a very sophisticated organization. But it was clear to me that the company had a long way to go regarding inclusion and diversity, and being young and impatient, I thought it best to look for new opportunities where I could flourish with less opposition. So who better to work for than myself?

I moved back to Vancouver and decided that, with my experience, education, and contacts, I was well-placed to start my own marketing consultancy focusing on providing integrated marketing services. That's what led me to launch Dorsey & Associates in 1996. (Interestingly, one of my first clients would be Bose.) For more than four years, I helped various organizations frame up their marketing strategies and develop creative campaigns.

In 1999 some of my former Bose colleagues gravitated to Seattle to senior management roles with a media start-up called PlayNetwork. They needed a VP-level marketing expert and creative director. Bingo! I had always wanted to test my mettle against the very best in the US, the biggest market in the world. After consulting for a few months, I was offered the job.

It was an amazing experience to work in such a pressure-filled environment—helping create value from nothing, an important marker for anyone looking to establish credibility in the start-up world. In my six years, we went from unprofitable to 3,300-percent growth and nearly $32 million in revenue. Our success was recognized industry-wide and by *Inc. Magazine* as one of the fastest-growing private companies two years running. This success was extremely validating for me, and would provide a solid foundation for my future endeavours.

I was at the gym early one morning, two years into my tenure at PlayNetwork, when all the TV monitors switched to footage of the World Trade Center in New York City. Heavy smoke was billowing from the upper floors of one of the Twin Towers. Apparently, a plane had accidently crashed into it. As I was pushing hard to finish my ride, I watched a second plane crash into tower number two. It was like watching a Bruce Willis movie. It didn't seem real. It couldn't be real. Suddenly, it was mayhem all around me. Phones ringing, people scared. America was under attack. I knew that some people on our team were currently in the air, heading to meetings across the US. My boss was married to a flight attendant who flew for United and was stationed on the east coast. We were told that other planes had possibly been highjacked. The threat and fear were palpable.

I arrived at the office about an hour later to find people crying, making calls, and doing whatever they could to find out about loved ones who'd been anywhere near Ground Zero. I made calls to friends in New York City and found some comfort knowing they were safe. Once my colleagues and I were able to account for everyone we knew, we were left to ponder what this all meant and what was next. I remember entering an office then, where some of my colleagues had gathered. What I heard next disturbed me to my core. "We should use our nukes and bomb all those fucking Arabs," one person said. Others chimed in, jumping on the hate-fuelled discussion. No one seemed to care that this "nuclear option" would cause the death of millions of innocent people—including children. The rest of the conversation was filled with the usual racist tropes: "They're animals, uncivilized!" "If it wasn't for their oil, they'd still be living in the stone age."

In that moment, they couldn't see past their rage and pain. In their minds, the US had been unfairly targeted without provocation. They wouldn't consider any rational argument as to why another country would want to attack America. Given the gravity of the moment and the fact that I was a guest in this country, I decided to keep my mouth shut. They were all understandably fired up, so trying to have a nuanced conversation in that moment would have been futile. Unfortunately, their stance didn't alter much over time.

The September 11, 2001, attacks would, of course, go down in the history books. The horrific series of airline hijackings orchestrated by militant Islamist terrorist group al Qaeda killed 2,977 people and changed our world forever. But as a Canadian who had studied history, I knew the story of America's interventionist track record over the centuries, and to me, an attack on the United States was not completely unexpected. The country had implicated itself all over the world in the interest of its own national security; had supported brutal dictatorships in places like the Middle East (such as Saddam Hussein in Iraq) and in South America, where the CIA helped overthrow democratically elected leaders and supported dictatorial regimes (General Augusto Pinochet in Chile comes to mind). History is rife with examples of America's negative impact—both direct and indirect—on the lives of millions of people across the globe.

Because of its many imperialistic interventions over nearly two hundred years, America had much to answer for. This did not make a terrorist attack on its soil right, but it did provide context for possible motives. That reality was a far cry from the most common refrain I heard during those early days post 9/11: "Why do they hate us so much?" It seemed devoid of any awareness of America's past actions.

American anti-Arab and anti-Muslim sentiment would become, in its own way, extremist. It would also linger in the collective memory. A poll was conducted by the Associated Press-NORC Center for Public Affairs Research ahead of the twentieth anniversary of 9/11. It found that over half (53 percent) of Americans have "unfavorable" views toward Islam[1]. This, according to Associated Press News, "stands in contrast to Americans' opinions about Christianity and Judaism, for which most respondents expressed favorable views. Mistrust and suspicion of Muslims didn't start with 9/11, but the attacks dramatically intensified those animosities." These post- 9/11 sentiments were amplified throughout American society and beyond by government leaders and the media, deepening an already pervasive racism. This widespread rise of Islamophobia mostly resulted in people of Arabic descent and/or Muslim faith "being ignored or targeted by low-level harassment." According to data from Brown University, hate crimes against Muslims skyrocketed 500 percent from 2000 to 2009.[2]

To contextualize the racist response to 9/11, consider the deadliest act of domestic terrorism[3] in the United States prior to September 11, 2001. Timothy McVeigh, a white, Christian American whom the *Guardian* referred to as "a disaffected veteran"[4] bombed a federal building in Oklahoma City on April 19, 1995, killing 168 people (including 19 children) and injuring 680. McVeigh subscribed to a racist Christian philosophy that advocated for the violent overthrow of the federal government that would eventually lead to a race

1   "Two decades after 9/11 Muslim Americans still fighting bias" by Mariam Fam, Deepti Hajela, and Luis Andres Henao, *AP News*, September 7, 2021. apnews.com/article/September-11-Muslim-Americans-93f97dd9219c25371428f4268a2b33b4

2   "What It Meant To Be Muslim In America After 9/11" by Jean-Francois Monier. *NPR*, September 9, 2021. npr.org/2021/09/09/1035578745/what-it-meant-to-be-muslim-in-america-after-9-11

3   "How Oklahoma City bomber Timothy McVeigh changed the fringe right" by Lou Michel, Dan Harbeck, *The Buffalo News*, April 19, 2020.buffalonews.com/news/local/crime-and-courts/how-oklahoma-city-bomber-timothy-mcveigh-changed-the-fringe-right/article_35958e7b-7e95-50d7-bb60-58473cebf002.html

4   "Oklahoma City bombing: 20 years later, key questions remain unanswered" by Andrew Gumbel, *The Guardian*, April 13, 2015. theguardian.com/us-news/2015/apr/13/oklahoma-city-bombing-20-years-later-key-questions-remain-unanswered

war.[5] For the most part, the media called the Oklahoma City bombing an act of "domestic terrorism" and did not link McVeigh's actions to the Christian faith or its 2.5 billion followers. In fact, early on, the mass media inaccurately communicated that the terrorist act had its roots in the Middle East because of a terrorist bombing at the Word Trade Center two years earlier, perpetrated by Ramzi Yousef.[6] "This is the deadliest terror attack on US soil ever. A US government source has told *CBS News* that it has Middle East terrorism written all over it," declared co-anchor Connie Chung the night of the attack.

The most overt recent example of systemic discrimination against Muslims in America was President Trump's 2017 Muslim ban, an executive order that banned people—including refugees—from seven Muslim-majority countries entry to the US. This blatantly racist order violated international law, demonized the vulnerable, and essentially held the 1.8 billion people globally who identify as Muslims responsible for the terrorist acts of a small group who adhere to an extremist form of the faith. The fallout of individual and systemic racism continues to negatively impact Muslims in America twenty years after 9/11. Canada is not immune to this discrimination, as evidenced by the murderous attacks on a Québec City mosque in 2017, which killed five people, and on a Muslim family in London, Ontario, in 2021.

≪≫

By 2006, I had grown weary of American politics and the country's continued decline towards divisive, right-wing, conservative values—the us-versus-them attitude—so I made the decision that my future was in Canada, where I would hopefully put down permanent roots, build a family, and pursue my entrepreneurial and creative passions. I quit my job, sold my condo, and left Seattle for Toronto.

When I'd lived there in the early 1990s, Toronto was characterized by its WASPy heritage and its institutions reflected that historical reality. Returning a decade later, Toronto had transformed into a vibrant, multicultural city. Citizens from over 230 countries and speaking over 170 languages had settled there, bringing with them their unique cultures, food, and traditions. This diverse population began to slowly move the racial discrimination dial in a positive direction—most profoundly in relationships between everyday people. In my own experience, it felt like there was an increased acceptance of others and less overt racism and discrimination. It felt like home.

---

5   "Why the Oklahoma bombing continues to cast a shadow over America" by Kesa White, *Open Democracy*, August 12, 2021. opendemocracy.net/en/countering-radical-right/why-oklahoma-bombing-continues-cast-shadow-over-america/

6   "Media fail: The flawed early coverage of 1995 OKC bombing," *The 1995 Blog*, April 19, 2015. 1995blog.com/2015/04/19/media-fail-the-flawed-early-coverage-of-1995-okc-bombingw

I had some early success in Toronto, landing a major international consulting assignment with an Australia-based company looking to grow in the North American market. We agreed on a six-month contract, and based on how that went, I might join the team full-time as the CEO for North America—a role that would see me also gain a minority stake in the company. I jumped in with both feet and after a couple months evaluating the Canadian operations and getting to know the team, I travelled to Australia—back to Brisbane, where I had worked nearly twenty years earlier—to fully immerse myself in the business and to understand how I could bridge that success to Canada and the US.

It was a whirlwind three-week tour that saw us travel to Sydney to meet with some of the company's largest clients in the banking sector. The company I was working with had developed a proprietary audio-based training program targeted at call centres. The program had been designed to deliver audio content, mixed with music, in order to boost employee energy and motivation.

My first client meeting turned out to be memorable, to say the least. After touring a nearly one-thousand-seat call centre, we met the client representatives in a large boardroom. Most of them were responsible for human resources for the bank's many call centres. Their biggest issues were employee turnover, motivation, and building positive team dynamics—pretty standard call-centre issues.

The CEO of our company was taking the lead in presenting; I was there to observe and learn. He proceeded with the usual introductions and then jumped into the slide deck. He started describing how the company curated the music and made sure that offensive language was edited out of the songs as needed. "You don't have to worry about any of that," he noted. "We'll remove any words like *fuck*, *bitch*, or *nigger*." I was still a little jet-lagged but that woke me up fast. I looked around the room to see what impact his words had made. As often was the case, everyone else in attendance was white. Not one of them had flinched. He moved onto the next phase of his presentation without skipping a beat, wrapping up the meeting about forty-five minutes later, and the CEO, COO, and I were out the door.

My mind was whirling, and my mouth was dry. I was stunned. As we arrived at our car, I had to say something. I asked my two new coworkers if that line was part of their standard pitch. They said yes. I told them there was no way we would be using that kind of language in North America—especially pitching to human-resources audiences. I explained how that line would probably cause meetings to come to an abrupt end. They were surprised, and claimed there had been no ill intent behind what they'd said, but remained oblivious as to why it had been offensive. I finished out my initial consulting agreement but in the end, I passed on the CEO role. I'd continue my search for a company that seemed to share my ideals or, at the very least, was willing to learn how to do better.

∞

The great recession of 2008 was unexpected and it created challenges for me. My traditional US–based opportunities dried up and I had to hustle to keep the lights on, fishing in many small ponds for creative projects. In 2012, as the global economy picked up steam, I partnered with a veteran advertiser to form a hybrid advertising/strategic consulting agency. We lasted three years before our partnership imploded. I decided to go forward on my own, and after rejigging my business model, creative and business engagements started to return to normal. The renewed stability allowed me to spend a little more time focusing on my other interests, such as community work and politics.

In 2018 Toronto went to the polls to elect new councillors, with the current mayor, John Tory, seeking re-election. In my ward, the incumbent councillor was seeking a fourth mandate. I did not agree with him on most policy positions and I found his approach to public service to be non-inclusive; he seemed focused on the past rather than on the issues affecting his changing constituency. So when I was contacted to see if I'd be interested in supporting a female Tibetan Canadian candidate with a robust social justice portfolio to run against him, I said yes.

It was always going to be an uphill battle, but since I'd been immersed in politics for more than a dozen years, I knew it was necessary for our candidate to establish a political base now to have a chance at a future win. We assembled a talented team and developed a solid marketing and communications program that demonstrated our candidate's credibility and viability. We had some key political strategists with experience running campaigns, and we went to it. There were nine candidates, including the incumbent. Our learned evaluation gave us confidence our candidate was in a solid number-three position and could possibility inch up to second place if we ran a great campaign. We knew we'd need a miracle to unseat the incumbent.

Suddenly, a new candidate emerged. Lawn signs popped up by the hundreds with a name I had never heard before—and I had lived in the neighbourhood for nearly a decade. He was a middle-aged white man who didn't live in our district and whom I had never met at any community meeting, sports event, school PTA meeting—nothing. He was a nice guy with a thin policy agenda (and that's being generous), but he was backed by serious political insiders with deep pockets. Many of my neighbours asked me who he was and whether I was supporting him. I shared that I didn't know him, but that I was supporting a candidate with amazing credentials, a track record of community engagement, and a passion for helping marginalized people—a true member of our community. Most told me emphatically that they would take a serious look at my candidate because, like many, they were disenchanted with the incumbent councillor.

When the votes were counted, the incumbent had been re-elected with nearly 45 percent of the vote. My candidate had done very well, garnering 14 percent support—about 5,500 votes to the incumbent's nearly 17,000. None of this was a surprise to our team. What shocked me was that the come-from-nowhere candidate, who offered little and had no real stake in our community, garnered more than 8,000 votes, finishing in second place. How could this be?

I reflected on my conversations with many of my neighbours and wondered what had swayed some of them. I asked some people who had put a sign for this unknown candidate on their lawn. Many explained that they simply had seen lots of his signs in the neighbourhood and had jumped on the band-wagon. I can't be sure of the nuances behind each individual's voting decision, but there is one key difference between these two candidates which I believe factored into their decision: some voted for this little-known candidate simply because he was white, and my candidate was a person of colour. While most would probably not have considered their choice racially based, they may have allowed their inherent biases to lead them to a "safer" choice. I wasn't alone in coming to this conclusion. A disturbing conversation a couple weeks prior to the election had informed my perspective.

In an effort to boost our candidate's chances, I'd started working the phones in our electoral district. My focus was primarily on younger voters, who tended to be more open to change and diversity, and I hoped they'd connect with our candidate's progressive platform. One memorable call was with a well-edu-cated twentysomething who lived in a well-heeled neighbourhood. We'd met at several political events in recent years. I cut to the chase and asked if he'd consider supporting my candidate and help rally other young people in his network. His reply surprised me.

"Do you really think diversity is going to resonate with people in my neighbourhood?" he asked. "No one cares about that here." I was taken aback that a young person—and a self-declared progressive—would express such a dismissive opinion so casually. I asked him whether he remembered that I was Black. He went quiet. I then shared that our team had canvassed heavily in his neighbourhood and that people seemed very receptive to my candidate. I thanked him for his time and hung up.

This entire electoral experience shook me up a little. It showed me that even people with good intentions and progressive politics often fall back on what feels familiar and safe, rather than following through on their ideals and intentions. For me, this speaks to the fact that we have much more work to do to convince many white people to move beyond conscious or unconscious biases, and encourage them to walk their talk—especially when it comes to electing people of colour to positions of power.

I was also becoming increasingly frustrated by the false narrative some white people were perpetuating—that racial problems were mostly a thing of the past—completely ignoring the current lived realities of BIPOC across North America.

Just a few months before I began work on this book, many of my friends and colleagues were shocked when I shared the racist vitriol I had experienced in the national media. In October 2020, my opinion piece "If Canadians Hope to Achieve a More Just Society, Let Us Eliminate 'White Advantage'"[7] was published in Canada's paper of record, the *Globe and Mail*. I received lots of congratulatory messages from family, friends, and peers, and some even admitted they'd gained a new level of understanding on the issues of systemic racism and white privilege. Of course, most people read my piece on the *Globe*'s website. I decided to check out the response to the article online. Against the warnings of many, I scrolled down to see nearly 180 comments. I had only read a few before my mood turned sour and I had to stop.

In the months that followed, I continued to reflect on the many conversations I'd had, the conversations I'd overheard, and the ongoing discourse in the media about systemic racism. I heard many people continue to claim it was mostly an issue of the past. Canada had made much progress; racism was on the decline. "Why do we have to focus on the past and not on how things are better today?" was the common refrain. A few months into my writing process for this book, I decided to go back to that article's online comment section and assembled all the posts into one document that I could read and reference more easily.

I expect that most readers of the *Globe* generally stay away from the *National Enquirer*. In fact, the *Globe*'s readership is made up in large part of well-to-do businesspeople.[8] Every person who decides to comment is identified by their online handle, so while it's anonymous, an enterprising digital sleuth could find out who these commenters really are. My personal take is that as soon as you've commented, you've decided that you're comfortable sharing your views publicly—seemingly without a thought for the potential consequences. (In fact, I wrote an article a couple years back that focused on how a growing number of professionals were posting their personal political

7   "If Canadians hope to achieve a more just society, let us eliminate 'white advantage'" by Stephen Dorsey, *Globe and Mail*, October 9, 2020. theglobeandmail.com/opinion/article-if-we-hope-to-achieve-a-more-just-society-canadians-must-stop/

8   *The Globe and Mail Media Kit 2021*. globelink.ca/wp-content/uploads/2021/01/Globe-and-Mail-Newspaper-MediaKit-2021.pdf

views—in some cases, seething diatribes targeted at public officials and political parties—on LinkedIn[9] with total disregard for how their actions might be alienating potential employers or clients.) I thought I'd share some of the *Globe* comments to shed some light on the reality of racism in Canada today. Here are the "greatest hits."

pioneer27

...why are non-whites so eager to live in White countries?... Whites, via mass immigration, are in the process of bestowing their homelands to non-Whites. Normally, living things fight over territory rather than cede it voluntarily.

nsouthway

This is all left leaning thinking... we did not ask your kind to come here...

nsouthway

This is a white country..Its not our problem if you cannot put up with the disadvantage if so just don' come here.

Nome Cognome

Presumptive, entitled authors like this one are doing more to create racism than any avowedly racist organization ever has. Does the author have any idea how ridiculous he sounds and how much resentment is created by his unwillingness to accept responsibility for anything?

ALK8343

I feel as responsible for slavery as I do for the Spanish Inquisition; not at all. This is just another in a seemingly endless series of opinion pieces by or on behalf of recent immigrants who haven't immediately risen to the top (many have but they aren't the ones complaining). Life is hard work, no one owes you anything, let's move on.

---

[9] "What's happened to LinkedIn?" by Stephen Dorsey, *Medium*, March 19, 2019. medium.com/@ dorseyondigital/whats-happened-to-linkedin-65304e70ce23

canadian patriot 55

Why isn't this anti-white proposal branded racist?

RondeauGuy

Get over it. There have been injustices the world over.

Richard--Vancouver

I don't doubt that a black person in Quebec in the 1990s experienced racism. Perhaps he still would. But most of Canada has moved on since then. I certainly see this in my young adult children. Please don't tax them and their diverse peer group, in order to give the money to Mr Dorsey's family to buy real estate. Blackness is, by the way, very hip in Vancouver these days, for a variety of reasons, including the fact that it's a quality shared by only about 2% of the community. Curiously, the dozen or so black people I know, including the two black families living on our block, are well able to own their own houses.

CookeV

Martin Luther King Jr had a dream that people should be judged by the content of their character and not the colour of their skin. And here is an author calling for the exact opposite of MLK Jr. dream: doling out cash not based on a competitive business plan, but based on skin colour. And only one skin colour to boot! This author's proposals are blatantly racist, and he isn't even trying to hide that fact. I can only imagine MLK Jr turning over in his grave.

midası

Merit: that's the only advantage. Go over the same hurdles the nation-builders went over, and work as hard as they did. Then you'll get what you deserve, and deserve what you get.

app_69507493

All the wining is always about victimology and income redistribution, that will never work. Here's a much better solution. Personal responsibility and a focuss on the family unit. 7 out of 10 black families in the USA don't have a real father in the family. Proper parental mentorship will never be replaced by even the best social workers in the world...Parents have to do it !! What a concept... Must be racist.

Johnboy88

Everybody is a victim now.

ALBERTA FIRST CDN FEDERALIST

Many other non-Whites demographics seem to be doing spectacularly in Canada.

Asians in particular seem to be able to educate their kids, start businesses, buy real estate and build wealth.

They do not seem to be disproportionately involved in crime.

Were they subsidized and coddled?

Are they asking to be?

Kirk21

It is human nature to blame one's failings on external factors or other people. What has changed recently is that now the media is legitimizing this as part of its obsession with "systemic racism". We are teaching a generation of children that if they do not work hard enough to achieve their goals, they can blame "the system" and still achieve the same end result. This is not a healthy state for a society. We are now into the stage where people are calling for reparations for things which never happened.

It really is time for the silent rational majority to speak up.

MyOwnAccount

It must be nice to know that any failure in your life isn't your fault.

pioneer27

We don't know for certain how Floyd died. It may yet be revealed that he died of a self-inflicted heart attack, brought on a fentanyl overdose. From the autopsy reports this is a very real possibility.

rmac

Canadian society as a whole is becoming "less" racist...the author trots out the usual grievances from years before...sometimes decades before...people are getting sick of hearing about their perceived "white privilege"I, like many Canadians (Black included) have worked hard for what I have and rightfully should not apologize for that...laughably, the author cites some think tank's recommendation to pay reparations to the descendants of slaves....issue cheques to those who were never slaves from those who never held slaves

HeavyJetCaptain

No society in today's world is perfect. Given my experience, Canada is as just as a society as any other in the world, perhaps even more so. Is it perfect no, but everyone regardless of race, sex, sexual orientation, religion or whatever is given every opportunity to be successful and prosper. Governments of all levels have extensive programs in place to ensure everyone is accorded the same opportunities. It is what people do with these opportunities is what is important and that seems to be missed in many articles such as this one. More often than not it seems racism is a convenient crutch to account for failure. It certainly gets a politician's attention. But no, it isn't always somebody else's fault.

Sledder1205

Boo hoo hoo. It is hard to be successful. White peoples have everything handed to them. Everything is somebody else's fault

mtyeo

We can be equals after I've shamed you for some magical benefit you get for being white that I've never demonstrated, and knocked you down a peg or two so that I feel better about things. THEN we can be equals.

It's an asinine argument.

comcon

They are an underperforming demographic and I think much of it is in their control, their lot due to their behaviours and choices. Too many aspiring "musicians". Forgive the bluntness and barely camouflaged mock, but I am sick of it.

These comments are from people who were motivated to make their views public. There are many others who choose to espouse their views in more private venues. The point is, this is the vitriol that Black people are subjected to on a regular basis. Imagine the impact of hearing that negative chorus every day. The "advantage" here for white people is that they are not subjected to this barrage of hate-fuelled narratives simply because of their white skin.

I often make my friends laugh when I tell them some of the things white people have said to me—often with no ill intent. I've heard, "You're so articulate," hundreds of times in my professional life. Of course I'm articulate—I am an educated, experienced professional. In contrast, what most white colleagues hear first are things like "great presentation" or "well done." The key difference here is the tone—it's a compliment that comes from a place of *surprise*—as if my achievement has been unexpected. The conscious and unconscious biases of many white people lead them to judge me against a prejudice that most Black people are not articulate, not well-educated. Whatever the motivation, as the person receiving these backhanded compliments, it's offensive. This is yet another pervasive kind of microaggression, and is just one example of the doublespeak that most Black people have had to endure over the years. Of course, most Black people in this situation would likely do what I've traditionally done—shrug it off, change the conversation, and move on.

As a Black man, how am I supposed to move on? How do we, as people of colour, ignore this added challenge in our lives? Black people are not a monolith; we don't all deal with racism in the same way. We are not even all the same colour. We are individuals with diverse views on an issue that unites us. White people who want to be allies need to keep this in mind. There is no one-size-fits-all approach to connecting with "the Black community" or to understanding the many diverse individuals within it.

It will take more effort, but I believe it's the best route to reaching more constructive and positive results. For those open to allyship, simply starting conversations with people from BIPOC communities is a good first step. (More on this in the final chapter.)

∞

The examples of racial discrimination I've noted in this chapter are meant to illuminate the reality of being Black in a white world. I'm not suggesting that I have not also had amazing experiences throughout my life and my career. Most of the time, I was welcomed warmly by white friends and strangers, forged long-time personal and professional friendships, and achieved success as a collaborative member of amazing teams.

That said, I have had to push back against much stronger headwinds than my white counterparts. But I've continued to work extremely hard because I enjoy what I do, and I am driven to achieve. Has that been twice as hard? Who knows? What I do know is that I've had to waste untold energy to navigate a path strewn with obstacles that should not have been there—obstacles that remain for many racialized people and communities within so-called advanced democracies like Canada and the United States. And they'll remain until we are truly seen, heard, and supported by those very systems that continue to disadvantage us.

Chapter Ten

Be Better. Do Better. Live Better, Together.

THERE ARE MOMENTS IN OUR LIVES, MOMENTS IN HISTORY, THAT AWAKEN US. As previously shared, my personal awakening was triggered by the racial reckoning of 2020 sparked by the killing of George Floyd. As an unarmed Black man killed by the excessive use of force by police, Floyd was but one link in a seemingly infinite chain of Black people who have had their lives cut short because of racism. But as we've witnessed, something was different in 2020—the access to instant "proof" of the crime, video of the gruesome event accessible to millions around the globe in a matter of minutes. Traditional media followed suit and this global spotlight was a catalyst for awareness. People of all colours and backgrounds began to see anti-Black racism in a new light. It seemed impossible, now, to deny the truth.

The global discourse conjured by this moment caused many non-BIPOC to become more aware of racial inequality; some, ingrained in the systems that traditionally enable many white people to stay in a bubble of unawareness, were now considering the issue for the first time. But for members of the Black community, the reality of anti-Black racism is nothing new. It has been a pervasive, everyday reality for generations all over the world.

So now, nearly two years later, where does this leave us?

As with all historical milestones, time and distraction have a way of dulling our collective memory. In a world dominated by twenty-four-hour news cycles and instant access to information, it seems to take the ripple effect of serial tragedy to keep our attention. The COVID-19 pandemic diverted attention from the Black Lives Matter movement and the call for equality, but we need to remember that racial inequity persists. We shouldn't have to wait for these tragic and unnecessary deaths to propel us into action.

We need allies. We need you.

Throughout this book, you've learned about the pervasive nature of systemic racism across North America, in everything from education to health care to the criminal justice system. You may be feeling overwhelmed by all of this—that's to be expected. You may be feeling like you can't do anything, but the reality is we all have something to contribute. We are all necessary to the dismantling of systemic racism. And when you act, you are signalling to others that change is possible.

Because we all understand information differently, it's important to try and unpack the issue of systemic racism in a way that works for each of us—to look at it through a lens that we understand well. For me, that's marketing. A few years ago, my friend Ron Tite published the bestselling business book *Think. Do. Say.: How to Seize Attention and Build Trust in a Busy, Busy World*. In it, he suggests how brands can earn consumers' trust–by first doing the work to rally their organizations around their true purpose (*thinking*); then by taking action by creating organizational systems to help achieve that purpose in an authentic and meaningful way (*doing*); and finally by communicating that purpose, in a relevant and engaging manner, to the marketplace (*saying*).

This framework resonated with me first on a professional level, as it aligned with my approach to positioning successful brands in the marketplace. But I was reminded of Ron's work when considering how to best rally people around gaining a more thorough understanding systemic racism, and inspiring them to take deliberate action.

Here's what I landed on: *Be Better. Do Better. Live Better, Together.*

To Be Better is to push ourselves to become more aware of systemic racism, to seek a more fulsome understanding of the lived realities of BIPOC communities, and to acknowledge the truth—and lasting impacts—of historical wrongs. Ideally, this purposeful journey of understanding will lead each of us to our own personal awakening, and will compel us to Do Better.

To Do Better is to *do the work*—and that means moving from thought to action. Actions can be small to start with, individual or collective, but the ultimate goal is to achieve tangible, long-lasting change, for a more just and equal society.

Living Better Together is the ideal outcome, a collective future we should aspire to once we have done the heavy lifting to dismantle systemic racism. It is about the promise of a better world, where we can all live in greater harmony, lift each other up, and celebrate each other's uniqueness. A world where no one is left behind because of the colour of their skin, their ethnic or religious background, gender, ability, or sexual orientation. You have to first imagine that world before you can work toward creating it.

∞

BE BETTER

Broadening Awareness

We can all be better versions of ourselves, and this starts with becoming more aware of the world around us through purposeful discovery. It takes more work to walk purposefully through life, aware of the bad, the unjust, the inequitable. But change doesn't come without awareness, and it is a *choice* that must be consciously made. As retired Canadian Senator Don Oliver (the first Black man to be appointed as a Senator in Canada) put it succinctly in his recently published, must-read book, *A Matter of Equality*, quoting Socrates, "the unexamined life is not worth living."[1]

In the wake of the Black Lives Matter movement and the George Floyd tragedy, many white people dipped a toe into the pool of anti-Black racism awareness; we now need you to jump in with both feet. Some have already moved beyond demonstrating their genuine support on social media and within their community and are now engaging more actively; they are reaching out to BIPOC people in their network to listen and learn, they're reading books and articles by BIPOC writers, and they're having difficult conversations with their peers, friends, and family, working to share what they've learned so far and further develop their own point of view. All good.

We need more non-BIPOC people to follow their lead. Systemic racism is not something we can fix overnight; it will impact all of us for their rest of our lives. Those just awakening to the harsh realities of the pervasiveness of racism need to work through their own pain in order to fully understand the issues at play, and to be a true ally to the BIPOC community. As noted previously, it won't be a one-approach-fits-all situation. We have to learn to communicate with each other on an individual, and communal, basis. It's going to be a heavy lift and it must be a collective, inclusive effort. And as it stands now, both public and private institutions are not keeping up.

So that's the big picture, at a national level. But we also need to encourage communities to engage at the grassroots level—in the neighborhoods where we live, where we play, and where we raise our families. We need to not only highlight the big issues but examine how they manifest in the very places where we are building and shaping communities. The question to ask ourselves is: where do I fit into this equation and what role can I play?

---

[1] *A Matter of Equality* by Senator Donald Oliver, Halifax: Nimbus Publishing, 2021.

I'll give you a personal example. In Toronto, we're lucky to have Business Improvement Areas (BIAs). A BIA is a collective made up of commercial property owners who work with the City of Toronto "to create thriving, competitive, and safe business areas" with the goal of attracting customers, tourists, and other new businesses.[2] The ultimate goal is civic improvement, and enhanced quality of life for the community. In 2020, my local BIA, Roncesvalles Village, formed a Social Justice and Anti-Racism committee, with the goal of helping to "remove barriers to equity, diversity and prosperity in our community, particularly for Black and Indigenous people and other marginalized groups."[3] The BIA focused on "creating and providing tools, resources and access to information...to empower business owners and community members to build a neighbourhood that celebrates unique voices and stands up to racism, hate speech, and social injustice.

In the past year, I've seen a tangible increase in local businesses visually expressing their support for the BIPOC community through themed window displays and postering of informative, anti-racist content—a small sign of increased awareness and tangible action.

This is just one example of a communal approach. Some people might seek out other community-based initiatives through rotary clubs, chambers of commerce, faith-based congregations, and local non-profit organizations. And let's not forget our places of work. Many companies lack diversity, equity, and inclusion (DE&I) mandates and training. Does your workplace have HR policies concerning DE&I? When's the last time they evaluated their hiring practices? Have you and other employees had access to anti-racism training?

Any corporation worth its salt is looking to Do Better. Maybe your workplace needs a nudge.

If you're reading this book, you're moving in the right direction. Keep going. Be the voice of change within your workplace, your community, your peer groups.

Acknowledging Truths

Achieving real change cannot be done without an acknowledgement of societal truths. This can be a difficult leap for non-BIPOC to make, especially given that some of the wrongs are deeply rooted in historical policies they may not be aware of. Because of this, when racism is raised people tend to deflect and become defensive, asking questions like, "I wasn't alive back then, so why are

---

2   "What is a BIA?" Toronto Association of Business Improvement Areas (n.d.). toronto-bia.com/whats-a-bia

3   "Social Justice and Anti-Racism Committee," Roncesvalles Village BIA (n.d.). roncesvallesvillage.ca/social-justice-anti-racism-committee

you blaming me?" Those who are just coming into an awareness of systemic racism will need to reconcile the reality that the very same institutions they perceived as doing good, may be perpetuating racism.

Unfortunately, acknowledging truth today seems to be negotiable. We have found ourselves at crucial crossroads where millions of people can't seem to agree on the same facts—let alone on what the truth is. As we've seen, this has created a dangerous situation in liberal democracies around the world, with some people refusing to acknowledge the results of an election and others convinced the COVID-19 virus is a hoax and that the science supporting the use of masks and vaccines is more about restricting civil liberties rather than saving lives. Regardless of where we stand, a lack of alignment on "truth" leads to disfunction, mistrust, and tribal behaviour. We've seen how this can manifest in extremist actions that endanger all of us—the assault on the US Capitol in Washington being a perfect example of how lies (in this case, that the election was "stolen") can have devastating consequences.

For members of the BIPOC community, the frustration around "truth" is exasperating. We are tired of hearing that there is no racism in Canada or America. Yes, not every Canadian or American is racist, but as the stories in this book reveal, to say that no citizens of these countries are racist, or that their systems do not disadvantage BIPOC, is false. To deny that systemic racism exists is to also ignore the mountain of data (some of which I've detailed in previous chapters) and the historical facts that validate the truth. Systemic racism, the most serious form of discrimination against marginalized communities, is baked into the foundations of the institutions that govern our society, including the criminal justice system.

When it comes to issues of race discrimination, convenient untruths—statements like "there is no systemic racism, it's just a few bad apples"—still too often win out the day; it is our job as allies to both acknowledge and remind others of the ugly truth. Easier said than done, I get it. But this step cannot be skipped. As the renowned twentieth-century Black American novelist, poet, and activist James Baldwin said, "Not everything that is faced can be changed, but nothing can be changed until its faced."

Your Awakening

As more allies acknowledge the truth of racial discrimination by actively listening, learning, and gaining a broader and deeper understanding of systemic racism, they will no doubt arrive at an inflection point in their own awakening. This is when there is a shift from being *not racist* to being *anti-racist*. The former is a passive state, while the latter is a proactive state that is characterized by action—doing or saying something when racism rears its ugly head.

I already see this happening in what you could call "early adopters." Their awakening is not so dissimilar to my own: a mixed bag of disparate emotions triggered by a realization—sadness and anger in realizing that racialized people, fellow citizens, continue to be disadvantaged in our "multicultural" country. When you look back through history, these watershed moments of collective truth-making, moments that mobilize and awaken, often occur.

In Canada, we recently observed this when the unmarked graves of 215 residential school students were discovered and the news was reported globally. But we need to learn our lesson from the silence that preceded this tragedy. It's not that Indigenous people hadn't told us for decades that thousands of children had disappeared in residential schools over nearly a century of oppression; many of us just hadn't listened. As with the response to George Floyd's murder, the heightened awareness of the "news" of Indigenous children dying by the thousands in Indian Residential Schools became a *collective truth*, one that was impossible to ignore any longer.

For some, this was the moment of their awakening. I heard many express feelings of shame after hearing the news—shame that the society they believed was a bastion of equality was, in fact, a whitewashed narrative told for centuries by the white elite who dictated their preferred version of the truth. They wondered why their government, their education system, the judicial system, and other institutions they had respected and accepted as good were in fact systemically complicit in the many lies. "How could this have happened?" I heard many ask. "I knew nothing about any of this," others claimed. I empathized with their sense of genuine disbelief.

I felt the same way regarding other issues of systemic inequality where race was not the central issue, and for the most part, did not affect me directly. As someone who came of age in the 1980s, I saw first-hand how women with the same skills and potential were not treated equally to men in the workforce. I never understood why this was, so I never gave gender a thought in my decades building teams and promoting talent. But I did observe how female colleagues' careers were hampered by the simple fact that they were women. It took another generational uprising via the MeToo movement to remind many of us that much more work still has to be done—including pay equity and the dismantling of gender-based power dynamics that continue to both disadvantage women and put them at risk.

There are many more examples of systemic inequality I have not touched on that continue to negatively affect women, members of the LBGTQIA+ community, and people with disabilities. And there's often overlap, or intersectionality, between members of these communities. That's why it's important for us to acknowledge and address systemic inequalities wherever they exist. To Be Better is an important foundational objective, but we must go further and Do Better.

DO BETTER

In former president Barack Obama's 2020 book, *A Promised Land*, he describes visiting a majority Black high school in Dillon, South Carolina. Like Vic High, it's a school that traces its history back to the nineteenth century. He reflects on witnessing first-hand the school's dilapidated state:

> What message had generations of boys and girls received as they arrived at this school each day? Except for the certainty that to those in power, they didn't matter. Whatever was meant by the American dream, it wasn't meant for them.[4]

The decades of neglect I highlighted at my former high school is a parallel example of the negative impact that such neglect imposes on the formation of a young person's identity. What struck me as we fought to seek equity for the socio-economically disadvantaged students in Victoria was the extraordinary efforts to which that the powers that be (the city, the school district) went to preserve the status quo. It didn't seem to matter that the policies they continued to champion advantaged some while severely disadvantaging others. And the members of the public who should have been asking the hard questions were either not paying attention or just simply not interested.

The latter really bothered me. I was perplexed by Victorians' apathy around this issue. We did rally more than a thousand people to sign our online petition and a few hundred more to support us on Facebook; a few journalists gave us ink and airtime, and a couple of trustees and city councillors let us know they were sympathetic. We had worked hard to make information readily available on social media, had made our case numerous times in mass media, and even took out a full page ad in the daily newspaper, publishing an open letter signed by luminaries from the worlds of sports and academia to share a message about the importance of providing equal opportunity and support to all students—not just those the system deems more deserving.

Systemic inequality in the city's education system seemed to be relative non-issue in the public eye—until the alert was sounded in a very public way in the summer of 2021. Tangible examples of systemic racism were made public by Indigenous leaders engaged with the school district, leading to a slew of resignations.[5] In fall 2021, I was pleasantly surprised to see parents (many of whom represented Parent Advisory Committees) rally to try to save music and art programs in Victoria when the school district made plans to

---

[4] *A Promised Land* by Barack Obama, New York: Crown, 2020.

[5] "'Pattern of systemic racism': SD61 Indigenous committee member resigns, calls for change" by Jane Skyrpnek, *Victoria News*, May 14, 2021. vicnews.com/community/pattern-of-systemic-racism-sd61-indigenous-committee-member-resigns-calls-for-change

eliminate them, citing budgetary concerns. It gave me hope that if we could raise awareness of systemic inequality, we could mobilize these same passionate parents to take action to help eliminate it.

Closer to home, I've always been inspired by the high level of engagement in my west-end Toronto neighbourhood. People show up to engage in civic affairs—especially when they believe policies may have a direct impact on their families and community. They support fundraising efforts for local parks and community centres and advocate for their children, and by doing so they keep the powers that be—local politicians, school boards, administrators—in check; by Doing Better themselves, they are asking those who control the systems to continually to Do Better, too. So now my question is: what stops some individuals and communities from jumping in full-force?

I must admit that I wasn't always aware of the severity of the socioeconomic inequalities experienced by generations of Vic High students. It's not that I was unaware of the growing income inequality in our society, but I was more focused on my own life and the community where I live, four thousand kilometres away. But then I started to pay attention. I had a desire to Do Better, and this awareness propelled me to understand the situation more fully and take action.

I asked myself: in what unique way can I help? What are the skills and the contacts I can contribute? I decided to use my experience as a communicator and strategist to organize and mobilize allies, and along with many others, to work to persuade the people in power to make change—to set aside their status-quo thinking and at minimum, acknowledge the realities of systemic inequality in their midst. And it didn't stop there; my new allies and I continue to advocate for change.

Now that you know more—even if simply from reading this book—how will you propel yourself to Do Better? Let's start here: I challenge you to identify three small actions you could take *right now*.

One way to Do Better and eliminate social inequalities is to demand that leadership Do Better, too! Part of Doing Better is holding others accountable—creating a community of care. When it comes to the politicians you support, ensure equity is one of their central concerns, and hold them to account: when they put forth policies, when they engage with private partners, and when they propose new plans for your community. You must make this your responsibility. Don't just leave it to others.

Now is the time to ask yourself some key questions. What matters to you? What do you stand for? What are you willing to put on the line for your family, for your fellow citizens? We don't all have the capacity to act in the same manner or perhaps with the same vigour as others, but we all have a voice, talents, and expertise; we can each do our part to bring about change.

What will inspire or move you to Do Better? What values do you live by that compel you to take action to fight for what's right, to help a friend, a family member, a stranger, people who think differently than you? Many people I know hold values that are rooted in their faith, which, from my non-religious (yet spiritual) perspective, can be summarized by the Golden Rule: Do unto others as you would have them do unto you.

What commitments to ending systemic racism are you willing to make based on your values—the commandments by which you live? How are you modelling those values in your family and in the wider community? How are you standing up for members of the BIPOC community in your everyday life? Do you say something when you hear someone say something racist, or do you say nothing and continue on your way? What happens at Thanksgiving when a relative recounts their racist joke for the umpteenth time in front of your children? Do you take another bite of your turkey, or do you say something? Will you speak out or worry more about making others at the table feel uncomfortable? Hopefully, letting things pass will become a thing of the past.

The Thanksgiving scenario seems to be a popular example, as it is where many of us often come face to face with racism in our own families. I know all about that. One effective response that I heard at a recent anti-oppression workshop[6] is, "That person is still learning." This simple phrase is a great way to say something in the moment while modelling to everyone around you that it's never okay to espouse racist sentiments—and that if you do, you will be challenged. It promises the possibility of better, of changing that person's attitude and behaviour. Remember that this is a journey—dismantling systemic racism is a life's work, and some of us are farther ahead than others.

In what other ways can you Do Better? If you're someone who owns rental property, consider renting to a racialized person—especially if you've never done so before. The hardware store owner in my own neighbourhood told me, "No person of colour has ever applied for a job in my store." If his answer resonates with you as a business owner, then perhaps you should specifically encourage qualified candidates from the BIPOC community to apply.

Another easy way of contributing is by paying attention to your purchasing power. We are all consumers, whether we like to admit it or not. We can very easily contribute to positive change in our communities by discovering, supporting, and promoting local BIPOC-owned businesses. What a great, tangible way to create and sustain more diverse neighbourhoods.

While it might seem like a small step, I believe that some of the most impactful change we can make is in our local communities. This is informed in part by my own lived experience. As a volunteer director of my

---

[6]   Anti-oppression Zoom workshop by Rania El Mugammar for Fern Public School parents, May 19, 2021.

neighbourhood's Friends of Sorauren Park (FOSP) group, I know first-hand how community engagement can enhance a community.

As in many cities across North America, Toronto's municipal government has scaled back funding for parks programming due to budget constraints. Non-profit community organizations across the city, like the one I am part of, have filled the gaps. Before the FOSP became involved, the park was actually a works yard for Toronto City buses. It was the community's years-long lobbying efforts that finally convinced the city to turn the land into a park.

The FOSP raised funds to purchase professional movie equipment and has hosted movie nights in the park for more than five years now, bringing the community together during the summer months; we've simulcast concerts and Raptors playoff matches, drawing thousands; we've fundraised to build an outdoor pizza oven; and for more than a decade, our volunteer "hosers" have maintained an ice rink all winter. What has surprised me over the years is how some of my neighbours continue to be unaware of how all these good things happen in our community. I let them know that while the City supports us, it's community volunteers doing the heavy lifting—neighbours just like them, who put in the time and effort to make these community activities a reality.

All of this is to say that you can't wait for others to do the work for you, and this is also true when it comes to addressing systemic racism and inequality. If you've never been involved in community-building, what better time to begin? We all have unique skills and expertise. If your skill is bringing people together, organize a neighbourhood group or a rally for change. If your skill is painting, make signs for the next rally in your neighbourhood and share them. If your skill is baking, consider hosting a bake sale and donating the proceeds to an organization pushing for change. You can also Do Better by diversifying your friend groups, your book club, your pickup hockey or basketball team. Take a course in Black history. Read BIPOC-authored books with your children. It will make a difference. Take that first step and engage with purpose. If you are a community leader, this is your opportunity to inspire others to take steps to address systemic inequality where you live. Bring diverse people together to share and learn. And if the space you wish for doesn't exist, gather some like-minded folks and create it.

Inevitably, as we collectively move forward to effect change, we will face some obstacles along the way. We'll have to overcome, maybe start again sometimes, but we need to keep moving forward.

How Governments Can Do Better

My perspective has also been informed by speaking with activists on the front lines, with academics and civic leaders, and by doing the research work for this book. COVID-19 was never far from my mind, and I couldn't help but notice the communication strategies Canada's federal and provincial governments used throughout the pandemic. A variety of campaigns to increase awareness, explain prevention, and address misinformation[7] were launched across the country through advertising, paid partnerships, social marketing, and targeted marketing to at-risk populations, with the ultimate goal of protecting Canadians.

Significant resources were invested in order to educate and inform people across the country about basic prevention methods, such as the importance of handwashing, social distancing, and mask-wearing. More complicated messages related to vaccination and vaccine efficacy followed and, in the summer of 2021, we started to see more customized messaging in an attempt to persuade vaccine-hesitant Canadians.

Why couldn't a similar communications strategy be undertaken to address systemic racism? Proactive, sustained, and multi-faceted communications programs are key to building a critical level of awareness across Canada, and can set the stage for more informed discussions.

We are seeing more large corporations, NGOs, and non-profits taking more substantive and determined steps forward to raise awareness of the importance of diversity, equity, and inclusion, and some are even modifying their guiding principles and business processes. We often hear how small businesses are the engine of the economy, but they should also be engines for change. Access to educational materials and tools to address systemic inequality—such as those the federal and provincial governments could create—would be of benefit for smaller organizations that don't have the resources or capacity to develop their own. NGOs, chambers of commerce, trade associations, and unions across North America could help raise awareness and educate their memberships so that they can in turn, better navigate the complex realities of systemic racism and its impact within their institutions.

In the US for example, a broad, bipartisan group of legislators in congress, led by Senator Cory Booker and congressional representative Barbara Lee, have rallied, endorsed, and promoted legislation since early 2021, based on the community-based framework "Truth, Racial Healing & Transformation (TRHT)," designed at the Kellogg Foundation.[8] At its core, the TRHT is a

---

7   "Coronavirus disease (COVID-19): Canada's response," Government of Canada (n.d.). canada.ca/en/public-health/services/diseases/2019-novel-coronavirus-infection/canadas-reponse.html#:~:text=Public%20education%20plays%20a%20critical,to%20at%2Drisk%20populations

8   "Truth, Racial Healing & Transformation," W. K. Kellogg Foundation (n.d.). healourcommunities.org

"comprehensive, national and community-based process to plan for and bring about transformational and sustainable change, and to address the historic and contemporary effects of racism." It is in part focused on creating "a narrative change" to redefine the stories of racialized people and propagate new understandings across all media channels, all with the goal of working towards "community-based change."

This aligns with much of what we've discussed: the importance of focusing time and investment on public education and awareness by broadly communicating the complete story (the truths) of our history. We are seeing some progress on this front already, but we need much broader action, and at an accelerated pace.

"Racial Healing and Relationship Building," another key element of the TRHT framework, is focused on collective healing from past wounds and the building of "mutually respectful relationships across racial and ethnic lines that honor and value each person's humanity."[9] In short, this is about how individuals can Do Better when they are offered a standardized framework and supported by community agents to take steps to bridge divides.

In Canada, the Canadian Race Relations Foundation (CRRF), an arm's-length Crown corporation, is the leading agency "dedicated to the elimination of racism and all forms of racial discrimination in Canadian society." As part of its mandate, the foundation is instituting a national framework in order to bridge governments, organizations, and leaders in order to "further anti-racism efforts and initiate and maintain meaningful partnerships."

It shares many elements with the TRHT framework, but includes the direct organizational and administrative support of the federal government. In 2020, the CRRF announced a grant program via its Community Mobilization Fund to support projects targeting anti-Black, anti-Asian, and anti-Indigenous racism. This includes grassroots and local not-for-profit organizations that may use the grants to advocate for racialized communities and create campaigns to raise awareness around racism. In April 2021, the foundation received a two-year funding commitment from the federal government of $11.2 million[10], part of which will support the Community Mobilization Fund's grant program. This was a "clear expression of confidence"[11] that the foundation's efforts to support advocacy and raise awareness about racism and inequality at the community level was making a positive impact.

---

[9] *Ibid.*

[10] "The Canadian Race Relations Foundation welcomes the announcement of an $11.2M investment from the Government of Canada," Canadian Race Relations Foundation, April 27, 2021. crrf-fcrr.ca/en/news-a-events/articles/item/27378-the-canadian-race-relations-foundation-welcomes-the-announcement-of-an-11-2m-investment-from-the-government-of-canada

[11] *Ibid.*

Some may suggest that this is just a drop in the bucket when we look at the work that must be done, but I'd caution against criticizing efforts of any kind lest we discourage others from stepping forward. We should encourage positive action, big or small, and then work together to advocate for much more. We need to begin somewhere.

Efforts to dismantle systemic racism at the community level will require support from governments that have the legislative power to provide the policy and legal runways for systemic change to take off. The community-based TRHT model was devised to build community momentum into a transformative national movement in the US, but it will require the support of government policy-makers and legislators.

In February 2021, US Congresswoman Barbara Lee reintroduced legislation to form a TRHT Commission. The objective is for legislators to assemble ideas on how government, working with grassroots organizations, can use TRHT as a roadmap for transforming various social systems—for example, to make the education system more inclusive of racialized students and faculty through the implementation of new curricula "establishing safe public spaces for cultural dialogue." And of course, the goal includes securing federal resources to "support and amplify" these community-led efforts.[12]

How Corporations Can Do Better

Outside of governments and communities, corporations in North America can also play a transformative role in society by embracing and incorporating diversity, equity, and inclusion (DE&I) within their organizations.

In late summer 2021 a colleague working with a major trade association asked me to recommend speakers to help lead an online seminar series on DE&I. This series would be targeted at mid-level professionals across Canada. I saw this as a good opportunity to "share and teach" while also getting a better sense as to how systemic racism was impacting businesses on the ground, so I investigated further. A couple of weeks later, I connected with the seminar organizer to convey my interest and learn more about the series. I learned that the initial focus was on finding speakers that could share the challenges and opportunities of "positioning" DE&I in the marketplace.

This started a very interesting conversation. I told her that I didn't believe I would be the right person for her specific needs as my focus was not on *promoting* diversity to consumers as if it were a product, but on helping clients

---

12 "'No healing without the truth': How a federal commission could help America understand systemic racism" by Rachel Ramirez, *Vox*, March 4, 2021. vox.com/22308043/truth-healing-commission-systemic-racism-barbara-lee

achieve deep and long-term allyship by aligning their corporate values with tangible organizational change that could help achieve DE&I objectives. More importantly, I suggested a conversation with seminar participants should begin with an examination of the corporate values within their organization. This resonated with her, and she admitted she'd received a similar response from the other leaders she had approached.

In the same conversation, I related an experience with one of my long-time clients, which had occurred just a few weeks after the George Floyd murder. Like many organizations, this particular client, who operates a successful franchise-based business in the GTA, wanted to convey their support for the Black Lives Matter movement. As a long-time strategic consultant to the company, I had become an integral part of—and the only person of colour on—the small management team.

One of my colleagues, Kim, a key senior member of the team responsible for elevating the brand, advocated for the organization to take a stand and do something rather than sit on the sidelines. At a management meeting just days after our initial conversation, it was agreed that I should take the lead, in collaboration with Kim, to define a path forward for the organization. We agreed that we should take the time to fully understand the reasoning behind our intended actions before making any public statements to ensure we stayed clear of "performative allyship," and that our actions would be seen for what they were—genuine.

My client, like many other successful businesses, had operated for years with no formalized guiding principles. That said, there was a genuine feeling that the brand should be a good corporate citizen, grounded in demonstrated positive values. Kim and I agreed that before the organization could take any action toward public support for the BLM movement, we should take the time to not only codify the organizational values but also secure a commitment from leadership; we had to know that it wouldn't just be *talk*—that leadership would stand behind those values and support them with adequate resources to ensure they were championed company-wide.

To his credit, the founder of the company immediately embraced the formal values we had defined as a team—including commitments to honesty, transparency, accountability, and authenticity—and committed to providing short- and long-term resources to achieve those objectives. A commitment to diversity and inclusion was now a core company value.

It was important to us to be transparent about the organization standing in solidary with the Black Lives Matter movement, but we also wanted to ensure we didn't take any action until the management team had taken time to fully reflect on the realities of diversity, equity, and inclusion within the organization. Only then would the company be able to take tangible steps toward positive change.

As a result of doing this critical foundational work, weeks later we were able to make public our plans to support key organizations in Toronto that were already making an impact in the Black community. We were also able to make clear the company's genuine commitment to do more in the long term by developing and implementing a diversity, equity, and inclusion practice as we grew and scaled the organization's operational capacities. The entire effort was authentic, grounded in a true desire to Do Better.

As I covered more extensively in a previous chapter, much of the change needed to eliminate systemic inequality will likely happen much faster in the corporate world than within public and governmental institutions. Corporations are nimbler and are better positioned to respond quickly to market forces, such as customers' evolving values.

Even before COVID-19, businesses seemed to be doing a lot more to attract the best talent—increasing minimum wages, benefits, and offering more flexibility on how and where employees could choose to work. A rise in social consciousness has led many workers to seek out organizations that demonstrate a commitment to diversity and inclusion—organizations that are walking the talk.

It's become a popular sport for Generation Xers and Baby Boomers to chide the Gen Y (Millennial) and Gen Z generations for being "entitled" and "unfocused," especially as it relates to career, loyalty to employers, or commitment to finding "fulfilling" work. But the reality is they are the generational underdogs. Elder Millennials came of age during the 2008 financial crisis, the Great Recession, which saw rising tuition costs and slow wage growth, leading them to become known as the "student debt generation."[13] There is also a large generational wealth gap between Generations X and Y. Consider the rate of debt-to-after-tax income in members of Gen X versus Gen Y. According to Statistics Canada, in 1999 the rate for Gen Xers was 125 percent, while in 2016 for Millennials it was 216 percent.[14]

Perhaps it is because they come from this socially marginalized perspective that these younger generations understood something early on that many of us missed or ignored. Studies have shown that Gen Z individuals in particular take a more "values driven" approach to their careers, and are more likely to seek out a workplace "aligned with their personal morals."[15]

[13] "Half of older millennials with student debt say their loans weren't worth it" by Abigail Johnson Hess, *CNBC.com*, April 8, 2021. cnbc.com/2021/04/08/older-millennials-with-student-debt-say-their-loans-werent-worth-it.html

[14] "Millennials & Debt: Dealing with the Millennial Wealth Gap, by Anna Guglielmi, Credit Canada, September 10, 2021. creditcanada.com/blog/dealing-with-the-millennial-wealth-gap

[15] "How Gen-Z Is Bringing A Fresh Perspective To The World Of Work" by Ashley Stahl, *Forbes.com*, May 4, 2021. forbes.com/sites/ashleystahl/2021/05/04/how-gen-z-is-bringing-a-fresh-perspective-to-the-world-of-work/?sh=68edbf5710c2

While "pay" is still the number-one job priority for Gen Z, they seem much more willing than generations past to consider their personal politics when shopping the job market. It would appear that they have a generational Do Better attitude, and they're changing their workplaces for the better because of it.[16]

In an era where corporations are now in hand-to-hand combat for global talent,[17] there is a real window of opportunity for workers to demand change to help transform the corporate world into a more equal and socially just pilar of modern society. No matter what generation you belong to, we can all take a page out of Gen Z's book. If you're just starting your career, seek out organizations with values that align with your own. Support businesses that champion equality and opportunity for all. Do Better by demanding better from the organizations you work with.

If you're someone in a mid-career role with a voice at the table, this is your time to push for action to accelerate change around DE&I. Demonstrate your leadership skills by ensuring project teams you are leading are inclusive and diverse. Embrace and advocate for racial-sensitivity training that could help transform your workplace into an agent for change.

If you're a corporate executive with the responsibility to define, implement, or drive DE&I change forward, you need to walk your talk. You need to champion leadership and mentoring programs for BIPOC and other traditionally marginalized employees. You must ensure that your pool of talent becomes more reflective of our diverse society. Institute a BIPOC sponsorship program, and celebrate successful client wins by diverse teams. Lead your organization by taking a public stand to support BIPOC communities and call out racial discrimination. Do so even if you believe it may be a risk to your brand. Be bold and courageous.

Just do it. Nike did.

In September 2016 Colin Kaepernick, then quarterback for the San Francisco 49ers, took a knee during the US national anthem before a game to protest police brutality and racial inequality. While the 49ers released an official statement recognizing Kaepernick's First Amendment rights, his protest sparked an intense backlash in the public—particularly from veterans and military supporters, who viewed the kneeling as unpatriotic.[18] By the end of the season, Kaepernick opted out of his contract and no other teams picked him up.

---

[16] *Ibid.*

[17] "In The War For Talent, Competition Has Never Been So Fierce" by Jon Bostock, *Forbes.com*, July 20, 2021. forbes.com/sites/forbesbusinesscouncil/2021/07/20/in-the-war-for-talent-competition-has-never-been-so-fierce/?sh=3ab0f268118b

[18] "The backlash over Colin Kaepernick is just Americans' refusal to acknowledge racism — again" by Victoria M. Massie, *Vox*, October 16, 2016. vox.com/identities/2016/10/13/12710860/colin-kaepernick-anthem-protest-explained

The NFL went on to impose a rule banning kneeling during the anthem in May 2018, attempting to put an end to the peaceful anti-racist protest.

Nike, a multi-billion-dollar corporation, made the choice to support Kaepernick by creating the social justice campaign "Believe in something. Even if it means sacrificing everything," calling for all to stand up against systemic racism. Many pundits said it was too risky for Nike and would harm its global brand. However, weeks after the campaign launched, Nike reported a 31 percent increase in online sales[19] and the brand has since become a textbook example of corporate social justice advocacy.

The NFL, also a multi-billion-dollar corporation, took a different approach entirely. Team owners worried more about lost revenue from angry fans than they did about the well-being of their players, over 57 percent of whom are Black.[20] It would take the George Floyd murder in 2020, and an ensuing firestorm of public criticism, to finally push NFL owners to voice support for the Black Lives Matter movement, and for the league's commissioner to issue an apology to players who risked their careers to protest racial injustice and police brutality. As of December 2021, Colin Kaepernick has yet to resume his football career.

My question to you is this: where, when, and for what will you be willing to take a metaphorical knee? Think about the organization you work for. Will you fight for the elimination of systemic racism and for more diversity and inclusion? It's game time.

And no matter what our professions, we as individuals have the power to shape government policies through advocacy and through our votes. Exercise your power and advocate individually or as part of a group. Meet directly with elected officials—start with your local member of parliament, school boards, and police commissions. Demand reform, and follow up.

We can also force ourselves to move beyond our "tribal" political allegiances to elect representatives who are prepared to champion policies to eliminate systemic inequality. It's time we collectively stop defending the status quo and protecting the advantages that benefit only some in our society. History is happening now. You have the power to change it.

For those of you most personally affected by racism and inequality who are going through your own process to deal with your lived realities—your own healing must come first. We don't live in a bubble, so non-BIPOC people will undoubtedly turn to you to engage, to ask questions and to have you "explain." I believe we should demonstrate openness in this regard, but it's important to encourage people to do their own learning, to do the work necessary.

---

19   "Despite Outrage, Nike Sales Increased 31% After Kaepernick Ad" by Gina Martinez, *Time.com*, September 10, 2018. time.com/5390884/nike-sales-go-up-kaepernick-ad

20   "Share of players in the NFL in 2020, by ethnicity," *Statista*, March 16, 2021. statista.com/statistics/1167935/racial-diversity-nfl-players

That doesn't mean we shouldn't celebrate allies who are taking steps in the collective effort to make change happen. Eliminating systemic racism and inequality must be an inclusive, collective, and collaborative enterprise if we are to be successful in getting us to a place where we can all Live Better, Together.

LIVING BETTER, TOGETHER.

To achieve the change we need, each of us must accept the reality that systemic racism and white advantage are real. I hope this book has more than proven that point. Wilful ignorance and lack of awareness are no longer excuses for supporting the status quo. Protecting unearned advantage by choosing to ignore difficult truths, or discounting facts because they don't align to your own lived experience, only fuels white advantage and systemic racism.

Reforming systems will require the support of white citizens who hold the levers of power. As former prime minister Pierre Elliott Trudeau, the architect of Canada's Charter of Rights and Freedoms, said, "The Just Society will be a united Canada, united because all of its citizens will be actively involved in the development of a country where equality of opportunity is ensured."[21] We are a long way from achieving that goal, but I remain hopeful that with continued momentum and leadership, and with white allies engaging with members of BIPOC communities, change is possible.

There are many more aspects of systemic racism and ways to bring about change that I haven't even touched on in this book. I encourage you to seek them out and to continue to inform and educate yourself. Speak with your friends, family, and neighbours—engage with members of the BIPOC community, and listen before offering your perspective. Learn as much as you can from BIPOC sources. Be prepared to change your point of view. Ultimately, change will happen through a series of small actions by people like you.

We can Be Better. We must Do Better. We can Live Better, Together.

There is something empowering and energizing in the pursuit of equality. The experience of writing this book has further ignited that in me. I hope that by sharing my own story, I've shown you that it's possible to heal and transcend negative circumstances. I truly believe that part of my own healing is rooted in shifting my mindset. As with any challenge to systemic racism, it begins with our own perspective. I decided to stop seeing myself as a victim and to work toward becoming an individual agent of change. This all started with changing how I saw and felt about myself and the world around me.

I'm strong. I'm worthy. I matter. I'm here.

---

21   "The Just Society" by Pierre Elliott Trudeau, *The Essential Trudeau*, ed. Ron Graham, McClelland and Stewart, 1998. (16–20.)

All those who say yes to change and are willing to take the necessary actions to make it happen can play an integral part in elevating our society to new heights in the years and decades ahead. I remain optimistic that we can get there together. As Martin Luther King Jr. said best, "We must cross the finish line hand in hand." Living Better, Together. Imagine that.

Imagine if Indigenous peoples didn't have to fight for their basic human rights.

Imagine if Black people didn't have to worry about their personal safety every time they left the house.

Imagine if women, from day one, had the same opportunities as men.

Imagine if religious minorities didn't have to choose between their faith and their careers.

Imagine how many more extraordinary people would be able to shine, innovate, and make our world better if we removed the societal barriers of prejudice and bias.

Imagine how we could transform our world—together.

This is the legacy we can leave our children, our grandchildren—a better world where they can begin their lives with more opportunity no matter where they were born, what they look like, who they pray to, or who they love.

Epilogue

In March 2021 we were still in COVID lockdown in Toronto and the pandemic was weighing heavily on me—the disaster of homeschooling my two young children, unending Zoom marathons, and missing much socializing important to my life and sanity. I mused about how wonderful it would be to fly to Paris for a week to write in some of the city's many cafés, drinking coffee and wine, watching people walk by, and channelling the many authors who, for centuries before me, had drawn inspiration from the City of Light. I wanted to connect to and be inspired by my French heritage. I would have returned to Montmartre, a charming neighbourhood that saw luminaries of the modernist era like Fitzgerald and Stein pen some of their most influential novels whilst immersed in the Paris of the 1920s. But alas, with the pandemic, it was not to be. And then I thought—why not find a little piece of Paris right here in Canada? In late July, I carved out a few days and flew to Québec City.

I met with my French tutor, Vicky, in the Montcalm neighbourhood where I was staying. Vicky had just returned to her hometown after a work holiday in Nicaragua and Mexico City, and we'd been conducting our French classes via Zoom. The next day, I walked around old Québec City, which, with its cobblestone streets and continental atmosphere, is as close to the feeling of Paris you'll get in North America. It was quiet compared to the usual summer tourist mayhem, and I was able to find a café where I could take in the scene and do a little writing. Later that afternoon, I drove to Île-d'Orléans, the island directly across from Québec City framed by the St. Lawrence River.

The island, now largely tourist-driven and agricultural, was once inhabited by mostly French colonial settlers, and as such was the home of many foundational figures of New France. And, as I mentioned earlier, it was the home of my ancestors, who emigrated from England back in the late seventeenth century. Although I had been to Québec City many times, this was my first time visiting Île-d'Orléans. I stayed in Saint-Pierre, a little village overlooking the St. Lawrence and the rolling hills and farms on the north shore. The island itself was postcard-beautiful, dotted with colourful homes—many, stone houses in the traditional Québec style dating back centuries. Vineyards, raspberry and strawberry fields, and art galleries and boutiques. Lots of little cafés and *casse-croûtes*—quintessentially Québec roadside diners.

I planned to let my days unfold organically, to write when I felt like it and explore the island in between. My first morning, I woke up at six, made coffee, and wrote for two hours. There was something about being in this place that made my own history feel like more than names and dates on paper. I rented an electric bicycle for a few hours on my second day, having again woken up at six, made coffee, and successfully written for two hours—inspired by my locale and the ability to focus completely. Riding was an amazing way to see the sites and stop at historical landmarks connected to my ancestors—churches, cemeteries, and even the plots of land where they once raised their families. Everywhere I went, people were warm and welcoming. Some, I sensed, were pleasantly surprised to hear me speak French so fluently.

As I rolled along, I thought of my long-ago ancestors and wondered if they could have ever imagined their bloodline would one day include a Black man. As I stood where they once stood, I felt overwhelmed that, if not for the concept of time, my ancestors and I could be occupying the same space, living our lives as neighbours. I wished I could see what they looked like, how they spoke, learn what they worried about, and even talk to them. I wanted to understand their motivations, their loves, their passions. What had prompted them to voyage to this new world, and what kept them going through hard times?

It made me reflect on how so much happens to a family, a town, a city, a province, a country over four hundred years. Technology advances, societal thinking evolves, laws change to accommodate new understandings...and some things stay the same. Unfortunately, as we've seen throughout this book, that includes some of the worst parts of us as a society. The racial reckoning laid this bare.

∞

I wrapped up writing my book in December 2021, after thirteen months of research and collaboration with my editor, Whitney, my translator, Aycha, and key advisors who generously lent their time and expertise. During the many months of writing, it was challenging to keep up with all the developments in North America related to systemic racism, but as I lived in this world of constant awareness, I made sure to set aside time to reflect on my own journey dealing with racism—both individual and systemic—and the effect it has had on my relationship with those at the core of my story.

My relationship with my mother continues to evolve. She turned eighty-five earlier this year and lives in our hometown of Longueuil, not far from the suburban house we called home more than forty years ago. She has some health issues but she lives a full life, spending time with her brother, sister, cousin, and my sister, Elizabeth, who live close by. My mother and sister returned to live in Québec a few years back after nearly a decade living in the small town of Pemberton, BC.

My mother remained with my stepfather until he passed away in 2007; they had spent nearly forty years together. In his final days, my mother reached out to let me know that he wanted to see me, but I chose not to make the trip from Toronto to Vancouver. I had cut off all contact with my stepfather in the late 1990s after years of trying to forge an adult relationship with him and failing. His lack of interest in addressing the issues of our past helped me make the decision.

My mother called me the day after my stepfather died. I asked her if she thought he would have apologized if I'd travelled to see him one last time. Would he have just simply said "Sorry," I asked? That would have been enough to bring me some closure. She said that he would not have; in his mind, he had never done anything wrong. His passing caused a tumult of emotions for me and my brothers. In a weird way, he was our first father figure, but he was also our most intimate source of racial oppression.

People who have been privy to my story over the years always ask me what my relationship is like with my mother today. I can tell you that it's been a journey of its own—with many conversations often moving one step forward and two steps backwards—but about two decades ago, I arrived at a place of forgiveness. She continues to express how sorry she is for the hurt she has caused me and my brothers. In short, I've told her that I have forgiven her but I will never forget.

In another twist of fate, my mother and Chris's foster mother, Sharon—the woman who alerted the authorities to my mother's neglect all those years ago—struck up a close friendship more than decade go. They even travelled to Europe together. Life is full of strange surprises.

When I told my mother I was going to write this book she was understandably apprehensive, but after many conversations, she told me I should do what I needed to do and agreed to let me interview her. My hope is that, while harsh judgement will no doubt come her way, some readers will also gain a deeper understanding of the complexities of human behaviour and how life experiences can sometimes lead us to making regrettable choices.

My mother is not evil. She knows that she will have to live with the consequences of her choices for the rest of her life. Over the years, she has put genuine effort into building relationships with me and my kids. We can never change the past, but we can create the future of our choice. Today, I still find it difficult to say "I love you" out loud, even when in my heart I want to. Hopefully I can get there one day soon.

In 2016, on my fiftieth birthday, I had the pleasure to reunite with my first foster mother, Edith Borge, who is now ninety-one, and with her daughters, Liz and Angela, and her son, Charlie, at the Bengal Lounge at Victoria's Empress Hotel. I was hosting a celebration with friends and family, and I took the occasion to thank them publicly for being there for me when I needed them most over thirty-five years ago.

Earlier this year, I came across the obituary for Arnold Frieman, the self-made electronics retail tycoon from Winnipeg I shared a moment with twenty-six years ago at the Kennedy Center. He passed away in early April 2019 at the age of ninety. A life well lived.

My foster mother Marion Vipond is going strong at eighty-eight, living in Victoria. She keeps busy visiting with friends and family, staying engaged with her church, reading to young kids at a local school, volunteering to deliver meals to shut-ins, and taking regular walks to keep herself healthy. We spent some quality time when I visited the city with my kids in the summer of 2021.

∞

On the government and political fronts, we've seen some progress and some continuing intransigence. Québec premier François Legault shows no sign of breaking from his untenable position that systemic racism doesn't exist in his province. In February 2021, the federal government announced a funding commitment of $2 million to Joyce Echaquan's community through the Conseil de la Nation Atikamekw and the Conseil des Atikamekw de Manawan, in support of Joyce's Principle, a brief presented in November 2020 to the Government on Canada.[1] The principle is a call to action that "aims to guarantee all Indigenous people the right of equitable access to all social and health services without any discrimination, as well as right to the enjoyment of the highest attainable standard of physical, mental, emotional and spiritual health."[2] As of December 2021, the Government of Québec still refuses to adopt the principle.

Symbolic measures are important, and governments in Canada and the US have taken recent steps to honour the continent's non-Euro-centric heritage. In 2021, President Biden officially made Juneteenth (June 19) a national holiday,

---

[1] "Government of Canada provides $2 million to the Conseil des Atikamekw de Manawan and the Conseil de la Nation Atikamekwfor the development of Joyce's Principle," Indigenous Services Canada, February 10, 2021. canada.ca/en/indigenous-services-canada/news/2021/02/government-of-canada-provides-2-million-to-the-conseil-des-atikamekw-de-manawan-and-the-conseil-de-la-nation-atikamekw-for-the-development-of-joyce.html

[2] Joyce's Principle by the Council of the Atikamekw of Manawan and the Council de la Nation Atikamekw, November 2020 (15). principedejoyce.com/sn_uploads/principe/Joyce_s_Principle_brief__Eng.pdf

commemorating the emancipation of enslaved African Americans.[3]

In Canada, on March 24, 2021, the House of Commons officially designated August 1 Emancipation Day to mark the day in 1834 that the Slavery Abolition Act of 1833 came into effect across the British Empire. The day is meant as one for reflection and engagement in the fight against anti-Black systemic racism.[4]

On June 21, 2021, Canada observed the first National Day for Truth and Reconciliation, and celebrated the twenty-fifth anniversary of National Indigenous Peoples Day, which the federal government describes as "a day for all Canadians to recognize and celebrate the unique heritage, diverse cultures and outstanding contributions of First Nations, Inuit, and Métis peoples."[5]

On June 21, 2021, the *United Nations Declaration on the Rights of Indigenous Peoples* (formerly Bill C-15) received Royal Assent and became law. The act "sets out Canada's obligation to uphold the human rights (including Treaty and inherent rights) of Indigenous peoples affirmed by the 2007 *UN Declaration on the Rights of Indigenous Peoples*,"[6] including the right of self-determination and the enforcement of treaties.

All of these are positive steps forward, symbolic though they may be. But everyday realities remind us of the obstacles still ahead of us. In June 2021, a man driving a pickup truck ran down a Muslim family in London, Ontario, killing four and leaving a nine-year-old boy an orphan. The government called it a hate crime—a terrorist attack. The Prime Minister, the Premier of Ontario, and many other leaders participated in a vigil to provide support to the Muslim community in London and across Canada. "Muslims are not safe in this country," NDP leader Jagmeet Singh declared in a speech from the House of Commons days after the tragedy.[7] "I love my home," he said, "but the reality is, this is our Canada."

This is our Canada.

But we are starting to see some real change within North American judicial systems. On August 23, 2021, the Nova Scotia Court of Appeal ruled unanimously to consider historic factors and systemic racism in the sentencing of Black offenders—a system that was already in place for Indigenous offenders.

3   "Juneteenth Is Now A Federal Holiday" by Alana Wise, *NPR*, June 17, 2021. npr. org/2021/06/17/1007602290/biden-and-harris-will-speak-at-the-bill-signing-making-juneteenth-a-federal-holi

4   "Emancipation Day — August 1," Government of Canada, July 30, 2021. canada.ca/en/canadian-heritage/campaigns/emancipation-day.html

5   "About National Indigenous Peoples Day," Government of Canada, May 21, 2020. rcaanc-cirnac.gc.ca/eng/1100100013718/1534874583157

6   "[UN Declaration on the Rights of Indigenous Peoples overview]," Assembly of First Nations (n.d.), afn.ca/implementing-the-united-nations-declaration-on-the-rights-of-indigenous-peoples

7   "Jagmeet Singh: 'Muslims are not safe in this country'" by Lorraine Carpetner, *Cult MTL*, June 8, 2021. cultmtl.com/2021/06/jagmeet-singh-muslims-are-not-safe-in-this-country-london-ontario-terrorism-canada

Trial judges will now be legally mandated to "consider the history of racism and marginalization that shaped [Black offenders] and do their utmost not to put them behind bars where appropriate."[8]

On November 24, 2021, an American jury found three men guilty of murdering Ahmaud Arbery. The twenty-five-year-old unarmed Black man had been chased down and trapped, then subsequently shot and killed, while jogging through a residential neighbourhood in South Georgia just a few miles from his home. As in the George Floyd murder case, the video evidence of the attack and murder went a long way toward securing a guilty verdict.

On April 20, 2021, the former Minneapolis police officer who killed George Floyd was convicted on all charges and sentenced to 22.5 years in prison. On the news of the verdict, Kamala Harris, the first-ever US Vice President of colour, said, "Today, we feel a sigh of relief. Still, it cannot take away the pain. A measure of justice isn't the same as equal justice. This verdict brings us a step closer, and the fact is we still have work to do."[9] A measure of justice.

There have also been some positive developments with police reform. On September 14, 2021, as part of an ongoing focus on police accountability at local, state, and federal levels, the US Justice Department banned federal law enforcement officers from using neck restraints during arrests and from using no-knock entries while executing warrants, except in rare cases.[10] A total of twenty-four states restricted or banned the use of chokeholds and other neck restraints between 2020 and 2021, and eleven states have made changes to no-knock warrants in that time. "[George] Floyd's case did bring to light a lot of very critically important issues as it relates to accountability for police," said Charles Ramsay, former Washington, DC, and Philadelphia police chief.[11]

In Canada, police reform is gaining traction despite the lack of cohesiveness, and the broad spectrum of urgency from one jurisdiction to another. Beyond the reforms the Toronto Police Services Board is working to deliver, we have also seen the federal government move to action. Public Safety Canada's 2021–22 departmental plan will introduce legislation to enhance civilian oversight of the Royal Canadian Mounted Police and Canada Border Services Agency to "improve transparency, combat systemic discrimination, and reassure the public that Canada's law enforcement system is being held to a high degree

8 "Nova Scotia Court of Appeal rules to consider history of racism, marginalization in cases" by Sean Fine, *The Globe and Mail*, August 23, 2021. theglobeandmail.com/canada/article-nova-scotia-court-of-appeal-rules-to-consider-history-of-racism

9 "Biden and Harris on the Chauvin Trial Verdict" by Doug Mills, *The New York Times*, April 20, 2021. nytimes.com/2021/04/20/us/politics/biden-harris-chauvin-verdict-transcript.html

10 "Bans on chokeholds for federal officers latest in nationwide push to hold police to a 'higher standard'" by Emma Tucker, *CNN*, September 15, 2021. cnn.com/2021/09/15/us/police-accountability-george-floyd/index.html

11 *Ibid.*

of accountability."[12] With a newly elected minority government sitting as of November 22, 2021, the hope is that this important legislation will be enacted as soon as possible.

In the meantime, Canadians agree that their country has a long way to go. In November 2021, the report of a nationwide survey conducted by the Canadian Race Relations Foundation (CRRF) and the Environics Institute for Survey Research revealed "an erosion in confidence related to race relations in Canada."[13] Discrimination and mistreatment based on race is reported to be experienced by one in five Canadians "regularly or from time to time," with the highest numbers reported by those who are Black (57 percent), South Asian (48 percent), or Indigenous (45 percent). The executive summary of the report puts it plainly: "Race relations in this country may now be at an important juncture, and the next two years might well prove to be a critical period of reckoning."

∞

With growing calls for fundamental change in our society, a backlash against eliminating systemic racism was not unexpected. After the 2020 death of George Floyd, a new conversation began in the United States. President Trump warned his federal agencies against the use of critical race theory (CRT), a graduate-level academic theory that calls into question "colourblindness" and instead "acknowledges that the stark racial disparities that have persisted in the United States despite decades of civil rights reforms, and...raise[s] structural questions about how racist hierarchies are enforced, even among people with good intentions."[14] It understands race as a social construct, not a biological reality. Trump called CRT "divisive" and went so far as to enact an executive order, barring any training that suggested the United States was "fundamentally racist."

As the executive order stated, "This ideology is rooted in the pernicious and false belief that America is an irredeemably racist and sexist country; that some people, simply on account of their race or sex, are oppressors; and that racial and sexual identities are more important than our common status

---

[12] *Public Safety Canada Departmental Plan 2021–22: Building a Safe and Resilient Canada*, The Honourable William Sterling Blair, P.C., C.O.M., M.P. Minister of Public Safety and Emergency Preparedness, Public Safety Canada, 2021. publicsafety.gc.ca/cnt/rsrcs/pblctns/dprtmntl-pln-2021-22/dprtmntl-pln-2021-22-en.pdf

[13] *Race relations in Canada 2021: A survey of Canadian public opinion and experience: Final Report* by the Environics Institute for Survey Research, in partnership with the Canadian Race Relations Foundation, November 2021. crrf-fcrr.ca/images/Environics_Study_2021/Race_Relations_in_Canada_2021_Survey_-_FINAL_REPORT_ENG.pdf

[14] "Critical Race Theory: A Brief History" by Jacey Fortin, *The New York Times*, November 8, 2021. nytimes.com/article/what-is-critical-race-theory.html

as human beings and Americans."[15] It reads as defensive and ignorant to the lived realities of BIPOC. A sad step backwards. CRT then becomes the perfect scapegoat for those unwilling to acknowledge the racist history of the United States, and its lingering impacts.

Opponents fear that CRT admonishes all white people for being oppressors while classifying all Black people as hopelessly oppressed victims. These fears have spurred school boards and state legislatures from Virginia to Idaho to ban teachings about racism in classrooms. There is a fundamental problem with the uproar: CRT does not attribute racism to white people as individuals, or even to entire groups of people. But this fact doesn't seem to get in the way of those fearing the reckoning on race.

Anti-CRT sentiments and propaganda have become the rallying cry for the powerful right wing in America—and for those who believe they are being attacked for simply being white—who are dead set against recognizing or eliminating systemic racism. I won't be surprised if we experience similar pushback in Canada.

∞

In Canada, the last day of September is Orange Shirt Day, a day to honour the lost children and survivors of residential schools, their families, and communities. On September 30, 2021, just days before Canada's first National Day for Truth and Reconciliation, the hardware store in my neighbourhood was once again in the public discourse. The marquee was refreshed with the words *Indigenous Lives Matter*—with the words *Black Lives Matter* still present on the other side. It's clear that the owner had not taken the time to reach out to the BIPOC community to better understand the context of his initial transgression. I was disappointed, but I haven't lost hope, because at least we're trying, and all we can do is keep reminding each other that much more remains to be done.

So let's get to work, together.

---

[15] "Why are states banning critical race theory?" by Rashawn Ray and Alexandra Gibbons, *Brookings*, November 2021. brookings.edu/blog/fixgov/2021/07/02/why-are-states-banning-critical-race-theory

Acknowledgements

THANK YOU TO MY AMAZING TEAM.

A special thank you to Samantha Haywood for taking me on as a Transatlantic client and for believing in my story and my abilities as a writer. Your expertise and hands-on guidance in securing my publishing deal were truly masterful.

And to Whitney Moran at Nimbus Publishing (and her amazing team) for taking a chance on a first-time author, believing in the purpose of my story, and for her generous approach to collaboration as my editor. You made writing my first book an enjoyable and unforgettable experience. Thank you.

It really takes a village. Thank you to Aycha Fleury for her beautiful French translation and for retaining the essence of my voice with her mastery of the French language. Vicky Drolet, my French tutor, for being an amazing sounding board and providing her valuable generational perspective. Kristine Irving (Coach KI) for keeping me mentally focused and resilient as I dove headfirst into the fray. You rock.

Thank you to all my amazing advisors who generously contributed their time and expertise—keeping me in check as I tackled challenging and complicated topics.

Gregory Lang, who deconstructed key sections of the Charter so I could better understand and more skillfully create a concise narrative.

Matthew Benedict, for his policy wonk superpowers and youthful perspective that helped me shape my Québec narrative; Michael Benedict, who provided much-needed historical context to my political and policy-related narratives and for his expert editor's perspective.

Thank you to Jennifer Quinton, for her generosity of time and ninja business-coaching skills that helped shape and organize some of my important themes around change, and for guiding me over the finish line when I needed that added collaborative support.

Brian O'Dea, for always keeping it real as we discussed the racial inequalities in the criminal justice system, and for his unique perspective rooted in his lived experiences.

Lisa Wilcox, for her patience and grace (and gentle scolding) in teaching me more about the culture and traditions of Indigenous people as I worked to integrate part of the Indigenous narrative around systemic racism into my story. I'm still learning. Miigwech.

And Cathy Duke and Sarah Beckett for their expert insights and perspective as educators, which helped me better understand the current realities of systemic inequality in the education system and how and where progress is being made.

And to my many friends, peers, and colleagues who were kind enough to engage in the many conversations that helped me sharpen my points of view. Sarah King, Colin Richards, Candice Digeso, Candice Alderson, James Ducommun, Jessica Gibbons, Patrice Butterfield, Sam Dunn, Lindsay Barrowcliffe, John Miller, Jesper Bendtsen, Joanna Matsoukas, Allan Britnell, Mackenzie Ewing, Gina Gillis, Tom Bendtsen, Wendy Von Bogedom, Hugo Hollander, Simon Hamlin, Kim D'Eon, Piya Chattopadhyay, Shabiki Crane, Jim Irving, Brad Foster, Angela Schwarz, David Amburgey, Janice Gurney, Andy Patton, Jeff Semple, Alastair MacBeath, Anna Henriques, Chris Dorsey, Elizabeth Lefevre, Cynthia Pacheco, Maureen Vipond, Paul Vipond, Nancy Moore, Sylvain Marchand. Luik Moore, Luc Charette, Marcey and Warren Reid, George Szasz, Peter Charette, Katie Gorman, Mark Campbell, Jorge Miguel, Donna MacMullin, Jessie Jutras, Joël Dubuc, Anna Ruth Henriques, Lyle Shipley, Darla Campbell, and Howard Brown.

Thank you to my family and extended family across the world for the encouragement and never-ending support, past and present. The Vipond, Moore, Charette, Lefevre, Barrowcliffe, Dorsey, Pacheco, Nichols, Champagne, Baker, Borge, Anderson, Irving, Reid, Sadler, Karlica, Foster, Marchand, Quesnel, Van Geijn, Macbeath, Hey, Maher, and Szasz families.

To my "Friends of Vic High" crew, Tak Niketas, Esther Callo, Chris Kelsall, Chris Siver, Richard and Sandra Hunt, Hans de Goede, Moe Elewonibi, Alex Niketas, Paloma Callo, Maureen Vipond, David Maxwell and Francy Pesek and many others for all your efforts in taking a stand to eliminate systemic inequality in Victoria's school system and advocate for the kids at Vic High.

Shoutout to my League of Gentlemen PC friends—Marcus Fraser, Peter Armstrong, Jesse Capon, Dom Bochenski, Nick Yap, and Aaron Solowoniuk, for creating a safe place to debate important ideas. Our "town square" gathering pushed me to go "all-in" and write this book.

And to my mother, for agreeing to be interviewed for this book and for understanding why I had to write it. With love.

In loving memory of Winston "Ralph" Vipond, Signe Charette, Oliver and Edna Holm, Fred Gaysek, and Bob Pelletier. You were along for the ride.

One love.
Stephen